Jeremy Black is one of the UK's rians. He is Professor of Histor... renowned expert on the history of war. His recent books include *A Brief History of Italy* and *The World of James Bond*, which offers a historian's perspective on the Bond novels and films. He appears regularly on TV and radio, including BBC Radio 4's *In Our Time*.

A BRIEF HISTORY OF

The Mediterranean

JEREMY BLACK

ROBINSON

ROBINSON

First published in Great Britain in 2020 by Robinson

1 3 5 7 9 10 8 6 4 2

A CIP catalogue record for this book is available from the British Library.

ISBN: 978-1-47214-440-9

Typeset in Scala by Hewer Text UK Ltd, Edinburgh
Printed and bound in Great Britain by Clays Ltd, Elcograf S.p.A.

Papers used by Robinson are from well-managed forests and other responsible sources.

Robinson
An imprint of
Little, Brown Book Group
Carmelite House
50 Victoria Embankment
London EC4Y 0DZ

An Hachette UK Company
www.hachette.co.uk

www.littlebrown.co.uk

For Adrian Stones

Contents

Preface

The grand object of travelling is to see the shores
of the Mediterranean.

Samuel Johnson, 1776

A leading stage for world history, the Mediterranean today is
the centre of the tourist experience for many, and notably so for
Europeans. With tens of millions of tourists, international and
domestic, every year, the sea and its shores record shifts in the
sources, interests and concerns of tourists. However, alongside
these shifts, there is the central focus on the Mediterranean Sea
itself, whether cruising the deep blue sea, lounging on the beaches,
or visiting the port cities. The sun-blazing Mediterranean repeatedly draws the eyes of those onshore.

This history will provide an account in which the experience of
travel is foremost: travel for tourism, for trade, for war, for migration, for culture or, as often, for a variety of reasons. Linked to this,
travellers had a variety of goals and situations, from rulers to slaves,
merchants to pirates. We will go from the Phoenicians travelling for
trade to the modern tourist sailing for pleasure and cruising in ease.

Throughout, the emphasis will be on the sea, on coastal
regions, on port cities visited by cruise liners, such as Athens,
Barcelona, Naples and Palermo, and on their connections. This
is not a history of the states on the shores of the sea, the centres of which are often far distant: France is run from Paris, not
Marseille, and Spain from Madrid, not Barcelona, while Turkey is
governed now from Ankara, and not Istanbul (earlier, Byzantium,
and, then, until the 1920s, Constantinople).

Of course, the history of a sea and its shores looks beyond and,
notably, to the other waters that flow into it, in this case the Black

Sea, the Atlantic, the Red Sea (over a narrow isthmus now crossed by the Suez Canal), and rivers, from the Ebro and Rhône to the Nile. Yet, the wider significance of the Mediterranean does not mean that we should be writing a history of the world. Readers know that Rome and Byzantium/Constantinople/Istanbul were the centres of major empires and of Christianity. They do not expect their history. We focus here, instead, on the sea and its shores. That, however, does not mean a lack of engagement with the wider world for much of western Eurasia and northern Africa played a role, directly or indirectly, in the fate of the Mediterranean. At times, that can make the history of the latter an account of conflict after conflict, but it is necessary to understand these wars in order to grasp the changing boundaries of the Mediterranean states, societies and religions, the buildings that have been left, and the peoples' culture, sense of identity and history.

Debts are obviously many. I would first like to thank my parents for taking me to the Mediterranean repeatedly when I was a child and for sending me on two Mediterranean educational cruises that took me as far as Israel and Lebanon. In turn, holidays with my family to France, Italy, Malta and Spain have taken me to many destinations. Academic life – the pleasures of research, particularly in Genoa, Lucca, Naples and Venice, and the more ambiguous lifestyle of conferences and lectures, notably in Barcelona and Naples, have been important, as have been family holidays and over a decade of lecturing on cruise liners for Martin Randall, Noble Caledonia, Swan Hellenic and Thomson. I also enjoyed leading a land tour for *History Today*. For an historian, it is striking that you can now be invited to a weekend in the Mediterranean as if you were going to London. Flying from Exeter to Malaga can certainly appear less difficult, and is definitely quicker for me.

I have benefited in particular from the advice of Luigi Loreto, Graham Loud, Ciro Paoletti, Peter Quartermaine, Guglielmo Sanna, Peter Wiseman and Patrick Zutshi on all or part of earlier drafts. They are not responsible for any errors that remain. I have also been helped greatly by Duncan Proudfoot, again the commissioning editor, and Howard Watson, the exemplary copy editor. For me, this is a great team.

It is a great pleasure to dedicate this book to Adrian Stones and thereby record a strong friendship and much good humour.

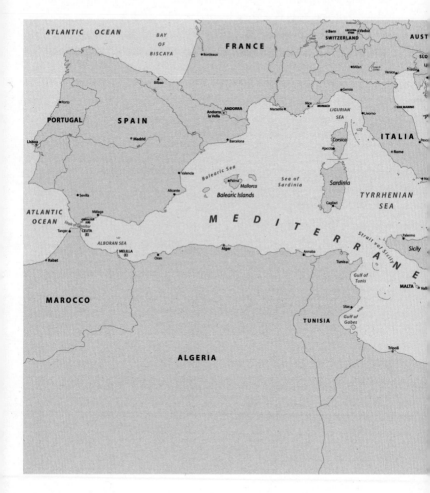

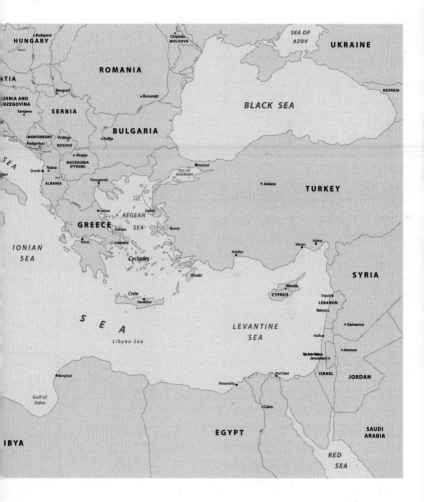

1. Sea and Shores

Thy shores are empires, changed in all save thee;
Assyria, Greece, Rome, Carthage, what are they?
Lord Byron, *Childe Harold's Pilgrimage*, 1812

The Atlantic waters breaking over the land lip at the western
end of the Mediterranean, the most vivid episode in its history, occurred before humans left records. For long earlier, the
Mediterranean, the creation of the separation of Eurasia from
Africa, was a shrinking enclosed sea, with the land joining
Spain to Morocco cutting it off from the Atlantic, while there was
another similar barrier from the Black Sea, rather like that which
survives between the Mediterranean and the Red Sea. The limited amount of water flowing into the sea from rivers ensured
that the water lost to evaporation was not replaced, and the lake
became increasingly saline, leaving salt deposits that were subsequently to be important. As a result, the basin emptied, and
the Mediterranean largely dried up in what has been termed the
Messinian Salinity Crisis, which began about 6 million years ago.

However, the raising of sea levels, combined with geological stresses, transformed the situation. The land barriers that
separated the Mediterranean from the Atlantic and the Black
Sea were breached. The former breach, the Zanclean (Pliocene)
Flood, probably initially began with water coming over the lip of
rock in the Strait of Gibraltar as a waterfall bringing a hundred
times more water per second than that at Lake Victoria, before
this lip was broken about 5.3 million years ago. First, in the
western Mediterranean, and then, after the Sicily Sill had been
breached, in the Eastern, the sea rapidly filled with the ocean's
water, possibly in a decade.

In the case of the Black Sea, there is the suggestion that Mediterranean seawater broke into the Black Sea, then a freshwater lake, about 7200 BCE. Other explanations suggest changes, for different reasons, variously in 17000–14000 BCE or 11000–8000 BCE. Certainly, the Black Sea has had a complex relationship with the Mediterranean, and the evidence for a traumatic flooding of the former is problematic.

This filling created a new system of flows and currents. Water evaporated in the Mediterranean, and the failure to replace it by rainfall and rivers meant that there is a flow in from the Black Sea and (far more) from the Atlantic. Shakespeare made reference to the former, drawing on the argument in Pliny the Elder's *Natural History* that, fed by the rivers that flow into it, notably the Danube, the Dniester and the Don, the waters of the Black Sea (the Pontic Sea) always flow into the Sea of Marmora (the Propontic) and the Dardanelles (the Hellespont), but never ebb back again. In *Othello*, when Iago tells the Moor that his mind may change, Othello replies:

Never Iago. Like to the Pontic Sea,
Whose icy current and compulsive course
Ne'er keeps retiring ebb, but keeps due on
To the Propontic and the Hellespont,
Even so my bloody thoughts.

This speech reflected the lasting knowledge of Mediterranean geography that stemmed from the writings of the Classical age, and especially once these works were printed in the Renaissance.

The flow of water in from the Atlantic is even greater because the saltier and heavier Mediterranean water flows out *under* the incoming Atlantic waters, thereby not creating resistance to the eastward flow from the ocean. This creates a navigational problem for ships trying to row or sail west; although this problem was in part circumvented by ships using an undertow along the northern shore that enabled them to move west. This expedient was employed by the Phoenicians and enabled them to establish a base to the west of the Strait of Gibraltar at Gades (Cádiz).

The pattern of Mediterranean currents is at once simple, yet also complex. The former is explained by the major current moving in a counter-clockwise direction eastwards along the coast of North Africa, then from south to north past Israel and Lebanon, before moving back westwards along the northern shores of the Mediterranean back to the Strait of Gibraltar. Yet, complex because the Mediterranean is in part a product of subsidiary seas – from east to west, the Aegean, Adriatic and Tyrrhenian – and there is significant disruption to currents and weather produced by major islands, such as Cyprus and Sicily.

These islands are the product of a varied sub-sea geology that includes flatter areas, notably the Cyprus and Ionian basins, and the Balearic Plain, as well as the opposite, particularly the Mediterranean Ridge. The combination of these with changing sea levels ensured past periods in which modern islands, for example Euboea and Sicily, were joined to the Continental land-mass, in their cases Greece and Italy; while some were joined to other islands as with Minorca and Majorca, or Corsica and Sardinia. On islands, animals living in isolation developed particular characteristics, becoming smaller or larger. Crete had a small dog-sized elephant, and still has distinctive goats; while Italy's Gargano peninsula, when an island, had giant hedgehogs, owls and dormice.

The melting of the ice sheets at, and after, the end of the ice ages affected sea levels, but far more than varying sea levels were involved in the changing physical history of the Mediterranean. In the shadow of the risk of volcanic eruptions and earthquakes, the Mediterranean had a precarious and volatile existence. There have been major earthquakes and volcanic activity in historic times, as in the major eruption on the Aegean island of Santorini

3

in about 1645–1500 BCE: the earthquake that wrecked the Italian city of Amalfi in 1343 CE, sending much of it into the sea; that in 1384, which killed the Duke and Duchess of Lesbos; the earthquakes in Calabria in 1793, Crete in 1810, Basilicata in Italy in 1857, the island of Chios in 1881, the western Peloponnese in 1886, Calabria in 1905, Messina in 1908, Izmir in 1928, Greece in 1932, Algeria in 1980, destroying 25,000 houses, and the 1980 earthquake that greatly damaged Salerno's Norman cathedral. Conspiracy theorists continue to argue that earthquakes or volcanoes are caused by hostile forces, although, by 2017, this took the shape in Turkey of claims that American and Israeli seismic ships were intentionally setting off earthquakes. The continuing nature of this precarious existence is abundantly clear, most obviously in the shadow of Vesuvius on the Bay of Naples, and again near Etna, both mighty volcanoes.

The relationship between the Eurasian and African tectonic plates, one that will probably bring the Mediterranean to an end in about 50 million years as the African plate continues to move north, is linked to continuing volcanic activity. This is really apparent at Mount Etna in Sicily, which is very active and where an eruption in 2014 forced the temporary closure of Catania airport. For tourists, past and present, visits to volcanic sites, notably Vesuvius, Etna and Santorini, were, and remain, a key part of the Mediterranean itinerary. On cruises, passing Stromboli, 'the lighthouse on the Mediterranean', in the Aeolian Islands (north of Sicily) at night, and seeing it lit up by volcanic activity, is truly dramatic. The volcano there erupted in 2002, and again in July 2019 when the island was covered in ash and a hiker killed while scores of tourists fled from beaches into the sea. Nearby, Vulcano is quieter though it has smoke, smells and sulphates, and the Grand Crater can be climbed.

Obsidian produced by volcanic activity has a hard and glass-like quality, can be fractured to produce sharp blades, and was an important working material for early human society. The islands of Lipari, Pantelleria and Milos had major deposits of obsidian, and these encouraged trade.

The past explanation of islands included an awareness of geological change. Strabo, a wide-ranging Greek geographer (*c.* 63 BCE–*c.* 23 CE), in his *Geography* (7 BCE) referred to Sicily as:

> rent from the continent by earthquakes ... the fire that was smouldering beneath the earth, together with the wind produced violent earthquakes because the passages to the surface were all blocked up, and the regions thus heaved up yielded at last to the force of the blasts of wind, were rent asunder, and then received the sea ... it is more plausible that the islands in the high seas were heaved up from the deeps, whereas it is more reasonable to think that those lying off the promontories and separated merely by a strait from the mainland have been rent therefrom.

Very differently, Strabo commented on what we would see as a tsunami near Tyre in Lebanon:

> A wave from the sea, like a flood-tide ... the ebb uncovered the shore again and disclosed the bodies of men lying promiscuously among dead fish. Like occurrences take place in the neighbourhood of the Mount Casius situated near Egypt, where the land undergoes a single quick convulsion, and makes a sudden change to a higher or lower level, the result being that, whereas the elevated part repels the sea and the sunken part receives it, yet the land makes a reverse change, and the site resumes its old position.

A tsunami of up to 30 metres (98 feet) was produced by a large earthquake at the island of Amorgos in the Cyclades archipelago in the Aegean Sea in 1956.

Alongside currents came the pattern of the winds, which changed very greatly by season and in response to weather systems. Thus, summer winds in the eastern Mediterranean tend to come from the north-west. Winds, such as the mistral, a southerly that blows onto the coast of Provence, made being able to take shelter in harbours very important. Before observing that 'along most of its coast it [Italy] is harbourless', Strabo focused on those sites that provided good protection from the waves, such as Brindisi, a key harbour on the route across the southern Adriatic to Greece, where the land, shaped like stag's horns, offered safe anchorage; whereas nearby Taranto 'because of its wide expanse, is not wholly sheltered from the waves', and there were also shallows in the inner harbour. His accuracy was high.

Issues for the traveller were far more challenging in the technology of the past. Galleys had a low freeboard and therefore were vulnerable to high waters in poor weather. As a result, autumn and winter weather were particular challenges. For example, the Turks allegedly lost sixty ships in a storm in late 1538. But, in practice, the entire year could be challenging, not least in terms of going aground. In May 1698, Robert Clayton, a British tourist, planned to sail from Naples to Sicily:

We had hired for this voyage a felucca with eight straight oars and . . . 16th in the morning we had a very clear sky, and a perfect calm; everything seemed to smile, and tempt us to the voyage, and promised a safe and quick passage to Messina. Accordingly about nine in the morning we put to sea . . . we rowed directly over the Gulf for the isle of Capri, and we were about twenty miles from Naples we felt a small breeze of wind, the sea began to swell, upon which our pilot steered directly to Massa a town near the point of the promontory and the nearest land we could make to. We had not rowed an hour but the sky grew cloudy and it blew very hard and the sea ran so high against us that we rather retired to Naples than advanced to Massa, and at last our oars became useless, which obliged us to put up our sail and endeavour to gain Capri, and so we beat for near an hour against the wind and sea both increasing still. Our vessel lay so much on one side that near a yard of the sail was continually under water whilst the sea ran over the other side of the boat and every wave seemed to threaten destruction. We are still 6 miles from Capri and found that we advanced but very little and that with great danger, and at last found no other security but to return before the wind to Naples . . . The weather continues still blustering . . . I shall lay aside all other points of pursuing this voyage.

Yet unpredictability could play to the advantage of the tourist. Writing from Sicily in April 1792, Thomas Brand, a 'bearleader' or travelling tutor, noted that, with his charge, Charles, Lord Bruce, he:

had a most prosperous sail of four nights and three days and a half cross Hesperian seas from Naples to Palermo . . . it was nearly a perfect calm – indeed it was much fitter for the revels of Aphrodite and her maids of honour than for any mortal expedition . . . The Sicilian packets are the most convenient things you can imagine. Each passenger has his cabin. They have a good dining room and the captains of both of them have had an English marine education.

However, subsequently that April, Brand was delayed at Messina because:

The wind is very contrary – Our original intention was to have returned to Palermo and have taken the packet there but we are sick of Sicilian roads and accommodations and as the north side of the triangle contains nothing worth seeing we determined to take the opportunity of a Neapolitan brig [boat] of good character and hope to be at Naples nearly as soon as this [letter].

As part of a world we have lost, Brand's use of Classical comparisons was commonplace for the period and across the arts. So were the references to storms in the Mediterranean. Indeed, Homer's *Iliad* and *Odyssey* played a significant role in élite cultural consciousness. It leaves its influence clearly in *Idomeneo* (1781), Mozart's Classical opera, one set in Crete on the return of the Greeks from the Trojan War. A harsh Sea God (Neptune), terrible storms over a deadly sea and a sea monster are all part of the action. Idomeneus was a figure in Homer's *Iliad*. This Mediterranean was certainly not solely the calm-sea background to the painting of ports and coastal scenes bathed in light by, for example, the French artist Claude Lorrain in the seventeenth century and his British counterpart Richard Wilson in the eighteenth. The Shipwreck Museum at Kyrenia in North Cyprus, which exhibits the remains of a Greek merchantmen of the fourth century BCE, provides an instructive view that can be amplified by the archaeological museum at Lipari in the Aeolian Islands, which contains well-displayed shipwrecked cargoes from Antiquity. There can still be storms today.

Vulnerability to the wind was a continual fear. It is not surprising that churches represented, or contained thanks for, survival. Allegedly, the cathedral at Cefalù in Sicily, founded in 1131 by Roger II of Sicily, commemorated his finding refuge from a savage storm at the port. Similarly, the sanctuary of Bonaria near Cagliari on Sardinia, was constructed by the Aragonese in 1325, and contains the image of Our Lady of Bonaria, which reflected the impact of a 1370 storm on a Spanish merchantman en route to Italy: an image of the Virgin Mary did not sink, but came ashore. As with many of the coastal temples of Antiquity, the image became a lodestar of protection to sailors, and was honoured accordingly.

The cathedral museum in Cagliari holds a collection of items seized from Pope Clement VII during the Sack of Rome in 1527 by rampaging unpaid mercenaries. The Catalan sailors who had them were engulfed in a savage storm, and, in thanks for their survival, handed them over to the Archbishop. The theme of safe voyages went on being significant, as in the marble murals of the mid-nineteenth century Notre-Dame de la Garde basilica in Marseille.

Problems certainly hit individual travellers. In January 1760, Edward Tucker, who had come the previous year by sea from England to Genoa, nearly being captured by a French ship off Corsica (this was during the Seven Years War of 1756–63), intended to spend only four or five days in Leghorn (Livorno): 'by the feluccas which (weather permitting) constantly pass and repass betwixt this and Leghorn every day – and for this month past have been in daily expectation of setting out for this place, but continual rain and hard gales of wind always rendered it impracticable for a felucca to put to sea till this I am now arrived in.'

In 1785, Charles Sloane had a quicker passage from Sicily to Malta, but: 'We got over in 12 hours, and had a storm astern most of the way. I was dead sick, and had I not been so, should have been greatly alarmed for my safety, as we were in a boat which six rowers called a sparonara.'

Naval operations were much affected by the weather in the Age of Galley and Sail. Fleets badly damaged in storms included the Persian fleet wrecked in the Aegean in a storm off Mount Athos in 492 BCE, that returning from the Eighth Crusade in 1270, which was hit off Trapani in Sicily, and Charles V's fleet off Algiers in 1541. The destructiveness of the last storm led to the end of the expedition. In September 1800, Vice-Admiral

William Young of the British Royal Navy wrote to his wife from Tetuan Bay in Morocco: 'We may truly be considered as a wandering army, at the mercy of the winds and waves – for we left Gibraltar merely on account of the anchorage there being unsafe, for a large fleet, in case of a Westerly gale, and if we should meet with a Levant, or easterly, wind here we must then weigh from this, and push out of the Streights.'

Shipboard life was generally difficult. In December 1801, John Hill of the Royal Welsh Fusiliers, who had served with the British army in Egypt, wrote to his mother from Gibraltar, 'on shipboard private soldiers suffer often times as much, almost, as before an enemy'. The accommodation was crowded and insanitary, and there was constant exposure to the weather and fear of sinking or falling overboard: few could swim.

Even if no storms were encountered, voyages could still be inconvenient. A British tourist who set off in September 1778 from Genoa for Livorno, recorded: 'Not being sure of the wind the next morning, and having passed a disagreeable uncomfortable night in the chaise [carriage] which took up too much of the vessel that there was no room to stir two steps we turned up the Gulf of La Spezia and landed at Lerici.' Putting the carriage on board, in order both to ship it and to provide accommodation, was normal.

The need to sail was not only a matter of voyages in which it was necessary to cross the sea, as to the islands in the sea, or between North Africa and Southern Europe. There were also the problems posed by the inaccessible nature of much of the coastline, the absence of roads along many shorelines and, linked to this, but also separate, the relative advantage arising from the greater directness, cargo-carrying capacity and speed that were possible by sea. As well as having few anchorages, the long, largely mountainous coast of Morocco and Algeria was particularly bad for road links, but it was not alone in this. On the European shore of the Mediterranean, the roads were especially bad on the Albanian, Dalmatian, Calabrian and Sardinian shores, for example that of eastern Sardinia; but not only there. In particular, there was no practical route along the Mediterranean coast between Marseille and Genoa until the nineteenth century, in part due to an absence of good roads in the county of Nice, which was part of the dominions of Savoy-Piedmont. An anonymous British tourist crossed the River Var between Antibes and Nice in 1754: 'But not without taking guides with us, who were always ready to wade through, find out the best fords for your chair, and support it, if there should be occasion: the sands move frequently, which makes the bottom extremely dangerous.'

In 1776–7, another anonymous British tourist noted: 'These torrent-courses are the roads, and, in some parts, the only roads of the country ... A road has been formed from Nice over Montalban to Villafrance, just practicable for a carriage, but so steep and so rough that it is scarcely safe; and a carriage is very seldom seen on it ... The road to Monaco is practicable only for mules, asses, or mountain horses; and in some parts is scarcely safe with any of them.' This road was so bad that he got off his mule and went by foot.

East of Monaco, the Ligurian mountains fell sheer to the sea, and it was not practicable to go by land to Genoa. The Grande Corniche road on the Riviera between Nice and Menton was not opened until Napoleon's time. Its construction reflected his political and strategic interest in better communications between France and Italy, and his control over the latter, one that was greater than that of any previous French ruler, even Charlemagne. Both men were crowned King of Italy in what proved highpoints in France's longstanding interest in Italy, one that was longer and greater than that of Spain.

To get between France and Italy, travellers had to choose between the Alps, via the Mont Cenis pass, and the Mediterranean. Both were hazardous and uncomfortable routes and each was greatly affected by the weather. The feluccas, the local boats, were small, vulnerable to storms and dependent on the wind. In 1723, John Molesworth observed: 'No mariners in the world are so cowardly as the Italians in general, but especially the Genoese; so that upon the least appearance of a rough sea, they run into the first creek when their feluccas are sometimes wind-bound for a month.' In 1734, Andrew Mitchell was 'detained some weeks longer at Genoa than I intended, and that by bad weather, for if it blows the least or if there is anything of a sea, the feluccas won't go out.' On 1 November, he sailed to Savona, but the next contrary wind obliged him to put into Loano and to have the felucca hauled onshore as there was no harbour: 'I was detained here a whole day by the laziness of the Italian sailors who chose rather to lie in the port and take their chance for a wind afterwards than to put to sea in fair weather. If there is the least swell in the sea they will by no means venture out.'

The situation did not improve until the Age of Steam. Indeed, the continued problems of sea travel contrasted with the gradual improvement in overland journeys as roads were constructed or improved. Travellers could cope with discomfort. Instead, it was the uncertainty that storms, contrary winds and calms brought to timetables that was the crucial problem. None was to be overcome until the nineteenth century when steamships developed and became effective and reliable. Sailing from Marseille to Civitavecchia in 1778, Philippa, Lady Knight, an impecunious widow travelling with her daughter Cornelia, observed: 'Our voyage was somewhat tedious, as we were, after seven weeks waiting for a wind, thirty days on our passage, putting into different ports.' Lady Elizabeth Craven was so fed up in September 1785 that she cut short her passage from Genoa to Livorno and, instead, landed in Viareggio in order to continue her journey by land.

There was also the question of the boat itself. Responses varied. John Holroyd had a pleasant journey from Genoa to Livorno in 1764: 'A felucca is a large sort of open boat which makes use of sails and oars. There was an awning to protect us from the sun and I had a good bench for a bed during the night. The expedition was very pleasant as we went close to the coast our Genoese boatmen having a very becoming bashfulness as to meeting the corsairs at sea.'

Eight years later, Philip Francis has a very different experience: 'Embarked [at Venice] on board a Roman trading vessel bound to Ancona ... passed the night in a hogsty (which the captain called his cabin) on a mattress, in the utmost misery. The vessel full of goods and stinking passengers. Calms or contrary winds all night ... continuance of misery. Godfrey eating, Francis spewing.'

He was then deterred from going overland to Naples by a route that avoided Rome: 'upon inquiry we found that the roads were impracticable, without posts or inns, and the people to the last degree brutal and barbarous. So we took the high road to Rome.' Few tourists toured the southern Adriatic or the matching coast of Italy.

The problems of travel help explain why Fernand Braudel, the great French historian of the sixteenth-century Mediterranean, referred to distance as the 'first enemy' and news as 'a luxury commodity', both longstanding issues. Rulers and ministers frequently complained that diplomats exceeded or, otherwise, misunderstood instructions; but it was difficult to provide orders that would comprehend all eventualities or, alternatively, to respond adequately to the pace of developments, including those caused by diplomatic negotiations and military moves. The slow and uncertain nature of communications ensured that considerable discretion had to be left to envoys if negotiations were to advance speedily. Special couriers could speed messages by land and sea, so that, in the sixteenth century, a message from Constantinople to Venice, sent on from the Venetian colony of Corfu by galley, could take twenty days. Communications, however, were not only slow by modern standards. They were also frequently uncertain such that information could only be confirmed by waiting for subsequent messages.

Moreover, uncertainty about the speed, indeed arrival, of messages ensured that they could be sent by separate routes simultaneously: notably from Constantinople to Paris via Marseille, the long sea route; and via the Adriatic, a shorter sea route, and Venice; and via Budapest, a route entirely by land. In 1731, in peacetime, the first route could take thirty-nine days or more. Two years later, when war with Austria broke out, Louis Sauveur, Marquis of Villeneuve, France's talented envoy in Constantinople from 1728 to 1741, preferred to send his mail to Paris across the Adriatic to Ancona in the neutral Papal States, a short crossing, rather than along the Adriatic to neutral Venice, a route that increased the risk of interception by Austrian ships from Trieste. On the Constantinople–Paris route in 1787, during a period of peace, reports by the French envoy on 25 April and 26 April, the second by sea, arrived on 20 May and 3 July respectively. Those of 11, 15, 16, 25 January, 10, 23 February, 10, 17, 24 March, 10, 25 May and 9 June 1787, arrived on 11 February, 6 April, 29 March, 26 February, 11 March, 25 March, 8 April, 31 May, 24 April, 9 June, 23 June and 7 July respectively. In 1755, due to contrary winds, the new French envoy had taken forty-nine days to sail from Marseille to Constantinople.

Such were the pressures that affected life and connections in the Mediterranean before the transformations to travel in the nineteenth century that were brought by steam, both steamships and railways. A very different view of the sea can be seen in Monaco's clifftop Oceanographic Museum where the display of species includes many Mediterranean ones. This serves as a reminder of the wonderful variety of that sea. To capture this variety, however, it is necessary also to look at its cultural resonances. Large ships at sea can be seen in the background of the *Triptych of the Virgin of Montserrat* painted, probably in 1470–5, for Francesco della Chiesa, a merchant from Acqui Terme in the present-day Italian region of Piedmont. He had settled in Valencia, where the work was painted and where the Virgin of Montserrat, venerated in a Catalan abbey, was called upon to watch over those involved in maritime trade. The painter, Bartolomé de Cárdenas (*c.* 1440–*c.* 1501), also produced stained-glass window designs for the merchants' exchange building in Barcelona, but it is the somewhat elusive ships in the triptych with their suggestion of voyages beyond that capture the memory.

2. Antiquity, from the Origins to 30 BCE

The *Odyssey*

Odysseus' fame as a traveller across the Mediterranean, on his ten-year return from the already-lengthy siege of Troy, the subject of Homer's epic the *Iliad*, was the subject of the sequel the *Odyssey*, the first Mediterranean travelogue, the earliest manuscript of which dates from the tenth century BCE. The joy and details of a successful voyage were mentioned:

> Flashing-eyed Athene sent them a favourable wind, a strong-blowing West Wind that sang over the wine-dark sea . . . The mast of fir they [the crew] raised and set in the hollow socket, and made it fast with forestays, and hauled up the white sail with twisted thongs of oxhide. So the wind filled the belly of the sail, and the dark wave sang loudly about the stern of the ship.

On Calypso's island, Odysseus (Latin Ulysses), the legendary King of Ithaca, builds a ship, cutting down twenty trees with a bronze-headed axe:

> He cunningly smoothed them all and trued them to the line . . . he bored all the pieces and fitted them to one another, and with pegs and morticings he hammered it together . . . he set in place the decks, bolting them to the close-set ribs, as he continued the work; and he finished the raft with long gunwales. In it he set a mast and a yard

arm, fitted to it, and furthermore made him a steering oar, with which to steer. Then he fenced in the whole from stem to steam with willow withes to be a defence against the waves, and covered the bottom with brush.

Homer offered details of navigation:

The comrades of Telemachus, drawing near the shore, furled the sail, and took down the mast quickly, and rowed the ship to her anchorage with their oars. Then they threw out the mooring stones and made fast the stern cables, and themselves disembarked upon the shore of the sea, and made ready their meal and mixed the sparkling wine.

Yet, there were also the justified terrors of 'the monster-harbouring sea'. These forced those planning a voyage to consider their options carefully. Thus, for the Greeks on the return home from Troy:

In Lesbos, as we were debating the long voyage, whether we should sail to seaward of rugged Chios, toward the isle of Psyria, keeping Chios itself upon our left, or landward of Chios past windy Mimas. So we asked the god to show us a sign, and he showed it us, and bade us cleave through the midst of the sea to Euboea, that we might the soonest escape from misery. And a shrill wind sprang up to blow, and the ships ran swiftly over the fish-filled ways, and at night put in to Geraestus. There on the altar of Poseidon, we laid many thighs of bulls, thankful to have traversed the great sea.

So far so good, but then for Menelaus' fleet on the route home to Sparta:

> Zeus ... planned for him a hateful path and poured
> upon him the blasts of shrill winds, and the waves were
> swollen to huge size, like mountains. Then he split the
> fleet in two, bringing some ships to Crete ... the ships
> the waves dashed to pieces against the reef ... the five
> other dark-prowed ships the wind ... and wave brought
> to Egypt.

The *Odyssey* repeatedly reiterates the hazards of maritime
travel. These hazards were human as well as natural:

> There is a rocky isle in the midst of the sea, midway
> between Ithaca and rugged Samos, Asteris, of no great
> size, but in it is a harbour where ships may lie, with an
> entrance on either side. There, in ambush, the Achaean
> waited for him.

The strange people and beasts Odysseus encountered, including the lethargic Lotus-Eaters, the cannibalistic Laestrygonians
and the Sirens, underline the strong fear of the unknown that
was an important aspect of a culture in which so much over the
horizon was a matter of rumour and supposition. The Strait of
Messina, between the eastern tip of Sicily and the western of
Calabria in southern Italy, was probably the source of the account
of Scylla, featuring a six-headed monster, 'with each head she
carries off a man', and Charybdis, a whirlpool, wrecking ships.
There is indeed a natural whirlpool in the strait, and the legend
testified to the travails of the sea and the anxiety aroused by
threats to navigation. Strabo later referred to 'a monstrous deep,
into which the ships are easily drawn by the refluent current of
the Straits and plunged prow-foremost along with a mighty eddy-
ing of the whirlpool; and when the ships are gulped down and
broken to pieces'. An ambitious, but very costly, project to build
a bridge across the strait, and thus replace the uncertainties of a

reliance on ferries in order to reach Sicily, was cancelled in 2006 and, anew, in 2013.

The *Isole dei Ciclopi*, the Islands of the Cyclopes, north-east of Catania in Sicily, were supposedly the rocks thrown at Odysseus' escaping boats by Polyphemus, the one-eyed giant he had just blinded. The enchantress Circe was a very different threat. Odysseus also repeatedly faced the attacks of wind and wave, as with the winds in Aeolus' leather bag and the thunderstorm caused by Zeus: 'The great wave struck him [Odysseus] from above, rushing upon him with terrible force, and spun his raft in a circle. Far from the raft he fell, and let fall the steering oar from his hand; his mast was broke in the middle by the fierce blast of tumultuous winds that came upon it, and far in the sea sail and yardarm fell.'

Being shipwrecked, there were also the problems of a hostile coast: 'the boom of the sea upon the reefs – for the great wave thundered against the dry land, belching upon it in terrible fashion, and all things were wrapped in the foam of the sea; for there were neither harbours where ships might ride, nor roadsteads, but projecting headlands, and reefs, and cliffs.'

Odysseus' journeys and, more generally, the Greeks' war with Troy, long set major themes for Western culture, and notably in painting. Neoclassical works drew greatly on both, as in Donato Creti's *Achilles dragging the Body of Hector round the Walls of Troy* and François-Pascal Gérard's *Achilles mourning Patroclus*. The vivid light from the rising sun in J. M. W. Turner's *Ulysses deriding Polyphemus* (1829) is absorbing. He visited Italy on a number of occasions from 1819 and was entranced by the Mediterranean's fusion of light and antiquity.

Early Man

The idea of early hominins originating in the Mediterranean region has been strengthened by analysis of the fragmentary

7.2 million-year-old primate *Graecopithecus* from Greece and Bulgaria. Recently discovered human-like footprints from Crete, analysed in the 2010s, also test the established narrative, as they are approximately 5.7 million years old. There has also been a dating of finds suggesting very early activity in North-West Africa, notably 'Ternifine Man' (*Atlanthropus*), the remains of which were discovered in Algeria in 1954. There was continuity between types of early man, both in terms of breeding and with reference to sites. Thus, in Gibraltar, the same cave systems were used by successive human species, both Neanderthals and early *Homo sapiens*. Evidence of the latter outside Africa has been found for earlier than previously thought, for example in Apidima Cave in Greece about 210,000 years ago, and in Israel about 90–125,000 years ago.

Judging from surviving remains, there was much activity later: there are numerous Palaeolithic and Neolithic sites around the Mediterranean. In particular, Neolithic funeral mounds can be seen across the Mediterranean, for example on the island of Pantelleria. In addition, Neolithic pottery was produced using obsidian from Lipari. The impressive archaeological museum in Ancona, an Italian Adriatic port that deserves more attention than it receives, includes not only Neolithic flint daggers, but also the *Venus of Frasassi*, which was carved in about 26000 BCE.

A barrier in the absence of boats, the early Mediterranean was also a source of protein to those who lived on its shores. Although most histories tend to emphasise land cultivation, early civilisations, not surprisingly, were often shore-based. Fish (both sea and river) and shellfish were very welcome, and the development of harpoons and bows and arrows helped in catching the former as did the adaptation of boats to particular maritime environments, for example *fassonis*, flat-bottomed, reed-built boats used to catch fish in the marshes and lagoons off the Sinis peninsula in Sardinia.

Similar boats were found in other locations, such as the Rhône delta. Protein from fish did not require the long processing needed to digest raw vegetables and fruits. The salt that could be obtained was also very welcome, as were edible marine plants. Early settlements, for example Phylakopi on the Aegean island of Milos, were often for fishing, in its case for tuna.

Around the Mediterranean, the warmer climate after the end of the last ice age in around 10000 BCE provided encouragement and opportunities for wildlife and its human hunters to move north. Rock paintings in Spanish caves show panthers, and those in North-West Africa depict elephants, giraffes and rhinoceroses. It is very clear that the range of animal life in the period was very different to that of today. This was linked to differences in the vegetation but also to human activity. The North African or Barbary lion stretched from Egypt to Morocco, only recently being wiped out. Many had been used for Roman gladiatorial 'games'. The North African and Syrian elephants were probably subspecies of the African and Asian elephants respectively. Both became extinct in Classical times.

Agriculture and Trade

Subsequent to the retreat of the ice, the spread of agriculture was gradually seen across the region. Large-seeded grains such as emmet and einkorn, early forms of wheat, were domesticated by about 9000 BCE in northern Syria. Their cultivation spread and by about 7000 BCE, farming, as opposed to hunter-gathering, had become the leading form of subsistence in South-West Asia. From there, farming spread, including into Egypt and (via Greece) southern Italy, and then to much of the Mediterranean by 5000 BCE. This spread was linked to population growth, the development of fixed settlements, for example with the Bonu

Ighinu culture of Sardinia, and the growth of specialist élites, including craftsmen, warriors, priests and aristocrats. Drawing on Plato, Strabo saw civilisation as resting essentially on the shore:

> Plato conjectures that after the time of the floods three kinds of civilisation were formed: the first, that on the mountain-tops, which was simple and wild, when men were in fear of the waters which still deeply covered the plains; the second, that on the foothills, when men were now gradually taking courage because the plains were beginning to be relieved of the waters; and the third, that in the plains. One might speak equally of a fourth and fifth, or even more, but last of all that on the sea-coast and in the islands, when men had been finally released from all such fear; for the greater or less courage they took in approaching the sea would indicate several different stages of civilisation and manners.

As society became more differentiated and surpluses were produced, so opportunities for trade increased. This trade helped produce networks that spanned the Mediterranean and linked it to other maritime centres. The wealth of some cities depended on trade rather than rulership. These included ports in the eastern Mediterranean, such as Byblos founded in about 3100 BCE, as well as Beirut, Tyre and Sidon, all cities in modern Lebanon that were collectively referred to as Phoenicia. As longer-distance commerce developed, so there were more cross-cultural interactions including trade to ports linking the Mediterranean to Eastern maritime centres, for example Dilmur (Bahrain) and Ra's al-Junayz (Oman). Trade also benefited from government, which provided security, not least by easing transactions through the means of law, coinage and the policing of markets.

Discoveries from Bronze Age Greece

Excavations since 2015 on the Aegean islet of Dhaskalio have revealed what appears to be a pilgrimage site from about 2600 BCE. Evidence of metal workshops and building with marble from the nearby island of Naxos has been found, and the marble would have required numerous voyages.

Egypt

The significance of the Mediterranean, as opposed to say the Baltic, was that major civilisations developed on, or near, its shores. The most prominent was Egypt. In contrast to the soil of much of North Africa, that of the Nile Valley, replenished by silt annually brought down by the river, was fertile, and the link between river and sea was good. Moreover, the centre of power in Egypt was close to the Mediterranean's porous intermediary, the Nile delta. Narmer, the first pharaoh or ruler of Egypt, who unified the country in about 3100 BCE, founded the mud-brick walled city of Memphis as his capital on the west bank of the Nile, south of the delta, not far from modern Cairo.

Egypt was a Nile power, expanding south into Nubia. It was also a Mediterranean one, with control west into Libya and north into the Near East where there were bitter struggles in the fifteenth and thirteenth century BCE over what is now Syria and Israel.

Bronze Age Greece

Very differently, there were civilisations without great territorial power in what is now called Greece. In the Bronze Age (c. 2200–c. 800 BCE), a series of societies using bronze, a more effective material than copper, emerged that traded widely in the Mediterranean, notably the Minoan civilisation of Crete and the Mycenaean culture of the Greek mainland. Palace-based societies emerged on Crete in about 2000 BCE, and the legendary King Minos provided the name for the civilisation. These societies were destroyed, possibly by a volcanic explosion in Santorini and subsequent tsunami on Crete, in about 1600–1627 BCE. The extensive ruins of the palace at Knossos are a testimony to the sophistication of this society and are the major tourist destination on Crete. There are other Minoan sites there accessible to tourists including Gournia and Malia. Santorini is a key Aegean site from this period, while Minoan pottery has been found in the Bronze Age village of Panarea in the Aeolian Islands north of Sicily.

Mycenae, an impressive palace-fortress, which dominated the main road in mainland Greece between the two great ports of Argos and Corinth, had already become prominent in about 1550 BCE, and, as Minoan culture went into decline, it then apparently took over control of Crete and the Cyclades islands. Mycenae, with its Lion Gate and its atmospheric view from the ramparts, has become busier and is best seen off-season. It is approached by cruise tourists as an outing from the port of Nafplio; so also with the theatre of Epidaurus, an impressive site that can be visited, as opposed to just seen.

Mycenaean Greece, a warrior society, is the basis for the story of the *Iliad*, the account by Homer of an expedition by the Greeks, in revenge for the abduction of Helen, to besiege the city of Troy near the Dardanelles, in modern Turkey. Honour was the key spur in Homer, honour in the shape of relations between men as well as control over a woman. Although the gods played the leading role in the story, pushing to the fore those humans who could interpret their messages, nevertheless humans, such as Achilles, made choices, including in response to divine injunctions, and took the consequences.

Mycenaean civilisation collapsed in about 1100 BCE, possibly as a result of invasion, part of a more widespread collapse that affected the eastern Mediterranean including the Egyptian and Hittite empires. The collapse was probably triggered partly by obscure invaders, aggregated sometimes in a misleading fashion as the Sea Peoples, by internal rebellions, and by the resulting crises in international trade and political control. This collapse, and the absence of a recovery, may also be linked to environmental problems, notably drought, and the effect of the entry of iron weapons into the region, which marked the start of the Iron Age around 1100 BCE.

The link between Mycenaean Greece and the Greece that resisted Persia in 490–479 BCE is obscure. There were 'Dark Ages' from about 1100 BCE until the eighth century BCE. Archaeological evidence for this period is limited. Nevertheless, the resumption of writing in the eighth century, as the Greeks adopted and adapted the Phoenician alphabet developed in about 1050 BCE, was linked to the rise of city-states in the Greek world, but also with the Etruscans in northern and central Italy, and with the Phoenician cities.

Phoenicia

City-states, centres of power and trade that dominated their hinterlands, had a significance that depended on their role as intermediaries with other societies. These networks varied with power politics, environmental shifts, such as harbours silting up, and changing trading routes. Cities were industrial sites largely processing and/or producing goods for their inhabitants and the surrounding area. Some, however, were also major industrial centres with their goods exported more widely. Strabo noted of Tyre, a major Phoenician centre and the leading one from the ninth century, 'the great number of dye-works makes the city unpleasant to live in, yet it makes the city rich'. For all cities, trade was essential, and this explained the importance of safeguarding maritime links, by force, negotiation and propitiating the gods: the economy was embedded in social, political and religious practices.

Protection was important due to the prevalence of piracy. To the Greeks, the Phoenicians, who appear in several stories in the *Odyssey*, were abductors and slave traders, as well as skilful sailors and purveyors of high-quality artefacts. In the 'Homeric Hymn to Dionysus', which dates from probably the sixth century BCE, there is a story about what happened when Etruscan pirates seized Dionysus under the impression that he was a king's son.

Ultimately, the most important Phoenician city was Carthage, which was founded, near Tunis, supposedly in 814 BCE and allegedly by Dido. In the western and central Mediterranean, the Phoenician settlements were subsumed by those of Carthage. The Phoenicians sailed further, indeed beyond the Mediterranean into Atlantic waters, both south along the coast of North Africa, although it is unclear how far, and, also, past a major base at Gades (Cádiz), north towards Britain. Along their routes, the Phoenicians founded trading bases or, at least, ports of call. In modern Algeria, there were Carthaginian posts in the bays of Annaba and Algiers, and on the island of Rachgoun, as well as Carthaginian-influenced settlements, as at Tiddis. Tunisian sites included not only Carthage, but also Althiburos and Utica. In Sardinia, there was Cagliari, Bithia, Nora, Monte Sirai, Sant'Antioco and Tharros. Pantelleria was colonised by the Phoenicians in the seventh century. Mdina, long the fortified capital of Malta, is Phoenician in origin, as was Carteia near Gibraltar.

The Phoenician presence across the Mediterranean was more widespread than often appreciated. It was also, correspondingly, more varied. This presence was a matter not only of trade but also of a power that seemingly derived from an ability to appeal to gods, such as Shadrapa, the counterpart to Dionysius, the Greek god of fertility and seafaring. Seafaring temples, such as the sanctuary of Ras il-Wardija on the Maltese island of Gozo, were designed to provide an aid to seafarers. There is no indication that the Phoenicians also used maps to assist their navigation, but they had considerable knowledge of the seas they sailed.

At the same time as similarities and links, the extent to which there was an ethnic self-consciousness as Phoenicians has been questioned. Instead, it has been argued that the category was a Greek one designed to provide cohesion to people who self-identified, instead, more commonly with reference to particular city-states, and who lacked unity, or a homogeneous religion, or consistent religious practices such as the child sacrifice employed in at least some locations. Textual evidence is certainly weak for the Phoenicians, and notably so from them themselves as opposed to hostile comment. The same is true for many ancient Mediterranean societies, for example the Illyrians in modern Croatia, the Etruscans in Tuscany, the Philistines in Israel/Gaza and the Nuragic culture on Sardinia.

On the other hand, archaeological evidence, for the Phoenicians and others, has become more plentiful since the 1980s. Archaeology will continue to fill in many historical and geographical blanks. Moreover the further incorporation of archaeological knowledge, for example of extensive early settlement in Malta and Sardinia, into general historical works will spread our understanding of early Mediterranean history.

Persia and the Greeks

Egypt, the first great Mediterranean empire, had succumbed in 525 BCE to another that was much more far-flung, that of the Persian Achaemenids, which was founded by Cyrus the Great (r. 559–530 BCE). Cyrus had advanced to the Mediterranean, conquering the Greek cities in Ionia on the eastern shores of the Aegean in 546–545 BCE: the besieged cities were surrounded with a rampart, an embankment was built up and the cities were stormed. In 539 BCE, he conquered Phoenicia. In 525, Cambyses II successfully besieged Gaza and defeated Psamtik III of Egypt at Pelusium near modern Port Said, before going on to besiege Memphis and annex Egypt. Cambyses benefited from the assistance of a Greek fleet under Polycrates of Samos: his fleet included triremes: galleys with three rows of oars, as opposed to the earlier penteconters (one row) and biremes (two), the latter of Phoenician origin. It is unclear whether triremes were originally Greek or Phoenician.

Under Darius I the Great (r. 522–486 BCE), the empire expanded further. Darius conquered Thrace in 513 BCE, and then gained control over the Greek cities on the northern shore of the Aegean, and made Macedon a vassal in 492 BCE. Modern continents, in this case Europe, Asia and Africa, did not determine political bodies and their boundaries in the past; and this was certainly so around the shores of the Mediterranean.

The Persians also used their conquests of Phoenicia and Egypt to build up a formidable navy, which they deployed to become a major force in the Aegean. The Greek cities in Ionia rebelled in 499 BCE, only to be crushed in 494 BCE at the battle of Lade, a naval battle off Miletus won by the Persian fleet. The rebellion ended the following year. Darius then decided to punish Athens and Eretria (on the island of Euboea), which had provided support for the rebellion. In 490 BCE, a Persian amphibious force conquered the Cyclades islands and then destroyed Eretria, before landing at Marathon on Attica. A rapid Athenian response, however, led to the defeat of this larger force, the battle becoming crucial to the Athenian sense of their special destiny. Not one to accept failure as anything bar a stage to revenge, Darius planned a return match, but postponed it due to a revolt in Egypt in 486 BCE.

Sparta and Corinth were key players in Greece as, from the 480s BCE, was Athens, which benefited from substantial silver mines, the basis for building up a large fleet. The development of specialised warships reflected the profit to be made from attacking or defending trade. At the 'high spectrum' end, oared vessels could be formidable, and modern full-scale reconstructions of triremes have helped greatly in understanding the options faced by the commanders of that period. The Athenians used the tactic of steering for an opposing trireme, then veering to one side just before colliding bow-on to break off the oars of their opponent, maiming or killing many of the latter's rowers in the process. This attack was followed by grappling and boarding. The success of this tactic led to it being copied by the other Greek and Persian navies. On their prows, galleys had rams, which could be used to devastating effect, but the preferred tactics were to bombard by catapults, arrows and javelins, and then board. Yet, variety was a key element of naval methods: whereas the Greeks and Phoenicians did not pack their galleys with troops and artillery, the Romans did.

The necessity for considerable manpower to propel these vessels by rowing them, however, greatly limited the cruising range of such ships, as they had to stop to take on more water and food. Combined with the absence of living and sleeping quarters, galleys therefore rarely abandoned the coastline and generally beached every night, a practice that exposed them to the risk of coastal rocks. Harbours and anchorages were of particular value if they had water. Thus, the Greek historian Polybius (c. 208–c. 125 BCE) in his *Histories* commented on the Carthaginian establishment of a position at Hercte, a fortified hilltop between Eryx and Palermo in Sicily: 'Hercte commands a harbour very well situated for ships making the voyage from Drepana and Lilybaeum to Italy to put in at, and with an abundant supply of water.' As a consequence of their inability to remain at sea for weeks at a stretch, the projection of naval power required safe ports as bases, without which it was impossible to blockade or besiege opposing ports.

Shipbuilding was part of a wood-based economy also seen in the central use of wood for construction, fuel, furniture and tools such as wagons. Access to and control over woodland therefore were important. Being built of wood, an organic substance which rots, and being dependent on slaves, who could be weakened by a shortage of food and/or illness, ships, however, were vulnerable. Indeed, the Athenian general and historian Thucydides (c. 460–c. 400 BCE), in his *History of the Peloponnesian War*, a key work in the development of Western historical writing, has Nicias seek aid from Athens for the force at Syracuse in these terms:

> Our fleet, as the enemy also have learned, though at first it was in prime condition as regards both the soundness of the ships and the unimpaired condition of the crews, is not so now; the ships are waterlogged, from having been a sea for so long a time already, and the crews have wasted away. For it is not possible to draw the ships up on shore and dry them out, because the fleet of the enemy . . . keeps us in continual expectation that it will sail against us.

Although modern concepts of control of the sea cannot be applied for this period, not least because ships could not remain at sea for long periods, fleets had great value. In combination with troops, they launched amphibious operations aimed at seizing positions, most famously Troy. This strategy brought profit and also limited the possibilities for naval action by opponents. Naval warfare played a key role in the fate of the Classical Mediterranean world, with the two crucial battles being Salamis (480 BCE) and Actium (31 BCE).

Salamis indicated the dependence of the Persian invaders of Greece on naval power. Having provided a bridge across the Hellespont (Dardanelles) in 480 BCE, a massive fleet of about 1200 warships supported the large Persian invading army, not least by escorting the supply ships. In the face of the Persian advance, many Greek states remained neutral or, as with Thessaly and Boeotia, allied with Xerxes. This threw the focus on Athens, the key source of resistance north of the Peloponnese. An attempt to hold the pass at Thermopylae against the Persians advancing south was outflanked thanks to advice on a route supplied by a traitor; and the Greeks withdrew, leaving a small, largely Spartan, rearguard under King Leonidas that fought to the death in the pass.

The Persians pressed on, capturing Athens. As the historian Herodotus noted, it was unclear what advantage the Greeks could derive 'from the walls built across the Isthmus [of Corinth] while the king [Xerxes] was master of the sea'. Instead, it was the 'wooden wall' of their warships that proved vital, an instance in which the ability to understand advice from the oracle proved crucial.

In the face of the larger Persian fleet (about 800 ships from Persia's subjects and allies, to the Greek 300), the Greeks decided to fight the Persians in the narrows of Salamis, rather than in the open water, as they correctly anticipated that this position would lessen the Persians' numerical advantage. The Persians indeed found their ships too tightly packed, and their formation and momentum were further disrupted by a strong swell. The Greeks attacked when the Persians were clearly in difficulties, and their formation was thrown into confusion. Some Persian ships turned back, while others persisted, and this led to further chaos, which the Greeks exploited. The Persians finally retreated, having lost over 200 ships to the Greeks 40, and with the Greeks still in command of their position. The battle had indicated that, as so often, numbers of warships alone were not the key issue.

As a result of defeat at Salamis, Xerxes returned to Anatolia (now Asian Turkey) with the remnants of his navy and part of his army. Yet, again, as is generally the case with the use of naval power, Salamis had not settled the war, as Xerxes left an army in Greece under his son-in-law, Mardonius. This army had to be defeated, as it was, at Plataea in 479 BCE. Moreover, threatened by the Greek fleet, the Persian fleet beached on the slopes of Mount

Mycale on the Anatolian coast opposite Samos. The Persians were then defeated on land and their ships burned, destroying their navy. In the aftermath of these defeats, the Persians not only lost control of the areas they had conquered in 480 BCE, but were also driven from Thrace, the Hellespont and Ionia.

The Greek World

Greek culture is very much seen in terms of the city, both a self-governing community of citizens, the *polis*, and a physical form with fortifications and an *agora* (forum). Cities developed from the ninth century BCE, although their political and governmental structure were often only formalised later. The urban-focus approach, however, underplays the role of the countryside, the sea and, separately, the extent to which, contrary to later idealised notions, Greek states were regularly imperialistic. Athens, Sparta, Corinth and Thebes proved some of the bigger players, although, compared to Persia, their resources and the scale of their imperialism were small. Alliance systems, such as the Delian League (founded in 478 BCE with its treasury on Delos), the rival Peloponnesian League and the Achaean League were, in large part, covers for the domination of one-city states: Athens, Sparta and Corinth respectively.

A common Greekness did not prevent important politico-cultural differences between the cities, and the attempt at a unifying Panhellenism after the Persian wars failed. Indeed, Thucydides described Athens as an economy, state and society transformed and empowered by maritime commercialism and presented its growing strength as a destabilising force in Greece. Its rival, conservative and landlocked Sparta, still agrarian and reliant on slavery, is depicted as unable to respond. Naval power provided Athens with the opportunity to dominate the Aegean, and, during the Peloponnesian War with Sparta (431–404 BCE), the fleet protected Athens's trade routes, notably its vital grain supplies from the Black Sea. In his *Hellenica*, Xenophon, in recording the last stage of the war, noted the significance given to controlling the grain trade: 'Agis, who could see great numbers of grain-ships sailing in to Piraeus, said, that it was useless for his troops to be trying all this long time to shut off the Athenians from access to their land, unless one should occupy also the country from which the grain was coming in by sea.' Fifteen ships were sent to Byzantium but, en route, three 'were destroyed in the Hellespont by the nine Attic ships which were continually on duty there to protect the Athenian merchantmen'. However, Athenian naval power could not be used to defeat Sparta, very much a land power, and, instead, led to the strategic overreach of the large-scale, but unsuccessful, attempt to capture Syracuse in Sicily (415–413 BCE).

The lengthy Peloponnesian War was destructive. For example, Athens was unwilling to accept the essential neutrality of the island of Milos and in 416 BCE invaded, offering the choice of alliance or destruction. Athenian victory over the obdurate inhabitants was followed by the killing of all the adult men and the enslavement of women and children. Athens settled colonists, only for them to be expelled by the Spartans in 405 BCE. Milos was then annexed.

Greek Expansion

The impact of Greece was spread with the establishment of coastal bases from the ninth century BCE. These reflected maritime links. Byzantium, controlling the Bosphorus and, thereby, the route from the Black Sea, was founded in about 660 BCE. Originally a colony of Corinth, Korkyra on Corfu was a major naval power in the fifth century BCE. Nearby Durrës (Durazzo) was established in 627 BCE.

On Sicily, Syracuse was founded in 734 or 733 BCE. Strabo recorded that the Greeks had long been 'so afraid of the bands of Tyrrhenian pirates and the savagery of the barbarians in this region that they would not so much as sail' to Sicily, but that, borne out of his course by the winds, the first Greek settler had found it safe, which had encouraged others to follow. Syracuse was not only to be a commercial and political centre, but also of cultural significance. Its expansionist tyrant (ruler) Hieron I (r. 478–467 BCE) was a noted patron of writers including Aeschylus and Pindar. At Himera, the first Greek settlement on the north coast of Sicily, which was founded in 648 BCE, an imposing Temple of Victory can be seen. It commemorates victory over the Carthaginians in 480 BCE, although, in turn, they destroyed the city in 409 BCE. Scattered around the Mediterranean are the remains of many ruined cities.

There was no comparable pattern of colonialisation into the interior, but the Greeks obtained raw materials, such as grain and amber, and exported their goods, such as metalwork, via their coastal bases. Greece played a major role in the transmission of developments across the Mediterranean, not least in that of writing and numerical systems from Phoenicia via Greece to Italy.

Sicily and southern Italy were a particularly important area of Greek settlement. For example, on Sicily, cruise ships stop at the port of Licata, ancient Phintias, founded by Greeks in 280 BCE, and, from there, tourists take a coach to Agrigento, which was similarly founded in 581 BCE. The *Valle dei Templi* at Agrigento offers a series of temples, the remains of the travails of history including Carthaginian attack. The archaeological museum is particularly impressive, with fifth century BCE finds from the temples. Metaponto and Policoro in the mainland region of Basilicata are less well-known sites of *Magna Graecia*, in large part because Basilicata is not a classic tourist destination, but Pythagoras founded a school at Metaponto. From Sicily, the Greeks spread further. Thus, in the Adriatic, Ancona was founded by settlers from Syracuse in around 387 BCE.

The Origins of Diplomacy

Diplomacy takes its name from the *diploma* (folded letter) of the Greeks. This inheritance included concepts such as neutrality, methods such as arbitration, and practices such as diplomatic immunity for heralds and providing envoys with credentials. The Greek god Hermes (the Roman Mercury) was for a long time to be linked with diplomacy as symbol and protector. The Greeks were also well-practised in the diplomacy of alliances, not least through the creation of leagues. Alongside special envoys, the Greeks used *proxenoi*, who were resident citizens of one city-state who would represent the interests of another city-state. However, diplomacy often consisted of threats.

Macedon

Athens's defeat by Sparta was followed by continued disunity in Greece, Sparta being the major power until it was defeated by Thebes at Leuctra in 371 BCE. In 338 BCE, with defeat at Chaeronea, the autonomy of the divided Greek city-states fell victim to a new imperial power, that of Macedon, to the north of Greece. Like the kingdom of Epirus to the north-west of Greece, Macedon was regarded as somewhat barbarian by many Greeks. This was an aspect of what is a consistent pattern in Mediterranean (and non-Mediterranean) history, namely a carefully granulated sense of difference between areas and people, one in which identity was largely constructed in terms of these differences.

Philip II of Macedon (r. 359–336 BCE), the key figure in the rise of his kingdom, remodelled his army and defeated Athenian attempts to control the coastline of northern Greece (359–354 BCE), following on by invading Thessaly to the south in 353–352

BCE. Victory at Chaeronea was succeeded by Philip creating, in 337 BCE, and then leading, the League of Corinth, which was designed as the basis for the invasion of Persia.

In the event, this was to be carried out, after his assassination in 336 BCE, by his son, Alexander the Great. He invaded Asia Minor in 334 BCE, defeating a larger Persian army at Issus (333 BCE), before turning south, via the Near East, to conquer Persian-ruled Egypt in 332–331 BCE. In the context of his campaigning, it is not helpful to think of Europe or its limits, whether geographical, political or cultural.

The Macedonians demonstrated the strength of land powers against those reliant on navies. In capturing Tyre (332 BCE) and defeating the Athenian fleet off Amorgos (322 BCE), they greatly benefited from their ability to deploy allied and captured naval forces. Amorgos is now a beach resort. Yet, the Macedonian advance on Egypt was overland and there was no prior equivalent to Augustus's naval victory at Actium in 31 BCE.

The empire of Alexander the Great was divided after his death in 323 BCE. His generals established a number of rival kingdoms from his empire, including Macedon (ruled by the Antigonid dynasty), Egypt (the Ptolemies), and Syria, Iraq, Persia and southern Turkey (the Seleucids). There was scant sense of subsequent geographical boundaries. Thus, Seleucus I Nicator, one of Alexander's generals, having gained control of the Asian territories, invaded Thrace in 281 BCE, also hoping to gain Macedon, only to be assassinated. The ruling families remained in control until Roman conquest, but, in the meantime, had their own wars against opponents, both foreign and domestic. Thus, in 166-158 BCE, the Jews of Israel under Judas Maccabeus successfully rebelled against the Seleucids. The Ptolemies had the strongest navy among the successor naval powers and projected their power as a result to Cyprus and the Aegean, notably in the 270s BCE, only to be defeated off Andros in 246 BCE and affected by the rise of Rhodes.

Macedon's dominance of Greece had been rapidly challenged by independent Greek states, some of which created leagues, notably the Aetolian League and, from 280 BCE, the second Achaean League, a rival to Antigonid Macedon that was supported by the Ptolemies of Egypt. Although the contexts and contents were different, this politics prefigured that which was later to be seen in the medieval and early-modern Mediterranean as Christian and Muslim powers both then sought support against rivals from within their own bloc by looking at the other. The capture of Corinth by the Achaean League in 243 BCE greatly weakened Macedon's allies in the Peloponnese. With the *polis* continuing in the Hellenistic world, Athens and Sparta were among the independent states. However, Macedon remained the key power, in part due to rivalries between the Greek powers, for example between the Achaean League and, first, Sparta and, then, the Aetolian League.

The Punic Wars

Further west, the Roman state for long did not place an emphasis on sea power, but, eventually, it had to do so in order to contest the Carthaginian position in the central and western Mediterranean. This initially was a matter of the waters off Sicily, where Carthaginian control was well-established. At the start of the three Punic Wars, in 264 BCE, Rome had no significant naval tradition, but, faced with war against Carthage, it developed successful techniques: in battle, the Romans rammed the Carthaginians, and then used the plank-like corvus, which had a spike that attached it to the enemy ship so that the latter could not escape, to bridge between ships and thus enable rapid boarding of the enemy vessel. War at sea was thereby transformed into land battle afloat, and the Romans used their skills in land fighting.

By 200 BCE, Rome had considerable experience in naval conflict, and had exploited its naval strength to project troops into Sicily, Sardinia, Corsica, Spain and North Africa, and, at the same time, had denied Carthage the ability to unite its disparate territories and campaigns. The Romans had also triumphed over the Carthaginians in major naval battles such as Ecnomus in 256 BCE and the battle of the Aegadian Islands off north-west Sicily (and now a tourist resort) in 241. In the latter, the Roman fleet under Consul Lutatius Catulus inflicted a defeat that led the Carthaginians to end what became the First Punic War and to leave Sicily to Rome. The remains of the sunken ships of both sides have been found by archaeologists and are displayed in museums.

The Punic Wars, which closed with the total destruction of Carthage in 146 BCE, were won convincingly by Rome. In part, this result was a testament to the ability of a traditionally land-based power to wield sea power with sufficient investment and dedication to its development and use. Earlier, Pyrrhus, King of Epirus, in crossing the Adriatic to invade Italy in 280 BCE, demonstrated anew that the sea was not a barrier to expansion or activity. Finally defeated by Rome in 275, he then returned home. At Carthage, tourists visit the extensive remains of the later Roman city, although they can see the remains of the impressive naval yard from which Punic Carthage could simultaneously launch many ships.

The Rise of Rome

The defeat of Carthage left Rome the leading Mediterranean maritime power, enhancing its central position, and also ensured a naval experience that was to be useful in subsequent operations, including Julius Caesar's expeditions against Britain in 55 BCE and 54 BCE. Whereas Athens had failed to capture Syracuse during the Peloponnesian War, the city was successfully besieged by Rome in 213–211 BCE.

Rome developed a considerable capability for force projection by sea, and this capability was closely linked to its ability to deploy effective armies, as with the successful conquest of Greece in the second century BCE. Not all this campaigning was easy. For example, eventual victory over Carthage led Rome to a permanent commitment to North Africa, initially entered into only in order to find allies. The Numidians, a Berber tribe that dominated northern Algeria, became an ally against Carthage in 206 BCE. However, disputes within the Numidian ruling house in the 110s BCE led to war between Jugurtha, one of the claimants, and Rome, which found it difficult to defeat him. It only did so in alliance with his father-in-law, Bocchus I, ruler of Mauretania, a state that covered modern north-west Algeria and northern Morocco. In turn, the rulers of the latter became Roman vassals in 27 BCE, and it was annexed by Rome in 44 CE.

The relationship between sea and land power was also the case with civil war in the Roman Empire, for example Caesar's conflict with Pompey (50–48 BCE), and that between the triumvirate that succeeded Caesar and the conspirators who had killed him (43–42 BCE).

The Siege of Marseille

Founded in about 600 BCE as the Greek colony of *Massalia*, Marseille is France's earliest city. Backing Rome against Carthage, Marseille later made the mistake in 49 BCE of supporting one of Julius Caesar's opponents in the civil war. Refused access, Caesar lay siege to the city, blockaded the port, and then compressed the soil for a mighty ramp on which two towers on rollers were placed. From them, catapults bombarded the city, while battering rams were also used. The towers were burned down in a sally, and inflammables and stones were dropped on the rams, but the inexorable effort that was typical of the Romans won Caesar success. He developed Narbonne as a port in opposition to Marseille.

The defeat of the conspirators who had killed Caesar was followed by the struggle between two members of the victorious triumvirate, Mark Antony and Octavian, later Augustus Caesar. This conflict is best remembered for the battle of Actium (31 BCE), which was fatal for Mark Antony because his naval breakout from blockade on the coast of Greece and flight to Egypt entailed the abandonment of his army there. Augustus's naval capability enabled him to exploit this victory by the conquest of Egypt in 30 BCE, which left Rome as *the* Mediterranean naval power.

This outcome was a key attribute of its geopolitical position and imperial strength. Rome's ability to control the shores and to dominate the sea were linked. The latter came first and very much so in the case of Egypt. The Romans benefited in part from an adaptability that was important to naval development. For example, campaigning against the *Liburni* (Dalmatians) on the Adriatic coast of modern Croatia, the Romans saw that the thin ships of the *Liburni* with their round hulls were good in the island-strewn coastal waters. The Romans developed ships called *liburna* to carry marines, who were intended for ship-to-ship warfare.

The Struggle against Piracy

The rise of an imperial power able to bring peace to the Mediterranean can seem inherently positive, not least thanks to the ending of pirate attacks which, in 69 BCE, had led to the enslavement of much of the population of Delos, after which the island was left nearly uninhabited. Six years earlier, the young Julius Caesar was captured by pirates for ransom, and not in the wilds, but in the Aegean at Pharmakousa between the islands of Samos and Cos.

In 67 BCE, Pompey was given command of the Mediterranean in order to overcome the pirates who were operating at a greater scale and becoming a greater threat, not only to mainland Italian ports, but also to the crucial grain trade from Sicily. Indeed, Pompey's appointment was followed by a fall in the price of grain in Rome. In control of 500 ships, Pompey divided the Mediterranean into thirteen districts and, with coordinated operations, cleared the pirates from west to east. He finally drove the pirates to the coast of Cilicia, a key pirate location, where the pirates surrendered off Coracesium, modern Alanya in Turkey. Pompey's willingness to show clemency to those who surrendered was important to his success.

Conquest and Enslavement

Enslavement and slavery, however, were also integral aspects of Roman power and trade. Capturing the city of New Carthage in Spain in 209 BCE, Scipio Africanus enslaved the men, the strongest as galley slaves, an arduous occupation, while Lucius Aemilius Paulus (Macedonicus) allegedly sold 150,000 of the population of Epirus (north-west Greece) into slavery after his victory over Macedon at Pydna in 168 BCE. Indeed, this war wrecked the cities of Epirus. Pydna was the key event in a series of wars between Macedon and Rome, fought in 214–197 BCE, 171–168 BCE and 150–148 BCE. Greek disunity provided a basis, first, for Roman intervention and then, in 148–146 BCE, for Roman conquest, which was demonstrated most clearly in the brutal sack of captured Corinth in 146 BCE. Ultimately, the establishment of the Roman Empire rested on force. Strabo recorded that the slave market at Delos handled 10,000 slaves a day in the boom years after the conquest of Macedon. Delos was referred to as the 'agora [market] of the Italians'.

The Balearic Islands: A Different History

The early history of the islands is unclear, but there are legends of Greek origins. The Bronze Age has left a large number of stone monuments, notably on Minorca, for example at Naveta d'Es Tudons. Their function is unclear, but it is believed that many were linked to funeral rites. The *Museo de Menorca* in Mahón is of interest for this culture. The Phoenicians ran the islands, and the art they left can be seen in the archaeological museum of Ibiza and the museum there for the Puig des Molins necropolis, which includes Phoenician funerary chambers and a bust of the goddess Tanit. The Balearics passed after the fall of Carthage into the Roman sphere, although the Roman conquest did not occur until 123 BCE. The Romans recruited men from the islands to fight with slings. Conquered by the Vandals in the 460s, and the Byzantines in the 530s, the islands submitted to a Muslim fleet in 707, but were sacked by Vikings in the mid-ninth century. The use of the islands for piracy led the Emirate of Córdoba to take direct control in 902. An independent *ta'ifa* (kingdom) from 1050, the islands were contested by the Almoravids and Almohads in the twelfth century, and an Italian–Catalan Crusade of 1113–15 had scant impact. In 1229–35, however, Aragonese forces conquered the islands. In the aftermath, churches were built, for example the cathedrals at Ibiza and Palma and the monastery of *Nuestra Señora de Lluc* on Majorca. On Majorca, there are a variety of architectural styles in the capital, Palma, but relatively few Muslim remains.

3. The United Mediterranean: The World of Rome, 30 BCE–630 CE

It happened, as he passed by the bay of Puteoli, certain passengers and soldiers out of a ship of Alexandria which was then newly arrived, decked also with garlands and burning frankincense, had heaped upon him all good and fortunate words, chanting his singular praises in these terms: that by him they lived, by him they sailed, by him they enjoyed their freedom and all the riches they had. At which he took great contentment and was cheered at the heart.

This episode from 14 CE, recorded in Suetonius's *Augustus*, was a fitting send-off as the Emperor died a few days later. There was no mention of the repression that was also a tendency of Augustus.

The Mediterranean was very much a known world in Ptolemy's *Geography*, a gazetteer produced by a Greek subject of the Roman Empire who lived in Alexandria in the second quarter of the second century CE. His knowledge, however, diminished beyond the boundaries of the empire and the routes of its trade. What is striking with his career, and also with that of the most famous thinker of the late Classical world, St Augustine (354–430 BCE), Bishop of Hippo from 396, is that both men were based in North Africa, Hippo being a maritime Phoenician city that became a Roman *colonia*, and which is part of the modern Algerian city of Annaba.

The history of the Mediterranean is generally told from the perspective of its northern shore. However, in Antiquity, the southern was long more important, in the shape of Egypt, or at least as significant when Carthage competed with Rome. Even when Rome ran North Africa, the southern shore was of major consequence.

Roman North Africa

Extensive archaeological remains include Leptis Magna (in modern-day Libya), an earlier city the Romans greatly expanded in 192–211 CE, Thysdrus and Carthage (both Tunisia), which they rebuilt. At Tipaza near Algiers, a site probably founded by the Phoenicians, the Roman ruins include an oval-shaped amphitheatre as well as the baths, a theatre, cemeteries and basilicas. At Djémila, a site reached from Béjaïa, the Roman port Saldae, there is an impressive Arch of Caracalla, a forum and temples, as well as striking mosaics in the museum. At Hippo, there is a large forum, a baths, mosaics from former villas now in the Basilica of Peace, and a museum containing mosaics including of the capture of lions and leopards for the circus. Large numbers of North African lions were captured and shipped to Rome.

North Africa had long been a conduit, both southwards to the Sahara and, through it, to the *sahel* region to the south, and, separately, northwards across the Mediterranean. This link continued while the Roman and then the Byzantine (Eastern Roman) empires occupied North Africa. The eventual outcome of the religious warfare that accompanied the Islamic conquest of the seventh century left North Africa in Islamic hands and, in contrast, Southern Europe under Christian control, changing the Mediterranean from a route of cultural transmission into a barrier. That, however, was no guide at all to the earlier situation.

Roman rule certainly brought peace to the Mediterranean and the wider region. Piracy had been a major problem, but Pompey made his name by crushing it. Subsequently, piracy overlapped with politics during the Roman civil wars, with his son Sextus Pompey playing a major role, one that leaves an echo in Shakespeare's play *Antony and Cleopatra*. Sextus occupied Sicily, cutting off the grain supply to Rome. However, Sextus was eventually crushed as a result of naval defeats off Sicily at Mylae and Naulochus in 36 BCE. As a result, the Romans were able to use the Mediterranean as a key trade system and with singularly low protection costs. Fleets based at Misenum near Naples and at Ravenna, supported by smaller squadrons around the empire including at Alexandria, Fréjus in France, and Seleucia in Syria, kept the peace. They were not much needed as the Roman Empire had made shipping safe. The unique circumstance of having all the Mediterranean under the same military and fiscal authority made large-scale overseas trade possible, whether of Egyptian wheat, North African pottery, Italian wine or Spanish *garum*, the fish sauce beloved by the Romans.

Grain from Egypt, Tunisia and Sicily was very necessary to feed the large population of Rome, and thus to preserve political stability there. Suetonius recorded of Augustus that to make Egypt 'more fruitful and better adapted to supply the city [Rome] with grain, he set his soldiers at work cleaning out all the canals into which the Nile overflows, which in the course of many years had become choked with mud'. Strabo described Sicily as 'the storehouse of Rome', and focused on the grain, cattle and hides it produced. The resources from the empire were obtained with relatively little provided in return, bar a security that in practice entailed coercion.

Fishing was another major source of food. The Mediterranean was not overfished, as it is now, nor affected by pollution.

Important Mediterranean fish included swordfish and tuna. Although it has been made industrial in some countries, notably Spain, fishing as a way of life leaves many sites for tourists, such as the picturesque fishing village at Paphos in Cyprus. In the main market at Thessaloniki in Greece, I can recall seeing a fish being cut up on a block with cigarette ash dropping on it from the fisherman. At Cetara near Amalfi in Italy, there has been a revival of the production of an anchovy essence thought to be *garum*. The village has an annual tuna festival and another for anchovy, which is fished at night from small boats equipped with lamps.

Mediterranean trade heavily rested on slaves, not only in harbours and ships, but also in regions producing goods to move to Rome, such as grain, wine and oil from Tunisia, grain from Sicily and Sardinia, and wine and olive oil from southern Spain, where there were large-scale estates. Yet, slavery covered many occupations, for example shepherds in Apulia. Alongside those enslaved through debt and judicial decision, and because they were the children of slaves, slaves were imported into the empire from across the Sahara and down the Nile and the Red Sea, into the North African part of the empire, and from southern Russia via the Black Sea. Slaves were also brought in from Germany and other lands to the north of the empire, largely through conflict. This was a bleaker aspect of Rome's new Mediterranean world, with the bleakness accentuated with the scarcity of the legal protections for slaves.

More commonly, control was in the form of taxation, conscription, justice, the imposition of a coinage as well as weights and measures, and the gathering of information on population and the land, by means of the census and land surveying. Rural areas were under city-based government. Indeed, Roman civilisation was based on an urban culture and forms of organisation. Many cities began as military bases or veterans' colonies, and therefore generally were inland, but port-cities were also significant.

In the eastern Mediterranean, some, such as Alexandria, were continuations of major pre-Roman cities. Spas were another significant reason for towns, as with Termini Imerese to the east of Palermo. The remains of an amphitheatre can be seen there. Roman buildings reflected an understanding of the arch and the vault. Vaulted brickwork was followed by the dome, notably with the Pantheon in Rome.

New Discoveries

The digging of Thessaloniki's new underground railway system since 2006 has uncovered about 300,000 archaeological artefacts, many related to Aphrodite, goddess of love. A key commercial centre, the city provided refuge for sailors and visitors, offering baths to brothels. In 2018, a 15-metre long, nearly 3-metre tall fountain from about 500 BCE was found. Other findings include fourth-century CE mosaics showing Aphrodite on a couch before a young Eros.

Less familiar Roman sites visited by cruises include Pula on the tip of the Istrian peninsula in Croatia. As Polensium, this city was built in the first century CE, and has a well-preserved arena designed to seat 20,000 to watch gladiatorial contests. Nearby Veliki Brijun in Croatia's Brijuni Islands, which is visited by small cruise ships, has a first-century CE Roman villa. Other Mediterranean coastal villas of note include the *Villa Roma Antiquarium* in Minori, east of Amalfi. Butrint in Albania, a UNESCO World Heritage site, is the remains of Roman Bouthroton, originally a Greek city, but much expanded before being hit hard by an earthquake in the third century CE. At Ancona, there is Trajan's Arch and the remains of an amphitheatre.

The distribution of Roman sites varies greatly. Thus, there are far more in wealthy Sicily than in Sardinia and Corsica combined. Sicily saw much cultivation, whereas Sardinia and Corsica were more pastoral. Nevertheless, in Cagliari in Sardinia, there are the remains of villas and a second-century CE amphitheatre, albeit one that suffered from the removal of stones in order to build churches.

The open nature of the Roman élite helped both the incorporation of territories and the response to social mobility. As a result, areas where there were relatively few cities, for example most of modern Algeria and Morocco, were less Romanised than Tunisia and eastern Algeria. Indeed, the Berbers proved rebellious from the second century CE, challenging the security of the local cities. Icosium (Algiers) was captured by the Berbers in 371.

When administration was divided, and a capital for the Eastern Empire established at Constantinople (and not, as originally considered, Troy), then grain movements from Egypt were again crucial in order to feed the population. The movement of grain helped explain the significance of Alexandria, Carthage and Rome's port, Ostia, and the major granaries found at the ports. At Ostia, construction of the *Grandi Horrea* in the first quarter of the first century CE was followed by subsequent modifications in response to public concern about the grain supply. The grain was unloaded from seagoing vessels, and then eventually transferred to river vessels. The storage capacity has been estimated at 254,000–375,000 *modii*, a *modius* being a unit of dry volume 8.8 litres, roughly equivalent to a peck. Alongside these and other journeys across the Mediterranean, there were also what Strabo called coasting voyages. They posed very different navigational challenges.

Ports were the foci of roads such as the Via Appia from Rome to Brindisi, where a Roman column survives to mark the end. Its pair was given to the town of Lecce in 1666 to thank the patron saint, Oronzo, for relieving Brindisi from the plague.

Ephesus

A key tourist site on Turkey's Aegean coast, Ephesus was built in the tenth century BCE by Greek settlers. Readily reached by cruise tourists via the port of Kuşadası, Ephesus had one of the Seven Wonders of the Ancient World in the shape of the temple of Artemis, the goddess of forests and hills who was worshipped across ancient Greece, including at Delos. The Ephesus temple contained a distinctive statue of Artemis with many breasts. The mysteries or rites of Artemis were observed there from the end of the fourth century BCE being supported by Lysimachus, one of those competing to succeed Alexander the Great. Political power and religious observance were closely aligned. By the mid-first century CE, the imperial cult was integrated into that of Artemis. As with much of the Roman Empire, the cult reached a highpoint in the second century, before falling victim in the third to a terrible earthquake and an invasion by Goths in 262. These disasters led to a collapse of confidence on the part of worshippers, which may have encouraged a move toward Christianity.

Ephesus holds a series of impressive remains, notably the Library of Celsus with its striking facade and the theatre, and it is a major Christian site where tourists visit the House of the Virgin Mary. At a distance from the major Classical sites, the Basilica of St John is less frequently visited, and is therefore particularly pleasant to tour. If you want to leave your tour of the major sites, taxis will readily take you to the basilica and then back to Kuşadası.

Ideas were also moved across the Mediterranean. Religious practices and ideas spread, not least emperor worship, Judaism, the worship of Mithras and Christianity. Although many individuals proved capable of adopting beliefs and practices from different religions, Christianity spread rapidly. It benefited from widespread links within the Mediterranean world, not least the extent of Hellenisation. Christianity became the official religion of the empire in the fourth century CE. Constantine I defeated his rival Maxentius at the battle of the Milvian Bridge in Rome in 312 and converted to Christianity. Constantine went on to become sole ruler from 324 until his death in 337, being baptised just before his death. A new capital, Constantinople (modern Istanbul), had been founded in 330 as a Christian city.

The monotheism it focused was a total rejection of the earlier religious practice of the empire, and, with the closing of temples and ban on sacrifices, greatly disrupted ideas of continuity. Divisiveness between monotheists and polytheists was accentuated with the adoption of Christianity. At the same time, at the individual level, there was also a degree of creative amalgamation and acculturation in terms of pre-existing local practices.

Alongside the move toward monotheism, there was also bitter division within Christianity, and over everything from doctrine to practice and organisation. As later with Islam, adaptations to earlier practices were a cause of dispute. Schisms included the Donatist one in North Africa in the fourth and fifth centuries; a schism that led to two rival churches, with Augustine of Hippo a critic of the Donatists and a supporter of Papal authority.

The spread of Christianity saw the construction of churches, often by changes to previous religious sites, as in Ancona where the cathedral was built on the site of a pagan temple. Many of these churches were subsequently reworked, while cemeteries were built over. Nevertheless, there are remains, for example the *Basilica di San Saturnino* in Cagliari. Christian sites and architecture drew on a number of traditions, both pre-Christian and Christian. This pattern also affected non-religious architecture, for instance through the use of Jerusalem as a device and vision in palace design and decoration, as in Constantinople and Ravenna.

Changing Functions

Visiting Thessaloniki on an Aegean cruise, I found the Rotunda of St George shut for restoration work after the 1978 earthquake. A helpful restorer granted me access. Built in about 306 CE, as a temple of Zeus or as the emperor's mausoleum, it was reconfigured in the fifth century into a church dedicated to the Archangels and subsequently embellished with mosaics, which were extended in the ninth century after an earthquake. Converted into a mosque under Turkish rule, the rotunda survives as a historic site. Alive with colour, the Byzantine mosaics are amazing.

In contrast to that of Christianity, a sinister spread was that of disease, which readily moved along Mediterranean trade routes. Plague swept through the empire in the 160s and 170s, as did a haemorrhagic fever epidemic in the third century. The very large crowded cities, notably Alexandria, Constantinople and Rome, were especially susceptible to disease and relied on a vulnerable food chain, while the empire's exposure to far-flung networks of trade, travel and migration exposed it to greater risks.

These problems were both those of activity and prosperity, and yet also major challenges to them. This difficult situation, which testified to the environmental strains of the period, was greatly exacerbated by the need to confront 'barbarian' attacks. Having long been an issue, these became more serious in the late fourth century. This situation challenged the legitimacy of emperors, which to a great extent was based on their ability to win military success.

The crisis began far from the Mediterranean, but it hit the latter hard as 'barbarian' groups, notably the Visigoths, moved to its shores in search of wealthy targets, especially cities. Led by

Alaric, they sacked Rome in 410 after the city was starved into submission. That was the most spectacular episode in what became a far more widespread crisis. The Visigoths moved on to establish themselves in Spain and southern France, but the Ostrogoths and, then, the Huns followed them into Italy. Meanwhile, the Vandals, having been defeated in Spain by the Visigoths, crossed into North Africa in 429. There, they overthrew the Roman world, capturing both Hippo (432) and Carthage (439), and depriving Rome of a key source of grain. Having suggested that the Vandal conquest had an ecclesiological dimension, St Augustine died in 430 during the lengthy siege of Hippo.

The Vandals, who had rapidly acquired proficiency at sea, also established control of the major islands of the western Mediterranean, including the Balearics, Sardinia, Corsica and western Sicily, and sacked Rome in 455. In 468, at the battle of Cape Bon, the Vandals, using fireships, defeated a large-scale Roman (both Western and Byzantine) attempt to defeat them in their base at Carthage. This failure was crucial to the fall of the Western Roman Empire, as it was the last chance to regain control over North African grain sources and to use Byzantine support.

Linked to the invasions, political instability became more serious within the empire. With civil conflict more acute, links between provinces declined, and the empire became less able to raise the taxation to defend itself against further incursions. In 476, Romulus Augustulus, the last Roman Emperor in the West, was deposed by Odoacer. From Pannonia and of Germanic descent, Odoacer was the commander of the German troops in Roman service and led the revolt that overthrew Romulus. Ostensibly a vassal of the Byzantine Empire, Odoacer conquered Dalmatia (coastal Croatia) in the early 480s, but was overthrown by the Ostrogoth leader, Theoderic, who had been encouraged to act by the Byzantine Emperor Zeno. Theoderic invaded Italy in 489, drove Odoacer to take refugee in Ravenna in 490, and, at a supposed reconciliation banquet in 493, killed him himself.

Theodoric ruled Italy until 526, as part of an empire that eventually included the Ostrogothic and Visigothic lands and, for a while, hegemony over the Vandals and Burgundians. This was presented by favourable writers as peaceful and prosperous. However, there are indications of considerable instability and violence, which would have contributed to the serious economic problems of the period.

In the East, the Roman (or Byzantine as it came to be called) Empire survived, and ruled the Mediterranean's shores from Greece round to Egypt inclusive. Constantinople itself may have had a population of as much as half a million by the fifth century. Visually, there was much continuity, in part because early Byzantine architecture substantially continued Classical models with its builders and their techniques. The change in this respect did not occur until after a period of transition in the seventh to ninth centuries.

Between 533 and 555, under the Emperor Justinian (r. 527–65) and his highly talented general Belisarius, and with their army benefiting from organisational reforms, the Byzantines reconquered much of the western and central Mediterranean: Tunisia, eastern Algeria, Sardinia, Sicily, Corsica, part of Italy including Naples, the Balearic Islands, and the south coast of Spain, were all brought under control. In addition, part of Dalmatia was reconquered in 535. Defeated in North Africa in 533–4, the Vandals surrendered and were expelled by the victors or absorbed into the Byzantine army. In 551, the Byzantine navy defeated that of the Ostrogoths at Sena Gallica in the Adriatic.

Military control brought political consequences. From 537 to 752, Byzantium appointed the Popes, or at least approved the choice. Byzantine influence can be seen most famously at Ravenna. However, there are other important and attractive sites, such as Poreč on the Istrian coast in modern Croatia: the sixth-century Euphrasian Basilica, a World Heritage site visited on small-ship cruises, is superb for its Byzantine art. Greek influence is readily apparent in parts of south-eastern Italy, for example the region of the Salentino centred on the town of Galatina and the Byzantine frescoes of the church of *Santa Maria del Casale* near Brindisi. Many later churches, for example the cathedral of Bari, are built atop earlier Byzantine ones. A Greek dialect is still spoken in part of Apulia.

Success, nevertheless, proved short-lived, as Byzantium was also under pressure from Avar, Hun and Persian attacks. Moreover, the achievements in the western and central Mediterranean were challenged by the Lombard invasion of Italy in 568, while the Visigoths drove the Byzantines from Spain by 624. Weakened by the plague, and in the bitter and lengthy conflict with the Sassanians of Persia, Byzantium could not devote sufficient resources to preserve its new position in the western Mediterranean. Nevertheless, the continued presence of Byzantium in the central Mediterranean helped ensure that the latter remained a frontier region irrespective of what became the border between Islam and Christendom. That situation underlined and sustained political fragmentation and overlapping identities in the region, and notably in Italy and Dalmatia.

The Byzantine revival under Justinian was impressive and, although short-lived at this scale, some of the gains were retained until the eleventh century. Even under Justinian, the unity of sea had been lost, and was never to be regained in the form of one territorial ruler. Yet, that did not prevent would-be great emperors of the future attempting to control the Mediterranean, nor, indeed, the more subtle imperiums of religion and trade.

4. The Divided Mediterranean 630–1453

The Book of Curiosities of the Sciences, and Marvels for the Eyes, produced between 1020 and 1050 by a Muslim scholar living in Cairo, probably for the Fatimid Caliph, contain maps that have recently been published in *Lost Maps of the Caliphs*. They cover the Mediterranean and include the earliest surviving maps of Cyprus and Sicily, and one of the no-longer extant trading city of Tinnis in the Nile Delta. A naval perspective is to the fore, as in the interest of the extent to which ports had a fort and the capacity to shelter a fleet. The Mediterranean also took a crucial place in the world map produced in the mid-twelfth century by al-Idrisi for King Roger II of Sicily. Both the commission and the map captured not only the place of Sicily as a cultural mixing point, but also the religious, political and commercial significance of the Mediterranean lands for both Christendom and Islam. Cairo and Palermo were key cultural and intellectual sites in a wider world of multifaceted interaction.

The millennium from the end of the Western Roman Empire in 476 to that of the Eastern in 1453 can readily be seen in terms of conflict, but only if that is not regarded as the sole theme. Conflict, notably between Persia and Byzantium, was already large scale prior to the foundation of Islam, but the nature and scale of conflict were certainly accentuated by the ideology and practice of early Islam, which saw rapid expansion within, and then from, Arabia. Muhammad's forces had captured Mecca in 630. South-western Asia and Egypt followed by 642. The latter led first to North Africa, where Tripoli fell in 647 and Carthage in 697, and then, in 711, to the invasion of Spain. Most of Spain and

Portugal rapidly fell, and this was followed by an Arab advance into southern France, where Narbonne was captured in 719, being held until taken by the Franks in 759.

With the Arabs in the direction of Anatolia essentially held at the Tarsus Mountains, Constantinople itself was besieged by amphibious forces in 674–8 and 717–18. They were aiming to deliver what would have been knockout blows. However, the defenders, with their strong walls, were helped by 'Greek fire', a combustible compound emitted by a flame-throwing weapon. This proved particularly effective against ships.

The Arabs indeed were not limited to land. Benefiting, as the Ottoman Turks were later to do, from their takeover of maritime territories, notably Phoenicia and Egypt, they were able to conquer Cyprus in 649, and to raid Rhodes and Crete in 654, and Sicily and Sardinia in 720. The 654 raids indicated that the Aegean was not safe, and those of 720 the same for the western Mediterranean. These islands proved precarious 'middle grounds' between Christendom and Islam.

Arab attacks and successful expansionism challenged the very survival of Byzantium, as well as its view of neighbours as barbarians, a view similar to that held by China. Byzantium sought to impress these neighbours with ceremonial and display, and, in doing so, to bind them within a subordinate psychological relationship in which they accepted the hierarchical notions of Byzantium. Yet, the Caliph claimed an authority that matched Byzantine pretensions. Also following a realist policy, creating a ministry responsible for foreign affairs and containing professional negotiators, Byzantium pursued a hard-headed, well-informed, and practical, diplomacy towards its neighbours. This diplomacy was largely based on the divide-and-rule principle, notably in Asia Minor, but also in the Balkans and, less successfully, Italy.

Byzantium's strong and deep identification with the Church in the Greek world was a key element of its resilience and strength.

Moreover, its army provided provincial élites with a way to link themselves to the imperial government. In contrast, in Italy and North Africa, the Church did not play this role for Byzantine authority and power, while the army was smaller.

The loss of territories to Arab conquest was followed by cultural consolidation by Islam. There was certainly a measure of continuity. Thus, for example, the Arab conquerors of Egypt made use of Byzantine administrative methods in order to consolidate their rule in the seventh and eighth centuries. Nevertheless, there was a fundamental cultural change linked to what was to be a permanent retreat for Christendom: from the Near East and North Africa. There was also the loss to the Christian world of Classical, notably Greek, information and ideas. Instead, the Islamic world acted as the prime source of knowledge for the Mediterranean, not least with information, ideas and methods flooding back from far-flung lands through conquests, trade and travel. The routes from the Mediterranean to the Orient, by both land and sea, now went via the Islamic world.

The rapid expansion of Islam meant that a Europe initially defined for Arabs as solely Byzantium became more extensive and complex. For a while, the need by the Islamic world to respond to this complexity was limited, as raiding and/ or conquest were to the fore. However, both taking control of Christian societies where conversion to Islam was often limited, and reaching buffers of expansion, however transient, forced upon Islam a more varied reaction to Christendom. This reaction included an understanding of its geography, society, politics and history, for example of Christian Spain. That was a major contact zone as, subsequently, although for a shorter period, was Sicily. Frontier zones saw pragmatic opportunities for links as well as conflict.

From the European perspective, a new world order appeared in prospect as a result of Muslim expansion, but the Muslim sphere was itself increasingly fractured by rebellions and civil wars. Indeed, the political unity of Islam ended in the mid-eighth century. Baghdad, the capital of the Abbasid caliphate from 762, remained a key centre until a devastating Mongol conquest in 1258. However, this division brought independent Islamic rulers to the Mediterranean world. First was the Umayyad Emirate of Córdoba, the capital of *al-Anda-lus* (Andalusia) in southern Spain from 756. Then came the Fatimids: having established a caliphate in Tunis in 910, they conquered Egypt in 969. The Fatimids were Shi'ites, so that Islamic heterodoxy was part of the mix.

These, and other, divisions led to repeated conflict. Thus, in the second half of the eleventh century, the Seljuk Turks defeated the Abbasids and the Christians of Byzantium, while the Fatimids competed with the Seljuks for control over the Holy Land. The major Seljuk victory over the Byzantines at Manzikert (modern Malazgirt) in eastern Turkey in 1071, with the capture of Emperor Romanos IV, was followed by their conquest of most of Anatolia (Asian Turkey) as the Byzantine army disintegrated. Separately, in the 1090s, Muslim *al-Andalus* was conquered by the Almoravids, Berber warriors from Morocco, who, in the 1140s, were brought down by another Berber movement, that of the Almohads. They were overthrown in the 1200s by yet another North African insurgent movement, that of the Marinids.

Such struggles between Muslim powers, and their counterparts between the Christian powers, interacted with those between Christendom and Islam. There was longstanding conflict in Spain between Christian and Muslim rulers. Separately, the islands of the Mediterranean, notably Crete, Cyprus, Sicily, Sardinia and the Balearic Islands, were particular foci of competition. The Balearics were conquered by the Arabs in 798, Malta in 824 and Crete in 827. Conquered for Islam in 827–965, Sicily was reconquered by Christians by 1091. In 1015, Pisa and Genoa intervened to thwart an Arab invasion of Sardinia.

The Arab Conquest of Sicily

A struggle within Sicily in 826–7 resulted in Arab intervention. On a pattern familiar from the Roman Empire, Euphemius, a Byzantine naval commander, rebelled against rule from Constantinople and proclaimed himself emperor. Resistance by some of the district governors led him to call on Arab help. The Arabs then took over. Palermo, which they captured in 831, was made their capital, in place of Syracuse, the Byzantine capital, which did not fall to the Arabs until 878. Taormina fell in 902 and the last Byzantine position, near Messina, in 965. The Arabs brought citrus fruit, rice and mulberries to Sicily, and used slaves to cultivate sugar cane there. Large-scale Arab immigration from North Africa and Spain created a new social and political élite, but the immigrants soon saw themselves as Sicilian, and ready to resist direction from North Africa. Many of the indigenous inhabitants converted to Islam, and, while elements of Byzantine culture survived, this was as part of a society that was Islamic and used Arabic. The late tenth century was a period of prosperity and autonomy. However, ethnic difficulties, notably between Arabs and Berbers, and between new immigrants and others, as well as political fragmentation in the eleventh century, prepared the way for successful Norman intervention.

The Byzantines had already regained the initiative from the Muslims in the tenth century. Thanks to a major effort, Crete was recaptured in 960–1 after expeditions in 911 and 949 had failed. In a formidable logistical achievement, the Byzantine fleet, which included purpose-built ships for horse transport, was able to carry an expeditionary force, and then keep it supplied while the capital Candia (Heraklion) was besieged over the winter. In Sicily, the Byzantines used the Normans to assist in the reconquest, notably during the capture of Syracuse in 1086. They were then, however, ejected by the Normans, who had conquered it by 1093.

A Norman World

The Norman takeover of Sicily and southern Italy was a triumph for entrepreneurial warriordom over the weak and divided states of the region. Norman mercenaries conquered the Lombard principalities of southern Italy and also Muslim Sicily, taking Capua (1062), Amalfi (1073) and Naples (1139). The Norman capital was in Palermo. Active patrons of the arts and sciences, the Normans left a distinctive style of architecture that drew on Arab influences. They also sought to expand into North Africa in the mid-twelfth century but, with important individual exceptions, the Norman kingdom did not show a comparable consistent interest in the Holy Land.

Bitter rivalry between Islam and Christendom took a commercial (as well as political and military) form with piracy and slave raiding; with seaborne raiders being especially important. Arriving at a distance by sea ensured penetration far from the frontier zone on land, as well as speed, surprise and the easy removal of gains. Whereas the Viking presence in the Mediterranean was episodic, this was very much not the case with the Arabs. From *Fraxinetum* (La Garde-Freinet) in Provence from 890 to 972, the Arabs raided southern France, notably the Rhône valley and northern Italy. The raiders had profited from the divisions in Provencal society, but kidnapping in 972 the Abbot of Cluny, the most important monastery in Francia, proved an action too far and led to a focus on destroying the base. Although the ruin that overlooks La Garde-Freinet is thought to be the remains of the Arab fortress, today the settlement is a quiet and breezy relief from the busy Provencal coast to the south. Similarly, the Adriatic was raided from the base at Bari between 841 and 871. Rome itself was raided from Tunis in 846.

Raiding was important to the economy of frontier regions, with the large numbers of slaves seized mostly being sold on to the slave marts providing for more settled Islamic societies, for example Alexandria for Egypt. Towns on the barren coast of North Africa, such as 'New Hippo' (Annaba), focused on privateering, which brought wealth and status.

In this context, it was difficult to establish friendly relations across the Mediterranean, but shared animosity by Christians and Muslims toward particular rulers of either religion played a role in creating transactional or opportunistic cooperation, as in Spain, for example with El Cid. Rivalries within Christendom between Byzantium and the Western princes who looked to the Pope in Rome were a long-lasting feature.

The Papacy relied on these princes, Adrian I appealing for the support of Charlemagne I (r. 768–814), ruler of the Franks, against the Lombards, 'barbarian' invaders whom he subjugated in northern Italy in 774. Charlemagne also subjugated the Lombard Duchy of Benevento in southern Italy in 787, and competed with Byzantium in Italy and for control of Dalmatia (Croatia). For him, there were no limits between 'France' and other dominions, and no ready division of the Mediterranean world. Helping Leo III against rebellion in Rome in 799, Charlemagne was crowned Emperor of the Romans by the Pope on Christmas Day 800, setting up two separate empires, each claiming the Roman inheritance. Charlemagne's interest in Jerusalem reflected his eschatological ideas, as well as his sense that the *Romanitas* of the Christian-imperial tradition now linked

Jerusalem to his capital at Aachen. This interest was to be taken forward with later writers claiming (falsely) that Charlemagne had travelled to Jerusalem, and had received jurisdiction over the city, and the submission of the Caliph. These ideas proved part of the background to later Crusading ideology.

There were also more specific political differences between Charlemagne and Byzantium in Italy, both for example claiming the Duchy of Venice. The Venetians looked more favourably on Byzantium: from its foundation, Venice was under Byzantium, which was why it was ruled by a doge, or duke, which was a Byzantine official. Total independence was reached step by step according to the weakening of Byzantine power. Byzantium, however, retained an important territorial presence in Italy into the eleventh century when it was displaced by the Normans.

Alongside conflict, the possibilities of profit encouraged links between Christendom and Islam. This, however, was in a commercial context that had shrunk since Roman days, not only due to war but also to economic decline and epidemic disease, notably the bubonic plague of the 540s. More specifically in coastal areas, there was the spread of malaria, in part because the irrigation and drainage systems of Roman times were neglected. Combined with a decline in the demand for food, due to the major fall in population, and the resulting lower availability of labour, there was a move from the intensive cultivation of coastal lowlands toward keeping animals on inland, upland pastures far from the attacks of coastal raiders.

More generally, the instability of the fifth and sixth centuries led to a marked sense of crisis, and certainly to a feeling of decline from the world of Western Roman Christendom. The written record is limited, and notably so for non-clerical material, while the uneven spread of the archaeological evidence reflects in part the varied pattern of excavation and fieldwork activity. It is far from clear how much continuity or discontinuity should be stressed between the Roman and post-Roman period. Moreover, it is difficult to distinguish between the consequences of the end of imperial Roman rule, and, on the other hand, that of the invaders who brought Germanisation or, in the Mediterranean, the later Arab attacks. The nature and extent of the damage represented by what can be termed transformation is open to discussion. However, in the Mediterranean, there were Germanic invasions in the late fourth and fifth centuries, Arab ones, and attacks by other invaders such as the Lombards, and these all involved damaging conflict and disruption.

Nevertheless, there is considerable potential in a long-term approach that understands the Dark Ages in pre-Roman terms. This approach involves viewing the earlier Romanisation as overlaying deeper rhythms of continuity in settlement, land use and trade. The interplay between deep structures and issues, and more limited episodes, is a matter of scholarly debate for this and other periods. Another variable would be to see Hellenism as lasting not only into the Roman Empire but, transformed by Christianity, into the Eastern Roman Empire. A different aspect of continuity can be found in accounts of Christianisation that downplay abrupt change and top-down direction, and, instead, emphasise, as for example in Egypt, a long process in which existing patterns of worship and belief were supplemented as well as adapted, with Christians practising as a consequence a religion of amalgamation, as much conscious as not.

At the same time as undoubted crisis and specific crises in the Mediterranean world, there were both continuity and areas of new development. The latter, both continuity and new development, were aspects of the significant transition seen in these centuries, and ones that qualify (without destroying) the view that the rise of Islam decisively disrupted Mediterranean unity. Instead, the impact of the conquests linked to the rise of Islam and of the subsequent warfare can be qualified by reference to intellectual parallels and overlaps, not least the role across the Mediterranean as a whole of Aristotelian philosophy, and the extent to which the monotheistic religions influenced each other. There was also a shared continuity with aspects of the Roman inheritance.

In addition, commerce continued. Trade across the Mediterranean no longer focused on the supply of grain to the major cities, but new causes and patterns of commerce developed. A major trade was that of slaves from Christian Europe to the Muslim world, in return for which gold and silver coins were obtained alongside spices, drugs and papyrus. From the late sixth to the eighth centuries, Eastern, not Western, ships dominated Mediterranean trade, which increased greatly in scale in the eighth and ninth centuries. At the same time, most trade was regional, for example, grain from Sicily to North Africa, rather than at the level of the Mediterranean as a whole. This was part of the more persistent interdependencies of local, regional and wider-ranging aspects of the Mediterranean economy.

Italy itself was no longer the centre of a mighty empire, but some cities survived there, notably Rome, Milan, Naples and Ravenna. Trade certainly faced far more disruption than when under the protection of the Roman Empire, but it still revived. Moreover, there was significant development in particular locations, especially Amalfi, which had a site relatively protected by mountains from attack by land, and which became an important maritime republic that operated widely in the Mediterranean. Its cathedral reflected cultural links across the Mediterranean, including the Sicilian Arabic-Norman style with its two-tone masonry, and the bronze doors made in Syria.

Cities were cultural and religious sites as well as commercial foci. Both aspects reflected links but also led to competition. Thus, cities vied to acquire saintly relics, and dedicated cathedrals and churches accordingly, as with the relics of St Mark in Venice, St Nicholas in Bari and St Matthew in Salerno. Protected in its case by its location in a lagoon, Venice followed Amalfi, as a major commercial centre, and to more lasting effect.

New developments included the establishment of monasteries, notably those of the Benedictine order launched by Benedict of Nursia in 529. He founded twelve monasteries in Italy, first Subiaco and, most famously, Monte Cassino. The Benedictines became the most significant monastic order and thus set the standard. The life of the monastery was organised in God's service, notably by prayer and work. There were many monasteries in cities, but urban life was affected more by the establishment of bishoprics. Bishops became key players in an urban world in which those appointed from outside wielded greater power than hitherto. Moreover, churches and, in particular, cathedrals became more important as the civic buildings and spaces of cities were transformed. Those on the standard tourist itinerary include the cathedral at Amalfi.

Across the Mediterranean, there was an interplay between the drive for greatness, including unity within a greater whole, and the strength of regional and local particularism. The former drive and unity were presented by Christendom, Byzantium and the Papacy, and they were to produce a clear consequence in the Crusades that began in the eleventh century. This situation, however, left much room for tension and disputes. These differences drew on the decentralised power structure of the post-Roman Mediterranean or, looked at differently, of the late-Roman Mediterranean that was part of the 'Dark Ages', which, in some lights, continued until approximately the close of the millennium. At the same time as these broad patterns, the central political questions of dynastic monarchies, both Christian and Islamic, the calibre of the ruler and the nature of the succession ensured a large degree of unpredictability, alongside the continuities and similarities offered by sacral monarchy, military leadership, ritual and the legacies of imperial Rome. So, even more, did conflict between Christendom and Islam ensure unpredictability.

Roger II of Sicily

Modern geographical distinctions and political boundaries were not of consequence in the past. Calling himself King of Africa, Roger took Tripoli in Libya (1146), Mahdia (1148), Sousse (1148) and Sfax (1148), while Tunis paid him tribute. Helping establish his position, native governors were left in power. The Almohads, however, drove the Normans out in 1158–60, with Christians and Jews given the option of Islam or death. Roger also harried the Byzantine Empire, his admiral George of Antioch in 1147 attacking Corfu and sacking Athens and Corinth. In 1149, George took forty warships to Constantinople, but was unable to land.

The Crusades

Rivalry between Christendom and Islam was both greatly expanded, and focused anew, as a consequence of the Crusades. The Seljuk advance against the Byzantines, and concerns about access for Christian pilgrims to Jerusalem, led Pope Urban II in 1095 to preach a holy war against Islam that became the First Crusade. It was the first of a series of Christian holy wars that were inspired by the potent ideal of fighting against the external or internal foes of Christendom.

Yet, at the same time, Christian and Islamic states, at least to a degree, continued the pattern of seeking to exploit rivalries among the other bloc by negotiating agreements. This was even seen with the First Crusade. After the Crusaders' capture of the city of Nicaea (today İznik) from the Seljuks in 1097, the Byzantine Emperor, Alexius I Comnenus, advised the Crusaders to send a mission to the Seljuks' bitter rival, Fatimid Egypt. In 1098, a Fatimid embassy returned to Antioch, the ruins of which are near modern Antakya. It had been seized by the Crusaders in June 1098, and the embassy appears to have come to a provisional agreement against the Seljuks. The Crusaders, however, broke this agreement in 1099 when they entered the Fatimid lands to seize Jerusalem. Its conquest was presented as a key episode in sacred history.

Although the Crusaders advanced overland through modern Turkey and Syria, they benefited from supplies brought in by sea, notably during the sieges of Antioch and of Jerusalem, for the second of which the ships arrived at Jaffa. These supplies were an aspect of the mixture of planning and adhocracy that is so typical of war as a whole, and that was to be significant throughout the Crusades. The commitment to religious goals did not mean a failure to engage with practicalities.

The Crusaders founded a number of states in the Holy Land: the Principality of Antioch (1098), the County of Edessa (1098), the Kingdom of Jerusalem (1099) and the County of Tripoli (in Lebanon, 1100s). However, they were not to gain any of the key Islamic centres in the region: Aleppo, Damascus and Cairo. As such, there was no strategic depth for the Crusader states. The Crusaders, nevertheless, developed a support system and extended their coastal control by seizing a number of ports, notably Caesarea (1101), Acre (1104) and Tripoli (1109). The naval dimension was important. In 1123, the Fatimid fleet was heavily defeated by a larger Venetian fleet commanded by the Doge Domenico Michiel, off Ascalon (Ashkelon) in modern Israel. The fleet then helped the Crusaders besiege Tyre, which fell the following year, the Venetians being rewarded with generous commercial concessions. They were very keen to insert themselves directly into the Middle East, and to ensure that they could trade there without intermediaries.

The Christian control of the coast made it difficult for the Fatimid fleet to replenish its supplies, notably of water, which was an issue when it moved north in 1126. The gain of the port of

Ascalon (1153), Egypt's major border fortress, after a difficult siege, expanded the Crusader presence in the eastern Mediterranean. The city's mosque was transformed into a church. This capture hit the Fatimid Caliphate hard and led to attempts to conquer Egypt itself. In 1167, an invasion by land by Amalric I, King of Jerusalem, was supported by a fleet, with Alexandria, however, unsuccessfully besieged. In 1169, a joint Frankish (Crusader)–Byzantine operation led to the unsuccessful siege of Damietta in Egypt.

Moreover, the early Crusades contributed to an expansion of Byzantine control in western and southern Anatolia, notably in 1158–61, although this faltered with the victory of the Seljuks at Myriocephalum in 1176. After defeat by the Seljuks at Manzikert in 1071, the Byzantine army was never again as large. In addition, Byzantium was under pressure in the Balkans, where the kingdom of Hungary gained Croatia in 1091, while, by 1204, the Bulgarians, having reasserted their independence, had conquered large areas of Thessaly, Macedonia and Thrace.

The success of the Crusaders depended in large part on the serious divisions within Islam. Strong Islamic rulers indeed proved able to dominate much or all of that part of the Mediterranean. This was particularly the case with Saladin (c. 1138–93), who rose to prominence in the service of his uncle, Shirkuh, whom he succeeded as vizier in Egypt in 1169. Two years later, Saladin, after the death of the Egyptian Caliph, abolished the Fatimid Caliphate, and in 1175 he was proclaimed the Sultan of Egypt and Syria. Saladin's forces pushed west to Tunisia, gaining access to wood from the Atlas Mountains of Morocco, Algeria and Tunisia for his new navy, and south into Sudan and Yemen. His conquest of Syria and northern Iraq, Damascus being captured in 1174, Aleppo in 1183 and Mosul in 1186, was an age-old goal of Egyptian rulers.

Proclaiming a *jihad* in 1187, Saladin crushed the Christian kingdom of Jerusalem. However, his new fleet was not strong enough to cover the siege of Tyre, let alone to thwart the Third Crusade. During the latter, Richard I of England, 'the Lionheart', helped capture Acre in 1191 after a two-year siege, and then used his fleet to support his army on the march to Arsuf where Saladin was defeated. Due to Richard's participation, this Crusade was the most famous in English history.

After the death of Saladin in 1193, the Ayyubid realm he had founded was contested among his family and by local Muslim dynasties. Tension between Egypt and Syria was exploited by the Crusaders. Thus, the Holy Roman Emperor Frederick II, who embarked on the Sixth Crusade in 1228, achieved in 1229, for ten years, the restoration to Christian control of Jerusalem (where he crowned himself king in 1229) as a result of a truce with Sultan Al-Kamil of Egypt.

There were other possible allies. The Crusaders made intense efforts to achieve an alliance with the Mongols against the local Muslim rulers, especially the Mamluk Sultanate of Egypt, which had overthrown the Ayyubid Sultan in 1250: the Mamluks were mostly ethnic Turks who served the Ayyubid rulers as an élite fighting force. The Sultan, Turanshah, was attacked at a banquet, escaped and was then murdered. Once in power, the Mamluks were riven by feuds, and there was much politics by assassination. At any rate, the Crusaders sought to profit from the rivalry between the Mongols, who overthrew the Ayyubid rulers of Syria, and the Mamluks. However, the Mamluks' sweeping victory over the Mongols at Ain Jalut near Nazareth in 1260, a key battle for the future of the Mediterranean, followed by a Mongol defeat at Homs in 1281, settled the matter. Baibars, who seized power in Egypt in 1260 after the assassination of the Sultan, ruling until 1277, built up an effective army. He failed to capture Acre in 1263, but took Arsuf and Haifa that year and Antioch in 1268. The population of the latter was killed or enslaved. Jaffa, Ascalon and Caesarea also fell. Pope Gregory X (r. 1271–6) died before he could bring his plans for a new crusade to fruition.

Thereafter, there was no significant effort to do so, and the last major Crusader position, Acre, fell to the Mamluks in 1291; Tripoli (Lebanon) had fallen in 1289.

As such, and these categories have to be adopted with care, a non-Mediterranean force, the Mamluks, that had become a Mediterranean one had succeeded over another of the same in the shape of the Crusader states. The Crusades fitted into a longstanding pattern in which local peoples were fought over by incomers, or the descendants of incomers. This had been seen, for example, in the struggle between Macedon and the Persian Achaemenids, between Rome and the Parthians, between Byzantium and the Sassanians, Arabs and Seljuk Turks in sequence, and, after the Crusades, was to resume eventually in the struggle between the Ottoman Turks on one hand, and the Habsburgs and Venice on the other.

As far as different Turkic peoples were concerned, the history of the eastern Mediterranean was in large part a product not so much of the power dynamics of that sea or of Europe, however defined, but, rather, of the Asian nomadic world, its longstanding pressures for expansion, and the opportunities for sedentarisation (settling down) offered by wealthier lands, notably Mediterranean coastal regions. This nomadic world had greater military resources than the Crusaders, and notably so once benefiting from the takeover of the wealthier lands. Local peoples, such as Syrian Arabs, Armenians, Copts and Jews, were frequently victims of this process. This approach can be taken further to note tensions between attempts within the Mediterranean to reach consensus across the confessional (religious) divide, for example in Spain, Sicily and the Holy Land, and the impact of outside groups, such as Seljuks or Normans, whose drive to establish themselves disrupted any such consensus. This element could then be taken further by emphasising the additional pressures stemming from those who deliberately rejected consensus, such as the Crusaders and the Almoravids. Moreover, these arrivals created new territorial links and routes, for example of the Almoravids from Morocco to Spain, and the Crusaders from Italy and France to the Holy Land, links and routes that put pressure on earlier ones.

Subsequent plans for Crusades to regain the Holy Land, for example by Marino Sanudo in 1321, got nowhere. This failure reflected political factors, in the shape of serious divisions within Christendom, but also the impact on society of demographic and environmental crises, notably the Black Death, with the resulting consequences for resources. Declining conditions for the soldiers have been linked to a deterioration in diet. Instead of fighting in the Holy Land, crusading became a matter of defending Western Christendom in Continental Europe.

Linked to the loss of the Holy Land, the military orders were reallocated. The Knights of St John (Hospitallers) established a new base on Rhodes in 1310, which they ruled until 1522. Alongside Rhodes the Knights held some neighbouring territories, including Halicarnassus (Bodrum) and, from 1374 to 1402, Smyrna (İzmir). Driven from the Holy Land, the Templars moved their headquarters to Limassol on Cyprus, but, keen on their wealth, Philip IV of France turned on the Templars in 1307 and this led to their suppression by the Pope in 1312.

The Fate of Byzantium

Earlier, the Crusaders had succeeded in capturing Constantinople in 1204 during the Fourth Crusade, ruling there until 1261, but failed in major attempts to conquer Egypt (1218–21, 1249–50) and Tunis (1270). The last, the Eighth Crusade, was seen as a means to move on to attack Egypt, but ended with an outbreak of dysentery that killed Louis IX of France and led to an abandonment of the siege. The contrasting fates of Constantinople and Egypt in part reflected contingency, a key element in the history of the Mediterranean.

Under Venetian influence, the Fourth Crusade first attacked the Dalmatian city of Zara/Zadar, a former possession of Venice now under Hungarian protection, in 1202, despite been ordered not to by Pope Innocent III. The Crusaders, who could not afford the cost of sea transport to Egypt, agreed with Venice, and the attack on Zara/Zadar was the return. The Crusaders were then offered money, help with the Crusade and the union of the Orthodox Church with Rome if they intervened in the increasingly vexed internal politics of Byzantium. Isaac II had seized power from the unpopular Andronikos I in 1185, and, that year at Demetritzes, had defeated a Norman invasion of the Balkans from southern Italy, only to fail to recover Cyprus and to be defeated by the Bulgarians. In 1195, Isaac's elder brother, Alexios III Angelos, overthrew, blinded and imprisoned him. Alexios Angelos, Isaac's son, used the Crusaders to have his uncle removed in 1203, but, as Alexios IV Angelos, was unable to fulfil his promises and was deposed and killed in an anti-Western rising. This led the Crusaders in 1204 to storm Constantinople with much devastation, to crown Count Baldwin of Flanders as emperor, and to partition the Byzantine Empire between them.

The Latin Empire in the East

The new Latin Empire, known as 'Romania', created in 1204, comprised not only the area under direct imperial rule, but also a number of feudal territories: the Principality of Achaia, which was most of the Peloponnese; the Duchy of Athens; and the kingdom of Salonica (Thessaloniki). In addition, the Venetians gained a number of strategic points on the mainland, notably Modon, Coron and Gallipoli, as well as many Aegean islands, including Crete, Euboea and those grouped as the Duchy of Naxos.

The Greeks were left with more peripheral parts of the Byzantine Empire, including Rhodes, Epirus (Albania), Nicaea and Trebizond. Power was fractured between these parts. The ruler of Nicaea, Theodore I Lascaris (r. 1204–22), son-in-law of Emperor Alexios III Angelos, was best placed to act, as its proximity to Constantinople meant that it was most able to challenge the Latins who, indeed, rapidly encountered problems. Nicaea, which absorbed Rhodes, overran the Latins' Asian territories in 1225. Meanwhile, in 1224, Epirus took Thessaloniki and made it the capital of the Empire of Thessalonica. The land route from Constantinople to Athens was therefore lost, and the Latin Empire became totally dependent on maritime links, which increased the already-strong influence of Genoa and, in particular, Venice.

Epirus, however, was decisively defeated by the Bulgarians in 1230, leaving the way clear for the Empire of Nicaea to claim the Byzantine mantle, while, with Thrace, Bulgaria acquired a Mediterranean coastline. Emperor John III Vatatzes of Nicaea (r. 1222–54) used his fleet to seize the islands in the eastern Aegean, including Lesbos, Chios and Samos, captured Gallipoli in 1235, and also overran the European shore of the Dardanelles and most of the shores around the Sea of Marmara. However, in 1235, his joint attack with the Bulgarian tsar, John II Asen, on Constantinople was repelled, with the Bulgarians abandoning the Greeks.

As part of the flow of conflict that explains why so many Mediterranean cities have both fortifications and a complex history, the Mongol invasion of Eastern Europe in 1241 severely weakened the Bulgarians. As a result, profiting from the weakness of a fellow Christian power, John III extended his territory deep into Thrace and Macedonia. In 1246, he entered Thessaloniki. Michael II, the Despot of Epirus, attacked John III, but was defeated in 1259 and forced to cede many of his territories, including Thessaly and the Albanian coast round Dyrrachium (Durrës). In 1262, the rest of Epirus became a Byzantine vassal state. Like the Muslim rulers and those of Catholic Europe, and undermining any idea of war being between civilisations, there was no unity among the Byzantine rulers. Indeed, conflict was incessant. As another instance of interacting struggles, the Mongol invasion of Seljuk territory in 1242 ended the Seljuk threat to Nicaea.

The Nicaean Emperor, Michael VIII Palaiologos (r. 1259–82), finally retook Constantinople in 1261. He did so with the support of Genoa, and burned down the Venetian quarter. Michael followed on by rebuilding and fortifying the dockyard at Kontoskalion. Latin rule, however, still clung on in parts of the former empire. Venice remained a major presence, while the surviving Latin principalities, Athens and Achaia, were driven to seek the support of Charles of Anjou, who is discussed in the next section.

The loss of Constantinople marked a major defeat for Western Christendom, for the Latin patriarch who had been installed in Constantinople was replaced by the Greek patriarch, now returned from Nicaea. The Bulgars, who had agreed to transfer their allegiance to the Papacy, in return for a patriarch of their own at Tarnovo, reverted to Orthodoxy in 1235.

Byzantium did not regain Cyprus, which had been captured by Richard I of England in 1191 during the Third Crusade; prefiguring the fate of Constantinople in the Fourth. He sold Cyprus to his friend Guy of Lusignan, and it remained under the Lusignan kings until acquired by Venice in 1489. This was an instance of the lasting damage to Byzantium caused by the Crusades as well as of their role in the growth of Venice.

The fall of Constantinople in 1204 reflected a rise of the West, in the shape of non-Byzantine Europe, that drew on a sustained period of population increase and greater economic activity. This rise led to an extension of cultivation, to more settlements and churches, and to greater trade. Politically, such activity was seen from the eleventh century, notably with the creation of the Norman kingdom of Sicily, forces from which invaded the Balkans, as well as with the Crusades, the development of Hungary, the increase of Papal assertiveness and the dynamism of Italian maritime power. This last was focused both on trade and on territory. Amalfi had been a key maritime city, but it was succeeded by Pisa and Genoa. In the Adriatic, Venice had developed with Byzantine help, in return providing naval assistance as well as trade links, but the relationship, like so many, was competitive as well as cooperative. Venice fattened itself on Byzantium's problems.

However, in the long term, growing Byzantine weakness was to make it difficult to resist the expansion of the Ottoman Turks, and thus, eventually, to challenge Western Christendom. The Ottomans replaced the Seljuks and benefited from the concern of the restored Byzantine Empire with its European dominions and conflicts. In the 1320s–30s, the Ottomans completed the overrunning of Byzantine Asia Minor, capturing Nicaea in 1331. Gallipoli, weakened by a destructive earthquake in 1354, followed in 1356, becoming the first Turkish conquest in Europe.

Divisions within Western Christendom

Italy, southern France and Spain saw much division between, and within, states. The authority and power of both the Popes and the Holy Roman Emperors were also at issue. Although much of their power and authority was based in Germany, the Holy Roman Emperors also had both in Italy and pursued expansion there. Control over particular territories, especially Naples and Sicily, was a focus of wide-ranging interests. They were brought under the rule of the German-based Hohenstaufen dynasty by Emperor Henry VI (r. 1190–7), who had the benefit of support from Genoese and Pisan warships. Naples and Sicily were key possessions of the Emperor Frederick II (r. 1220–50), the most famous member of the dynasty. As a reminder of the range of stories in which individuals were located, which helps to make Mediterranean history multifaceted and fascinating, Frederick has already featured with the Sixth Crusade and was intended as the head of the Fifth, that to Egypt in 1218–21. In Italy, he faced opposition from the Papacy and from Italian opponents.

After Frederick's death, Hohenstaufen control over Naples and Sicily was contested by Angevin (Anjou) and Aragonese expansion. Frederick II's grandson, Conradin, was defeated and executed in 1268 by Charles of Anjou, who had been made King of Sicily by the Pope in 1266. This defeat ended the Hohenstaufen state in southern Italy, and thereby the German link and, indeed, the Northern European one that had begun with the Normans. Charles, brother of Louis IX of France, was Count of Provence (1246–85), which he acquired by marriage, forcing Marseille to acknowledge his suzerainty. Having conquered southern Italy, Charles was creating a new empire. He developed a navy, with galleys built at Marseille and Messina, and arrived in Tunis in 1270 during the Eighth Crusade. With southern Italy as his base, Charles sought to create a second Latin Empire in the eastern Mediterranean. He gained Corfu and the Latin principality of Achaia in 1267, and was proclaimed King of Albania in 1272 after he won control of Durazzo and much of Epirus. Planning in 1281 to invade the Byzantine Empire, a goal that proved repeatedly attractive from the late eleventh century to Italian rulers, Charles provided an instance of the openness of the Mediterranean to ambition.

Louis IX had developed Aigues-Mortes as an embarkation port for the Seventh Crusade in 1248 and the Eighth in 1270. It remains an impressive fortified position, albeit cut off in the Camargue from the Mediterranean by the marshy delta of the Rhône. The Camargue is usually visited by cruises as a trip from a Rhône river stop at Arles, rather than from liners on the Mediterranean, although it can be a tour from liners docked at Sète on France's Languedoc coast. Earlier known as Cette, it is referred to as the Venice of Languedoc due to its canals.

In 1282, in an episode known as the Sicilian Vespers, Sicily, angered by Charles's financial demands, rebelled and drove out Charles, who had failed to manage its politics. Instead, Sicily turned to the house of Aragon, the rulers of eastern Spain. As a result of defeat at Muret in 1213, they had lost their territory north of the Pyrenees to expanding French power and were focusing, in its place, on Mediterranean expansion. The Aragonese had already seized the Balearic Islands and Valencia from the Moors. Charles of Anjou resisted the Aragonese, who had also seized Reggio in Calabria in 1283. Having unsuccessfully besieged it in 1284, he died the following year.

His son, Charles II (r. 1285–1309), continued, after war with Aragon and Sicily ended in 1295 and 1302 respectively, to hold southern Italy and Provence. However, the wider Angevin Empire proved ephemeral and the economic links within it, not least from the export of Italian grain, could not sustain political relationships. Charles II sought to force the Jews in his territories to convert to Christianity and introduced the Inquisition into Naples. His successor, Robert the Wise (r. 1309–43), fought on behalf of the Popes against Holy Roman Emperors seeking to extend their power into Italy. His heir, his granddaughter Joanna I (r. 1343–82), faced opposition from her husband, who was murdered in 1345. She then married a key general, Louis of Taranto, while her ex-husband's brother, Louis of Hungary, invaded Naples in 1347. She fled to Marseille but, in 1348, regained power in Naples where the Hungarians had become unpopular. Urban VI, who opposed Joanna because she backed a rival as pope, declared her dethroned in 1381 and gave the kingdom to her relative Charles who overthrew her with a Croatian force in 1381. The imprisoned Joanna was murdered.

Charles III of Naples in turn claimed the Hungarian throne as the senior male in the Angevin dynasty, overthrowing his relative, Mary of Hungary, in 1385 only to be murdered two months later. His son, Ladislaus (r. 1386–1414), an active campaigner, fought off attempts by the junior Angevin line to take over Naples and, in turn, tried and failed to take over Hungary. His sister, the childless Joanna II (r. 1414–35), was the last in the senior Angevin line of Naples.

The Angevin would-be empire ended with claims, but little of substance bar some interesting artistic legacies including in the impressive church architecture of Naples. René of Anjou (1409–80), Joanna's designated successor, might be titular ruler of much, including Jerusalem, but he was only briefly able to control Naples before it was conquered by Alfonso V of Aragon in 1442, the city falling after a six-month siege.

The Aragonese were to go on to conquer Sardinia, enslaving many of the native Sards in the fourteenth century. Cagliari was captured from the Pisans in 1326, and Aragon won control over the entire island in the 1440s. An attempt to establish themselves in Naples failed in 1422–4, with Genoese warships backing the Angevins, and again in 1435, with the Genoese fleet intervening, but, subsequently, Alfonso V won ground in a long war. Prior to that, Palermo was hit by no longer being the capital for mainland southern Italy as it had been under the Normans. Palermo had also been affected by the loss of its Muslim population, apart from those kept as slaves.

Meanwhile, Aragonese power had extended to include the Duchy of Athens, albeit only from 1379 to 1390, and again in 1451 to take Albania under vassalage as part of the lengthy resistance there to Turkish expansion. Again, the ability to create political connections across the Mediterranean was striking. Sicily gave the Aragonese state dockyard facilities in Messina and Palermo to add to their naval arsenal at Barcelona and to the naval facilities, variously for shipbuilding, supply and basing, at Blanes, San Feliu and Valencia on the Spanish coast and at Palma in Majorca. The ownership of galleys could be state or private, with the use of both depending on whether it was wartime or peacetime. So also with harbour facilities, whether or not referred to as arsenals. Aragonese imperialism was a key background to the expansion of Catalan trade, notably by the merchants of Barcelona.

Divisions within Western Christendom included those over the identity of the Pope, as Holy Roman Emperors supported their own candidates, only to be accused of heresy. These divisions had serious consequences in terms of the rivalries between, and within, Italian ruling houses, cities and aristocratic families. Thus, Joanna I, Queen of Naples, was in part deposed during the Great Schism (1378–1417) because of her support for one of the Papal claimants, while, in 1420, Pope Martin V backed Louis III of Anjou against Joanna II.

Rivalry between the major Italian trading cities was also important. In the western Mediterranean, Genoa and Pisa competed, notably over control of Corsica and Sardinia, particularly over the port of Sassari in the latter. Galleys replaced lateen-rigged ships in the Italian war fleets in the early thirteenth century. The Pisan fleet was heavily defeated by the Genoese at Meloria in 1284, a battle settled by ramming and boarding, and Pisa's navy declined. Genoa captured Porto Pisano, Pisa's port, and filled up the harbour which, anyway, suffered from alluvial deposits. Pisa was to be conquered by Florence in 1406 and, having bought it from Genoa in 1421, Florence used Livorno as its major port.

Genoa was a leading commercial centre with a prominent lighthouse, but unlike in Venice, the galleys were not built by, nor belonged to, the state. Instead, private individuals, such as the Doria family, did either building or owning, or both. Genoa and Venice fought four wars between 1253 and 1381, with Venice finally victorious. A sense of distinctiveness is preserved in the annual Regatta of the Four Ancient Maritime Republics, held on the first Sunday in June. It rotates between Amalfi, Genoa, Pisa and Venice. Of these, Genoa is the city least well-known by tourists, but it has much to offer, both its medieval core and early-modern palaces enriched with great art.

Most of the Mediterranean coastline, however, came under the control not of mercantile city-states but of princely territorial states. Thus, the ruling house of Savoy gained control of Nice in 1388, holding it, with the exception of the French Revolutionary and Napoleonic interlude, until 1860. France took over Languedoc (1229) and Provence (1481), Roussillon following in 1659. This was part of the consolidation of states and fixing of frontiers that was more generally seen in Europe.

Alongside divisions within Western Christendom, there was the strength of the Christian presence, which greatly expanded with the *Reconquista* in Spain, including the Balearics. These centuries have left an imprint in the shape of numerous churches across the Christian Mediterranean. Alongside prominent sites, mostly but not only in towns, there is the widespread legacy across the countryside of churches, shrines and other Christian sites. Moreover, the impact of Christianity was not simply a matter of the institutions, structures and life of the clergy, which displayed great vitality with the foundation and spread of the Franciscan and Dominican orders of friars. *San Domenico Maggiore* is a legacy of the latter that is worth seeing in Naples, not least the sacristy with the royal tombs.

There was also a powerful lay component. The Crusades were one indication. Another was confraternities in which the laity took a role in religious tasks such as charity. Clergy and laity joined in worship and in much that went with it, such as interest in saints, and also moral injunctions and policing.

The institutional structure of Christian life and worship, with the emphasis on the intercessionary role of the clergy, had a pronounced international character. This was true both of the Orthodox world and of its Catholic counterpart. Episcopal systems were structured accordingly, as were monastic counterparts and those of the friars. These organisations helped ensure a focus on Constantinople and Rome. Judicial and educational authority were aspects of these structures. The nearest Muslim counterpart in the Mediterranean world was Cairo. The nature, extent and role of these systems enhanced the wider significance of the Mediterranean, while also providing links within the Mediterranean, albeit a sectionalised Mediterranean. Clerics and others had to travel widely to maintain these links, and correspondence was important to them.

The Black Death

The Mediterranean was to face a formidable crisis in the fourteenth century in the shape of the Black Death. This outbreak of plague entered the Mediterranean world via Crimea in 1347. Genoese merchants fleeing the Mongol advance westwards into Crimea brought the disease, probably on rat fleas living on black rats on their ships, although the roles of infected birds, and of fleas and lice on humans, have also been discussed. Its spread reflected trade links, first to Byzantium and then, via Alexandria, around the eastern Mediterranean. From Messina in Sicily, the plague circulated around the western Mediterranean. Alongside rapid transmission and high mortality, the death rate varied, but, around much of the Mediterranean, was at least a third and, in some areas, about a half. Moreover, this was not a one-off loss, as, drawing on incubation, the plague was to recur with heavy casualties, for example in Sicily in 1360.

Alongside recourse to prayer and despair, the Black Death ensured the establishment of quarantine regimes, which originally meant forty days of preventive isolation. At Dubrovnik, a regime of thirty days was introduced for suspect travellers in 1377. In 1390, a Health Office was established in order to enforce the regulations, although plague hit again there in 1426, 1457, 1482 and 1526–7, the last leading to the death of maybe 20,000 people, a quarter of the population. In 1575–7 about the same proportion died of plague in Venice.

Exacerbated by the deterioration of the climate and by widespread political instability, the Black Death forced landlords, merchants, peasants and townsmen to respond to a very new economic context. The pressures upon rural and urban society stemming from the Black Death increased social strains and in places led to a measure of proletarianisation. At the same time, the response to new circumstances resulted in a measure of economic recovery in the fifteenth century, not least as the requirement for subsistence agriculture declined. This recovery was a context for the Renaissance, and the rising wealth of the period had even more of an effect due to the extent to which there was no major conflict in Italy between the Peace of Lodi (1454) and the French invasion (1494).

Trade

If the Black Death weakened the Mediterranean world, hitting for example the profitability of Catalan merchants operating in newly conquered Sardinia, it was as part of a broader crisis in Eurasia. At the same time, the existing commercial networks continued to respond to opportunities, and as part of a system in which activity and specialisation were symbiotic aspects of the continuation of the availability of information and of trade.

The extent of the slave trade was an aspect of this ongoing ability to react and profit. The slave trade from outside Christendom was notably to markets in the Mediterranean, as the practice of slavery retained a stronger grip there than further north in Europe where, in contrast, serfdom was more important. The Islamic Mediterranean obtained slaves from many sources, including from sub-Saharan Africa to North African slave markets such as Tunis and Tripoli; and, in the ninth and tenth centuries, from the Balkans, which reflected the lack of a strong Balkan power, and the linked openness of the Balkans to raiding; and from Western Europe via traders in Marseille and Venice. The last source was stamped out by the Church.

In Mediterranean Christendom, more particularly Sicily, southern Italy, southern and eastern Spain, Crete, Cyprus and the Balearic Islands, slavery was ubiquitous and provided labour for agriculture, industry, mining, transport and household service.

This was a consequence of the combined legacy of Classical slavery, the experience of conquest from Islam, and the availability of new slaves as a result of privateering and other attacks on the Islamic world. These areas contained a form of hybrid Christian–Muslim society.

Raiding and trade produced slaves. Thus, in 1135, as part of a process of Norman power projection in North Africa, Roger II of Sicily invaded the island of Djerba off Tunisia, killing or enslaving much of the population. In 1310, when Djerba unsuccessfully rebelled against rule by Aragon, three-quarters of the population was enslaved. In 1287, when Minorca and Ibiza were captured by Alfonso III of Aragon, much of the Muslim population was sold into slavery, especially at such major markets as Palma, Palermo and Valencia. Drawing on the Arab slave trade across the Sahara, Catalan merchants imported slaves from North Africa, via the entrepôts of Tunis and Tripoli, to Spain where Barcelona, Cartagena, Valencia and Palma were major markets. Others went to the leading Sicilian slave market of Palermo. However, the key sources of supply to the Christian Mediterranean were further east, especially the Balkans, the Black Sea and Anatolia. Byzantium valued slaves from Arab cities as skilled craftsmen.

The sources of slaves for the western Mediterranean expanded and became more profitable as a result of the Fourth Crusade in 1204, which led not only to the establishment of the colonial style Latin Empire in the East discussed earlier in the chapter, but also to Italian participation in the existing slave-trade economy based on the Black Sea. Slaves from there were exported to the Mediterranean, and to both Muslim and Christian areas. This trade continued after the fall of the Latin Empire in 1261, as the revived Byzantine Empire looked to the Venetians and Genoese, each of whom had an important base in Constantinople, for much of its foreign trade and naval protection. Venice kept a *bailo* there, his function that of commercial and diplomatic agent.

Italian merchants were important in London from the late thirteenth century, when they started to sail to England directly through the Strait of Gibraltar; although the number of ships coming direct from the Mediterranean was limited. The Italians were primarily in England to buy wool to export to the Low Countries and northern France, but were engaged in a wide range of trading and financial activities. However, London's key economic links remained with the Low Countries, notably Antwerp, Bruges and Ghent. The Italian search for products and markets was important to the integration of regional economies into a wider one. This integration was linked to the development of industrial production, for example with better-quality textiles, and to the establishment of banking systems. Such activity helped produce the wealth that financed the Renaissance, the cultural movement focused on Italy in the fifteenth and early sixteenth centuries.

Underlying the economy, whether confined to the Mediterranean or broader ranging, was a highly inegalitarian society, and the harshness of onerous labour stemming from limited technology. Sardinia produced grain, salt and silver, but each entailed hard physical labour in challenging circumstances. In Cyprus in the fifteenth and early sixteenth centuries, unfree peasants had an annual labour service of 111 days.

Culture and knowledge were aspects of trade: in goods, people and ideas. What was new and current included the rediscovery of Classical Greek and Latin knowledge, which was of increased significance in Italy from the fourteenth century. This rediscovery both validated practices and goals in terms of the authority of the past, and provided knowledge, styles, language and form for a range of subjects, including medicine, philosophy, history, literature, patristics and cartography. In part, this cultural renewal represented a 'joining' across the Mediterranean and, more particularly, the Greek/Latin divide. It was also a renewal that drew on the pattern by which Muslim and Jewish science and philosophy, in large part of Greek origin, greatly enriched Christian Europe.

This factor was by no means alone in terms of a background to, and context for, the Renaissance. Another significant element, already referred to, was the division between the Holy Roman Emperors and the Popes, and the opportunities this created for Italian cities and aristocratic families to manoeuvre to advantage. With their independence established and/or preserved, and their autonomy enhanced, they were able to retain control over their wealth, and were encouraged to take part in a process of competitive cultural patronage.

The Venetian Adriatic

Tourists can visit many sites on the Croatian coast that reflect Venetian expansion into what was termed Dalmatia and is now mostly Croatia, although there is a small Slovene section in northern Istria. In particular, the city of Zara (Zadar) was a Venetian possession from 1202 (when captured in the Fourth Crusade) to 1358, and, after a short period of Hungarian rule came back to Venice from 1409 until 1797; Ragusa (Dubrovnik) from 1205 to 1358; and Spalato (Split) from 1327 to 1358. From the 1420s until 1797, much of Dalmatia was Venetian. Further south, Durazzo (Durrës) in Albania was Venetian from 1202 to 1268 and 1394 to 1501; while Corfu was bought from the Angevins in 1386. Attractive Venetian island sites in Croatia include Cherso/Cres, and ports such as Rovigno/Rovinj in Istria. Slovenian sites with strong Venetian influence include the port of Piran, which was Venetian from 1283. Dalmatia was valuable to Venice, not least as a source of timber for shipping and sailors, and also as a buffer zone on land and for maritime routes. In particular, it was necessary to keep the ports out of potentially hostile hands.

Naval building in Venice was focused from 1302 on the *Arsenale* where galleys were built. A new large basin soon followed, so as to increase the number of galleys that could be constructed or refitted, and the *Arsenale* included the necessary ancillary buildings. There were important supporting naval facilities in the Venetian empire at Candia, Corfu, Zante, Zara and Retimo (Rethymno).

Navigation and Ships

Navigation in familiar waters was a matter of experience, memory and oral culture, including tales of past voyages. Acquired and accumulated knowledge were crucial, notably about currents, shoals, winds, safe anchorages, watering places and pirates. However, the means to disseminate such knowledge, other than by verbal tales, was limited, which helped ensure an emphasis on older and experienced captains and sailors who had sailed particular waters before. There was also the development of portolan charts, which supplemented sailing instructions by offering coastal outlines in order to assist navigation. Their name was derived from the Italian for pilot books with sailing instructions. The charts came to be covered in a dense network of rhumb lines: radiating lines showing, first, wind directions and, later, compass bearings. A guide to anchorages and sailing directions, these charts became more accurate with time.

These charts were not alone as instances of tools for navigation, and thus means to record position and direction, and to assess the impact of wind and tide. The use by Westerners of the compass for navigation had begun in the twelfth century, providing a new form of information. The compass, however, was not a one-stop change. Initially a needle floating in water, it became a pivoted indicator and, by the fifteenth century, there was compensation for the significant gap between true and magnetic north. Nevertheless, the capability to measure the distance travelled by sea remained an issue.

Developments in rigging, including an increase in the number of sails per mast, and in the variety of sail shapes, permitted greater speed, a better ability to sail close to the wind and improved manoeuvrability. An increase in the number of masts on large ships expanded the range of choices for rigging.

Alongside charts, the Mediterranean had a presence on maps because of interest in the Holy Land. The Bible was a significant inspiration for mapping, and the medieval traditions of wall decorations and manuscript illumination provided opportunities for scriptural mapping. The centrality of Jerusalem was seen in Christian *mappae mundi*, world maps. These depicted three continents – Asia, Africa and Europe, with the Mediterranean as the key divider between them.

After the failure of the Crusades, pilgrimages to the Holy Land continued, generally by sea from Venice. For most pilgrims, this was their first exposure to sea travel and many became seasick. Continued concern about holy sites was reflected in the reproductions of holy landscapes that were created in Christian Europe and in devotional literature that enabled would-be pilgrims to stay at home. Sacred landscapes were both real and a potent part of the imaginary world, locating belief, identity and interest, not least across a range of the arts.

The Fate of Constantinople

A large Portuguese amphibious expedition under John I (r. 1385–1433) seized the city of Ceuta in Morocco in a surprise attack in 1415, beginning what was to be a major commitment to conquest there as well as to expansion down the west coast of Africa. Tangier, after a Portuguese attack in 1437 failed, followed in 1471; while, further east, Spain conquered Melilla in 1497, Mers el Kébir in 1505, Oran in 1509, Tripoli in 1510 and Bône (Annaba) in 1535.

To European contemporaries, however, it was the expansion of the power of the Ottoman Turks that was more significant and ominous. In the late fourteenth century, the Turks overran much of the Balkans, making Adrianople (Edirne) their capital in 1363. This process subsequently continued, notably with the capture of Thessaloniki from the Venetians in 1430, and with the conquest of the Peloponnese in 1446–7 after the wall across the Isthmus of Corinth, the *Hexamilion*, had been breached. Building on the earlier turn to the Mongols, Christian Europe had attempted to win the support of Timur (Tamerlane) in the 1390s and 1400s against the Turks. Timur, indeed, heavily defeated the Mamluks in 1400, conquering Syria. He smashed the Turks at Ankara in 1402, capturing Bayezid I, and went on, that year, to overrun Ionia and besiege Smyrna (İzmir), where he beheaded the defending Knights Hospitallers after its fall. The King of Aragon sent an envoy to Timur, an indication of the significance attached to him on the other side of the Mediterranean and of the wide-ranging pursuit of alliances. Timur, however, died in 1405, and his empire rapidly collapsed. Dying in captivity in 1403, Bayezid was followed by a destructive interregnum as his sons fought for control, with Mehmed I (r. 1413–21) finally victorious. His successor, Murad II (r. 1421–44, 1446–51), sought to regain what had been lost after the 1402 defeat. He fought rebels as well as Christian neighbours and independent Turkish states in Anatolia.

Constantinople was now the reduced imperial capital of a much sliced empire. Hit by the Fourth Crusade, it had recovered as a state and was still an impressive city. Cristoforo Buondelmonti, a Florentine monk, produced, in his *Liber Insularum Archipelagi* (1420), a bird's-eye view that is the only known representation of the city before its capture. He accurately showed the fortifying encircling walls of Theodosius II, built in 412–13, and the city's location on a promontory bounded by the waters of the Golden Horn, the Bosphorus and the Sea of Marmara. North of the Golden Horn was the commercial entrepôt of Pera (now Beyoğlu), which, with its great Galata Tower built in 1348, was the concession made to Genoese traders. Open to tourists, the nine-storey tower, with its restaurant, café, nightclub and lifts, today offers a great vista of historic Constantinople to the south. Within Constantinople, Buondelmonti depicted the remains of the Roman Hippodrome next to the majestic and dominant Hagia Sophia, built for Constantine the Great, with the monumental column of Justinian. This was one of the remaining elements of the Mese, a great processional way leading to the imperial palace.

The Byzantine position was under growing pressure, both external and internal, although the continuing rituals of empire served in part to disguise the damage suffered. Domestic instability remained a problem and one that encouraged foreign interventionism. In 1354, Emperor John V (r. 1341–76, 1379–90, 1390–1) seized power from his co-emperor and father-in-law, John VI (r. 1347–54), with the support of Francesco Gattilusio, a Genoese privateer who, in 1355, gained Lesbos as a Byzantine vassal and as a dowry for John V's sister. In 1366, Gattilusio helped in the recapture of Gallipoli from the Turks. Lesbos itself provided wealth from crops, alum, salt and piracy. Aside from civil wars, John V's reign saw the Black Death and the advance of the Turks, including into Europe itself. Indeed, in 1371, John V recognised the suzerainty of Sultan Murad I. Gallipoli was returned to the Turks in 1376. The Byzantine rulers were reduced to largely fruitless attempts to win support from elsewhere in Europe. In 1425, having failed to win such support, Manuel II agreed to pay tribute to the Sultan.

In 1453 came the dramatic fall of Constantinople. A centre of power that had resisted non-Christian attack for nearly a millennium, including Turkish sieges in 1394–1402 and 1422, finally fell after fifty-four days of bombardment and attacks. There was no repetition of the rebellion elsewhere that had cut short the 1422 siege. Turkish numerical superiority (about 80,000 Turks to 10,000 defenders) was crucial, but so also was the effective use of gunpowder weaponry thanks to the skilful direction of Sultan Mehmed II. The artillery, including about sixty new cannon cast at the efficient foundry at Adrianople, drove off the

Byzantine navy and battered the walls of Constantinople, creating breaches through which the city was stormed. Moreover, building on the achievement of Bayezid I who, in the 1390s, had built dockyard facilities at Gallipoli, providing a safe anchorage and necessary storehouses, Mehmed created a fleet to help prevent Constantinople from being relieved. During the attack on the city, he also moved ships overland to the Golden Horn, from which waterway they could bring further pressure on the walls.

Although the rest of Christian Europe had sent little support, the fall of Constantinople inflicted a bitter psychological blow on Christendom, shattering the shared heritage of East and West. With Emperor Constantine XI (r. 1449–53) dying in the defence of the city, the Eastern Roman Empire was reduced to fragments that would soon fall, such as the Peloponnese in 1460. The Greeks were left to hope that Constantine would prove the 'Marble Emperor' who would awake from the cave where he had been placed by an angel and drive the Turks away.

As well as making their empire contiguous by the capture of Constantinople, and gaining a major commercial and logistical base, the Turks won great prestige in both the Muslim and Christian worlds from this capture, and took over a potent imperial tradition. Their capital moved to Constantinople where it remained for the rest of the imperial period, while Mehmed took the sobriquet 'the Conqueror' and the Byzantine title of 'Caesar'. The political order of the Mediterranean world had been totally recast.

5. The Early-Modern Mediterranean, 1453–1600

Narrowly escaping Mediterranean shipwreck as a baby, she later avoided murder, only to be seized by pirates and sold to a brothel in Mytilene on the Aegean island of Lesbos. Fact? Fiction? We are talking of Marina in Shakespeare's *Pericles*.

Shakespeare and the Mediterranean

Travel experienced at second hand is crucial. It is a key way in which the responses of those who have not yet visited, indeed may never visit, are prepared for, guided and understood. The travel described is in part imaginary, in part an account of what has actually happened; and, as with the *Odyssey*, this distinction is frequently not an easy matter to chart. Similarly, the script-writing and production issues of modern works, such as the film *Mamma Mia!* (2008), are not brought to the fore, although in that case a setting supposedly on an Aegean island was in fact on a Croatian one.

For the early-modern period, the most resonant travels, and not just for the British, are those of the characters in Shakespeare's plays. Storms and shipwrecks in the Mediterranean played a role in a number of plays, both by Shakespeare (who had never been there), including *The Merchant of Venice, Twelfth Night, A Winter's Tale, Pericles* and *The Comedy of Errors*, and by other playwrights. In *The Tempest*, King Alonso of Naples, thanks to magic, is ship-wrecked by Prospero on his return from marrying his daughter Claribel to the King of Tunis, who, when Shakespeare was writing, would have been a Muslim. The evil Antonio rejects Claribel as a plausible successor to Naples on the grounds that she 'dwells ten leagues beyond man's life'. Very differently, in *The Winter's Tale*, Antigonus's boat is wrecked off the coast of Bohemia with all hands in a storm, bar Antigonus who, ashore, is eaten by a bear. As was clearly shown by contemporary maps, such as Mercator's *Map of Europe* (1554), Bohemia, however, is far from the coast.

Apparent shipwrecks are the cause of the action in *The Merchant of Venice*, for they destroy (another) Antonio's prospects and, therefore, make his bond fall due. His trade includes a ship from Tripoli. Risk destroys credit, a situation that Shylock exploits in what was in truth a very limited insurance market. The episodic character and inherent precariousness of trade are amply demonstrated because Antonio, as a result of his stake, faces the prospect of the loss of his life. Information about trade was a crucial part of Mediterranean life, as was that about privateering and fleet movements.

A terrible storm is also important to the plot of *Othello*, in that the destruction of the Turkish fleet preparing to invade Cyprus leaves the Venetians sent to help defend the island free to pursue the obsessive jealousies that Iago builds up. Had Othello, the general, instead had to fight the Turks, as he had successfully done earlier, then the plot would have been very different and his martial character would have been to the fore. In reality, Cyprus had fallen in 1570–1, but *Othello*, probably written in 1603, was based on *Un Capitano Moro*, an earlier work by 'Cinthio' (Giovanni Battista Geraldi, 1504–73). At the beginning of Act Two of *Othello*, Montano, the Venetian Governor of Cyprus, gazes at the sea where the First Gentleman can see nothing bar 'a high-wrought flood' or turbulent sea. Montano provides a vivid account of the vulnerability of wooden ships:

Methinks the wind hath spoke aloud at land;
A fuller blast ne'er shook our battlements.
If it hath ruffianed so upon the sea,

What ribs of oak, when mountains [mountainous seas]
    melt on them,
Can hold the mortise? What shall we hear of this?
SECOND GENTLEMAN: A segregation [dispersal] of the
    Turkish fleet:
For do but stand upon the foaming shore,
The chidden billow seems to pelt the clouds.
The wind-shaked surge, with high and monstrous main,
Seems to cast water on the burning Bear
And quench the guards of th'ever-fixed pole [Pole Star].
I never did like molestation view
On the enchafed flood.
MONTANO: If that the Turkish fleet
Be not ensheltered and embayed, they are drowned;
It is impossible to bear it out.
THIRD GENTLEMAN: News, lads! Our wars are done.
The desperate tempest hath so banged the Turks
That their designment halts. A noble ship of Venice
Hath seen a grievous wrack and sufferance
On most part of their fleet. (II, i)

Thus, as was the case in Classical Greek drama, and, more
generally prior to cinema, the language of report has to make up
for the drama of show. Storms and shipwrecks were both important, indeed crucial and decisive, plot devices, and the occasion of
dramatic scenes and of vivid and often harrowing speeches. In
the second scene in *Twelfth Night*, the Captain remarks:

. . . after our ship did split,
When you and those poor number saved with you
Hung on our driving boat. (I, ii)

Later, Antonio refers to 'the rude sea's enraged and foamy mouth'
(V, i).

In *The Winter's Tale*, the Clown observes from land a ship-wreck in the stormy sea:

O, the most piteous cry of the poor souls!
Sometimes to see 'em, and not to see 'em; now
The ship boring the moon with her mainmast,
And anon swallowed with yest and froth, as you'd
Thrust a cork into a hogshead . . . to make an
End of the ship, to see how the sea
Flapdragoned [swallowed] it; but, first, how the
Poor souls roared, and the sea mocked them. (III, iii)

Winter voyages were harshest and most dangerous. This was true not only of long journeys, but also of the numerous shorter trips that were so important for trade and transport. More generally, journeys, both at sea and on land, that could be undertaken in the summer might be impossible (as opposed to just unpleasant) in winter, and to a degree that is not true today. This could reflect snow on land, freezing on rivers or different wind patterns at sea. Shorter days in the winter also posed a problem for navigation in coastal waters.

Making the situation even more treacherous, coastal charts were frequently imperfect or non-existent, and lighthouses absent or inadequate. Accurate timekeeping, and thus navigation, were very difficult without the instruments that were to be developed later. As a result, knowledge was unfixed, in the sense that it could not readily be related to such maps as might exist. Experience, in the shape of the views of long-lived members of the crew, was a crucial element in knowing how to understand and respond to circumstances.

Alongside a quest for practical solutions, there was a belief that witches and other occult forces could direct winds. This belief was noted in *Macbeth* when a witch promises revenge on a sailor, en route from London to Aleppo in Syria, for the rudeness of his wife. The role of the occult, and, indeed, of religion in response in propriating bad spirits and bringing good fortune to voyagers went back to Antiquity, and was linked to the location and alignment of many shrines.

Shipwreck was a frequent reference in Shakespeare's plays, and even in plays set far from the sea, as in *Two Gentlemen of Verona*:

Go, go, be gone, to save your ship from wrack,
Which cannot perish having thee aboard,
Being destined to a drier death on shore. (I, i)

The following scene has Julia refer to 'the raging sea' (I, ii), as she later does to 'the wild ocean' (II, vii). In *The Two Noble Kinsmen*, the jailer's daughter, gone mad, imagines a shipwreck (III, iv), while, in *Richard III*, the imprisoned George, Duke of Clarence envisages drowning at sea shortly before he is drowned in a butt (barrel) of wine in the Tower of London. In *Measure for Measure*, set in inland Vienna, Angelo's jilting of Mariana is explained in terms of a shipwreck in which her brother was drowned and her dowry lost (III, i). This explanation captures the many vulnerabilities of characters; vulnerabilities that were particularly present in the case of women. Those who were well-born had furthest to fall in fortune, a point demonstrated in a number of the plays.

The broader Mediterranean also features in Shakespeare's plays in a way that connects with the news. The Prince of Morocco is an unsuccessful suitor of Portia in *The Merchant of Venice*: Morocco had totally routed a Portuguese invasion in 1578, a major event in Mediterranean and global history as the balance between Islam and Christendom was then essentially fixed in the western Mediterranean until the French invasion of Algeria in 1830. Furthermore, thanks to a successful invasion by Philip II of Spain, Portugal, ruled by the kings of Spain from 1580 to 1640, never really recovered its impetus. Elizabeth I subsequently sought an alliance with Morocco against Philip II and supplied gunpowder to it.

A far less attractive account of North Africa was offered by Shakespeare in *Titus Andronicus*, in which the Moorish Aaron, the black servant and lover of Tamora, Queen of the Goths and new Empress of Rome, suggests the rape of Lavinia and the murder of Bassianus, and wrongly blames Titus for the murder. The play ends with the new Emperor resolving that justice be meted out to Aaron, 'that dam'd Moor', and the cause of all the mishaps.

The Turkish Advance

The fate of the city was ominous: the Turks were in Italy and to deadly effect. In 1480, a 12,000 strong force, convoyed by a fleet of 132 ships, landed at Otranto in south-east Italy, within campaigning distance (335 miles/540 kilometres) of Rome. The town fell, with its people slaughtered or enslaved. The Western Roman Empire had been extinguished in 476, just over a millennium earlier, and a new conquest of Western Europe appeared imminent. In 1463, Kritovoulos, Governor of Imbros, had noted that Mehmed II had decided to build up a fleet 'because he saw that sea power was a great thing'. His success in doing so reflected Mehmed's ability to develop a governmental system that had bureaucratic characteristics. In part, this success rested on incorporating Byzantine practices, but there was also a transition in Turkish culture and government from a tribalism to a state system, albeit a transition that faced resistance, leading to rebellions, as in Anatolia in the 1600s.

Providing a sense of inexorable advance, the Turks had captured Corinth (1458), Lesbos (1462), Negroponte on Euboea (1470), the last island the key source of grain for Rhodes, Cephalonia in 1479 and Albania, after a long struggle, in 1478–9. The fall of Negroponte greatly alarmed the Venetians and led to the enlargement of the *Arsenale* in Venice. Ragusa (Dubrovnik, Ragusa was the official name of the Republic in Dalmatia) came to a different conclusion, agreeing in 1458 to pay an annual tax/tribute to the Sultan, and receiving a beneficial trade treaty in return. This relationship lasted until the city lost independence in 1808, becoming part of the Napoleonic kingdom of Italy: French troops had taken control in 1806.

Otranto demonstrated that the Adriatic was no barrier and appeared to offer a parallel to the invasion of southern Italy in 280 BCE by Pyrrhus, King of Epirus. It was easy to understand why war, one of the four horsemen of the Apocalypse, was frequently presented as a Turk, as in Albrecht Dürer's woodcut of *c.* 1497–8. This fear increasingly coloured the humanist culture of the Renaissance, and notably so in Italy.

Cannon played a significant role in the Turkish advance. The fall of Mytilene on Lesbos and of Negroponte owed much to breaches made by Turkish cannon. In contrast, Turkish failure at Rhodes in 1480, and that of the Neapolitans to recapture hastily fortified Otranto the same year, were probably due to the limitations of the artillery, which was inflexible and had a slow rate of fire. In the event, as an instance of the fratricidal practice of Turkish dynastic politics, the new sultan, Bayezid II, faced opposition from his brother Jem, who took refuge in Christendom. Bayezid, therefore, adopted a cautious international stance. Otranto was retaken in 1481 by Neapolitan troops, commanded by Alfonso of Aragon, son of the King of Naples.

The Northern European, Christian, perspective on the Turkish advance and the Mediterranean understandably focuses on campaigning on those shores and islands. In practice, however, what was really impressive about the Turks was their ability, by 1520, to have gained control over the shoreline of the eastern Mediterranean, thus recreating the dominance that Byzantium had shown until the Muslim expansion of the 630s onwards. Issues of legitimacy and prestige, as well as stability, were posed by relations with other Muslim rulers, which brought together dynastic, ethnic, political and other concerns, and all within the extraordinary diversity of Muslim identity and expression.

The leading Islamic rival of the Turks was the Mamluk sultanate of Egypt, which also ruled the Near East and the Hejaz (western Arabia). The Mamluks were still a vital force, able to campaign successfully against the Turks in what is now south-east Turkey in 1465–71 and 1485–91. The key battles between the two powers occurred in 1516–17. They were on land, because Islamic powers focused their strength there; but the results affected the situation across the Mediterranean. In 1516, the opponents of the Turkish ruler Selim I the Grim (r. 1512–20) – the Mamluk Sultan, Qansuh al-Ghuri, and the Persian (Iranian) ruler, Shah Isma'il – moved close. Selim marched east, unsure which of his opponents to attack, but Qansuh's advance to the city of Aleppo in northern Syria led Selim to attack the Mamluks. At Marj Dabiq on 24 August 1516, one of the decisive battles in Mediterranean history, the Mamluk army was totally crushed. Selim then moved south to overrun the Near East, before conquering Egypt in 1517. This brought control over Mecca and Medina, and thus their pre-eminence in the world of Islam.

When Selim died in 1520, he was building up a fleet, presumably against the Knights of St John on Rhodes, which threatened the sea route between Constantinople and Egypt. The conquest of Egypt had made power in the eastern Mediterranean a far more significant factor in Turkish geopolitics, as well as greatly increasing the number of Muslims under Turkish control. In contrast, earlier Balkan conquests had reduced the percentage of Muslim subjects. Egypt and Syria produced about a third of the empire's income, and the Arab influences they encouraged led the Turks to become more clearly Muslim in their practice of statecraft.

From Egypt, the Turks extended their power along the coast of North Africa, where the authority of Selim I was accepted in Algiers in 1517 by Oruç, a leading privateer who had seized control there the previous year. After he was killed by the Spaniards in 1518, his brother Hayreddin 'Barbarossa' (c. 1478–1546), inherited his position as governor. The mutually beneficial relationship extended Turkish power as well as greatly reducing the flow of slaves to Western Europe from North Africa. 'Barbarossa' both raided the Christian Mediterranean and captured Spanish positions in North Africa, including Bône (Annaba). By helping Moors escape from Spain, 'Barbarossa' strengthened his position in North Africa. In 1529, the Spaniards were driven from the *Peñón* (Rock) of Algiers (the island of Amiraute), and in 1533, 'Barbarossa' was appointed *Kapudan Pasha*, the Grand Admiral of the Turkish fleet as well as Chief Governor of North Africa. Under Spain from 1510, and, once transferred (with Malta) by the Emperor Charles V, under the Knights of St John from 1530, Tripoli followed into Turkish control in 1551.

Naval strength entailed a commitment of resources that was often greater than that required for warfare on land. Warships were costly, as were food and wages, because fleets could not live on local resources as armies did. Facing challenges akin to those of crossing deserts, fleets had to be provisioned and watered, needs that made the size of the crew a particularly serious matter.

Competition for foodstuffs as well as the high price of grain supported the attempt to protect trade and to hinder that of opponents. The conquest of Egypt facilitated and encouraged a major growth in Turkish naval power and in the merchant marine, as links between Egypt and Constantinople were only really viable by sea, a situation that was even more true of North Africa. Mehmed II attacked Lesbos in 1462 in part because it provided a base for Catalan pirates who were slave raiding on the coast of Anatolia. Whereas the Egyptian (Mamluk) fleet had been defeated by Western pirates off Ayas in 1510, the Turks proved able to dominate the eastern Mediterranean. Selim I expanded the naval arsenal at Galata (on the other side of the Golden Horn to Constantinople), which became a major centre for shipbuilding. The conquest of Egypt led to the end of the annual state convoys of Venetian ships for the Levant. Venetian trade was now dependent on the Turks, but, less positively, the extent and development of the empire contributed to the spread of plague.

Turkish mapmaking developed to help this naval activity. Piri Reis, an admiral, born in about 1465 in Gallipoli, produced the *Kitab-i Bahriya* (*The Book of Seafaring*, 1521), a treatise on marine navigation that contained more than 200 maps, including nautical charts, coastal plans and city plans. He described coastlines and cities, for example Venice, as far west as southern France and Spain. More than thirty original manuscript copies survive.

The Turks, meanwhile, benefited from the decline of Genoese and Venetian naval power. In a war with Venice in 1499–1503, the Turkish fleet was more powerful. In the pattern of navies of the period, the Turkish fleet was intended to support amphibious operations, rather than to seek battle, and its operations combined with the heavy siege cannon moved by sea: they could not be fired from the ships due to the recoil. Lepanto (Návpaktos) fell in 1499, and Modon (Methón) and Coron, 'the eyes of Venice'. in 1500. These were stopping points en route to the Venetian island colonies of Crete and Cyprus, as well as the advance positions for the Venetian possessions in the Adriatic. The Venetian response was inadequate: their fleet was defeated at Zonchio in 1499 and failed to capture Mytilene (1501). As a result of these setbacks, fear of the Turkish fleet became more potent in Venice. The latter itself was heavily distracted by power politics within Christendom in the shape of the Italian Wars (1494–1559).

In the Aegean, Karpathos and the northern Sporades in 1538, and Naxos in 1566, were captured by the Turks from Venice; and Samos in 1550 and Chios in 1566 from the Genoese. Neither Venice nor Genoa now had the capability to protect such exposed positions, which was a far cry from the naval reach enjoyed by both powers during the Middle Ages, a reach that had extended into the Black Sea. Turkish expansion was partly by conquest and partly by a coerced enhancement of control, as with Chios, where the Turks moved from tribute-takers to direct occupation;

or Naxos which, in 1538, was allowed to recognise Turkish sovereignty and pay an annual tribute. Subsequently, it was brought under direct rule. The unity of the Aegean, lost by Byzantium in 1204, and largely restored by the Turks in 1470, was now completely reunited under the Turks.

The Siege of Rhodes, 1522

The base of the Knights of St John had survived siege by the Turks in 1480, as Constantinople had not done in 1453. However, Süleyman the Magnificent (r. 1520–66) launched a major attack in 1522, and his presence helped ensure commitment. In the meanwhile, the Knights had built large bastions that provided effective enfilade fire along the ditch, although they were not angled ones. They had also strengthened and widened the walls to create a terreplein, which allowed them to move their artillery easily along the walls. In 1522, the heavily outnumbered Knights resisted assaults and bombardment with great determination, inflicting very heavy casualties, but the Turks made impressive use of mining despite extensive countermining by the defenders. The Turks also used gunpowder to create a smoke screen behind which to attack. Affected by their gunpowder running out, the Knights were given reasonable surrender terms. The siege enhanced their prestige within Christendom.

While the Turks came completely to dominate the eastern Mediterranean, a counter-force also capable of mobilising unprecedented strength developed in the western, albeit, due to French opposition, it lacked the same dominance. The Habsburg, Burgundian, Aragonese and Castilian inheritances fused in the person of Charles I of Spain, who became the Emperor Charles V (r. 1519–56). His Spanish grandparents, Ferdinand of Aragon and his wife Isabella of Castile, had driven the Moors from Spain and conquered southern Italy. The fall of Granada in 1492 had brought Moorish Spain to an end, and in the Italian Wars, Spain, repeatedly defeating France, established and retained control of Naples and Sicily. This involved conflict on land and at sea. Gaeta, a key coastal fortress that protected the route to Naples from the north, was captured by the French in 1495 and 1501, being recaptured by the Spaniards in 1496 and 1504. The parallel with the struggles between Islamic powers is instructive, and can be pushed further as these wars involved a range of participants, causes and consequences. Thus, organising a coalition against Venice in 1507, Pope Julius II excommunicated the city.

There were, moreover, factions within individual cities. Thus, in Genoa in 1528, the Doria family changed side from backing France to supporting Charles V, drove the French out, and created a more oligarchic constitution, which was maintained against conspiracies in 1547 and 1548. As well as the Doria, Genoese financiers and merchants became key supports of the Spanish system, notably in finance and trade, and in the kingdom of Naples, where they were major traders, landowners and tax collectors. In part, this activity was a response to the detrimental impact of the Turkish advance on Genoese opportunities in the eastern Mediterranean. In turn, the French sought Turkish support, sending an envoy to Constantinople in 1535.

Alongside their divisions, France, Spain and the Italian states all opposed the Protestant Reformation. It spread, as Christianity had earlier done, with individuals, groups and writings pressing for aspects of Protestantism, but in the Mediterranean, unlike in Transalpine Europe, they did not have political support. This helped ensure vulnerability to the Inquisition, which was deployed by the reviving Papacy.

Presenting Venice

In 1500, Jacopo de' Barbari produced an aerial view of Venice. He used a careful survey of the streets and buildings, plus elevated viewings from different tall towers (using each tower as a survey point, the cityscape was spatially divided into sixty parishes), which means that the map is the product of an innovative proto-digital approach: he created a composite view from multiple partial views. The map is also loaded with symbolism. The presence of Neptune and Mercury suggests that the city has been divinely blessed with control of the seas and the wealth to be derived from commerce. The city was also presented in the shape of a dolphin, which had both Classical and Christian symbolism. The republican community was dominated by an oligarchical élite, but included the 90 per cent of the population who were *popolani* or commoners. The Venetian Patriciate, their names inscribed in the 'Golden Book of Venice', controlled the Senate and public administration. The 'Red Book' listed the *cittadini*, citizens who were the middle class, who did not belong to the élite. They included merchants, lawyers, doctors and sea-captains. The people, in the strict sense of the word, were not inscribed in any book.

In response to the Turkish advance, Charles V, Venice and Pope Paul III deployed a combined fleet in 1538 against the Turks in the Adriatic, where each had coastlines; but the Turks were able to check them at Preveza on 27 September. The battle demonstrated the importance of tactical problems in naval warfare and also the grave difficulties of arguing from them in order to assess general capability, as tactical issues played out in terms of the specific circumstances of particular engagements. Forcing battle is a key issue in naval warfare. Galley conflict in particular depended on fortified ports and anchorages, which often gave the advantage to the defenders.

This proved to be the case at Preveza where the Turks had withdrawn their galleys onto the beach under cover of their fortress guns, with their forward galley guns facing out to sea. The situation immediately robbed the Genoese admiral, Andrea Doria, of the initiative, as his crews were consuming their food and water as they tried to hold their station outside the port on the open sea. He had the choice of attacking the Turks in their fixed position, with the Turks able to fire from stable gun plat-forms with a secure retreat, or landing troops and attempting to storm the fort and its outer defence works with inadequate siege equipment. As neither option offered much prospect of success, Doria's only realistic option was retreat. However, the moment he began to withdraw, the great point of weakness in such conflict, Doria exposed his sailing vessels to the Turkish galleys, whose fresh crews were able to overhaul and board them.

Instructively, accounts of the battle vary, which is more gener-ally true of naval (and land) battles in this period and thus make it difficult to judge the particular factors that led to successful capability. Recriminations among the mutually distrusted allies were linked to these different accounts. However, one of the tech-nological successes at Preveza was the ability of a single, large, Venetian galleass to hold off the sustained attacks of the Turkish galleys and to make good its escape. The Venetians built more galleasses as a result, and these were to prove crucial at the battle of Lepanto in 1571.

In 1541, as part of a conscious struggle between the two empires that focused on the Mediterranean and sought to recre-ate a realm similar to that of the Roman Empire, Charles V led a crusade against Algiers, the key Muslim naval position in the western Mediterranean. This large-scale amphibious expedition, in which Charles coordinated forces from Italy and Spain, was a considerable logistical achievement: 65 galleys, 450 support vessels and 24,000 troops sailed from Majorca in mid-October. However, while landing the troops, the fleet was badly damaged by a protracted autumnal storm and, with about 150 ships lost, the troops were soon re-embarked. Thus, the expedition failed, unlike that which Charles had led against Tunis six years earlier. These were both very much the Emperor as war leader.

In 1542–4, 'Barbarossa', with 110 galleys, cooperated with the French against Charles V, raiding Catalonia (1542), capturing Nice (1543) and harrying the Italian coast (1544). These successes were made possible by the use of Toulon, supplied by France, as a base to winter in. Tripoli fell to the Turks in 1551 when they also raided the Italian Riviera, and in 1552, when Henry II of France attacked Charles V, the Turks sent about a hundred galleys to the western Mediterranean under Dragut (Turgut Reis), Turkey's leading mid-century naval commander. Born near Bodrum, he became a skilled gunner and a protégé of 'Barbarossa'. Governor of Djerba from 1538, Dragut harried the shipping and coasts of Christian Europe. In 1552, he raided Sicily, captured Pantelleria and defeated the smaller Genoese fleet under Andrea Doria at the battle of Ponza off Terracina. This increased the vulnerability of the western Mediterranean to Turkish attack. The Turks went on to attack Majorca (1552) and, with the French, to invade Corsica (1553), launching a conflict that continued until France returned Corsica to Genoa in 1559 as part of the peace treaty.

Each year until 1556, and again in 1558, the Turks sent out large fleets, although, for logistical reasons they returned every winter to Constantinople. The significant naval forces that operated from Algiers and the North African ports still remained in the western Mediterranean, but this return gave their opponents opportunities to contest the sea, so that when the Turks invaded Corsica, the Genoese were able to mount a counterattack in 1553. Corsica was at the limit of the Barbary vessels. Nevertheless, in 1557, the

Viceroy of Sicily noted a new integration of Mediterranean power politics:

> Things are different today from what they were thirty or forty years ago. Back then we talked about the Turks as if we were talking about the Antipodes, but now they come so close and they are so familiar with the affairs of Christendom that what happens in Sicily is known as quickly in Constantinople as in Spain; and it is normal for their fleet to sail by this island every year.

Turkish attacks had a terrible impact. Thus, in 1446–7, Murad II enslaved maybe 60,000 people when he overran the Peloponnese. In 1535, in revenge for Charles V's success in taking La Goulette near Tunis, a success in which the centreline cannon on the galleys had played a role, 'Barbarossa' raided Minorca, killing or enslaving the 5,000 inhabitants of Mahon. In 1544, he is rumoured to have taken up to 10,000 from the Aeolian Islands as slaves. In 1554, the raiding of the Maltese island of Gozo, a possession of the Knights of St John, was accompanied by the seizure of much of the population as slaves, such that the island became largely depopulated. Nicolas de Nicolay's mid-century account of slave dealers parading their captives naked to show that they had no physical defects, and so that they could be examined as if they were horses, with particular reference to their teeth and feet, referred to the large numbers of Christians sold at Tripoli having been captured from Malta and Sicily. This element tends to be forgotten in modern discussion of slavery.

There was also Christian raiding, notably from Malta which, from 1530, was under the Knights of St John and, thanks to their displacement of the old feudalism, was a more enterprising society. This was seen in the commercialisation of agriculture but also in raiding. The capture of individuals at least helped the transmission of information, some of which was printed, as with Leo Africanus's *La Descrittione dell'Africa* (1550).

Fortifications were built or restored to protect the Christian Mediterranean from attack. Many were a continuation of earlier works. Thus, the two-stage Moorish fortress complex continued to dominate Malaga. At Bari, Spain added bastions to a Norman fortress built over a Roman fort and strengthened in the early thirteenth century by Emperor Frederick II. The twelfth-century Norman tower in Lecce was surrounded by modern fortifications, and Charles V also improved those at Otranto and Trani. Thus, the supply of Apulian grain to Naples and Venice, and for the Christian fleets, was protected. These defences were also a response to the Turkish capture of Otranto in 1480. At Le Castella in Calabria, the seaside fortifications were on a site originally fortified in the fourth century BCE in order to protect the nearby town of Crotone. At Milazzo in Sicily, the castle built by Frederick II on the site of a Greek acropolis was enlarged by Charles.

There were also new-style fortifications along the coasts of Italy, including at Civitavecchia in 1515, Livorno between 1518 and 1534, Ancona in 1536, Genoa in 1536–8, Messina in the 1540s, Gaeta and on Venice's Lido. At Gibraltar, the Algerine privateering attack in 1540 was successful in part because the position was protected from the north, but not from the south, the direction of attack. As a result, Charles V had new bastioned fortifications built there in the 1550s. Elsewhere, along Italy's Tyrrhenian and southern Adriatic coasts, as well as Sicily, Sardinia and Spain's southern coast, watchtowers were constructed. Also in the 1550s, Fort St Philip was built on Minorca. Nevertheless, the decision by Venice to rebuild totally the defences of Nicosia in 1560 was relatively unusual, as, even more, was the scale of the work, with a three-mile walled circuit and eleven fully angled bastions.

Unlike their attacks on Rhodes (1522), Malta (1565) and Cyprus (1570), the Turks did not use their expeditions into the western Mediterranean to seek to accumulate conquests that might establish a permanent position, but the expeditions created grave problems for the articulation of the Spanish Empire as well as for the coastal communities in the region. During the period 1540–74, the number and scale of amphibious operations mounted in the Mediterranean by all of the major combatants were impressive. The size of armies that were transported, the distances they were moved and the speed of transit were all striking, and highlighted a degree of competence and capability that was largely due to the experience of the commanders and sailors involved.

In 1559, Charles V's son, Philip II of Spain (r. 1556–98), launched an expedition to regain Tripoli, lost by the Knights of St John in 1551, but delays in assembling the forces meant that the expedition did not sail until late in the winter, and it became stormbound in Malta for ten weeks. When the expedition eventually sailed for Tripoli in mid-February 1560 it was driven back by bad weather, and, instead, occupied the low-lying island of Djerba, which lay to the west of Tripoli. Djerba had previously been used by 'Barbarossa' as a base for his privateers, and was flat and interspersed with sandy lagoons. The Spaniards began to construct a fortress on the island, but chose to fortify the old town, rather than building a fortress next to the beach where the original landing was made. Dragut was well aware of the preparations and pleaded for immediate assistance from Constantinople. This was provided and a fleet left the city and arrived at Djerba twenty days later, on 11 May, an astonishing feat that took the Christian forces by surprise.

As a result of the surprise attack, a large proportion of the galley fleet was destroyed or captured, although, thanks to the leadership of the younger Andrea Doria, a number of Genoese galleys extricated themselves from the unfolding disaster and reached safety. The fortress was blockaded, with all of the wells outside the fortress being captured. The water cistern within the fortress had run dry by July, and the garrison was soon forced to surrender.

More generally, besiegers had to control the surrounding sea area of their target port in order to ensure unhindered logistical support for their own force and to thwart relief attempts. This factor was significant at Rhodes, Tunis, Bonifacio (in Corsica, besieged by a Franco-Turkish force in 1553), Tripoli, Djerba, Malta and Famagusta.

Seeing the Mediterranean in Venice

The *Sala dello Scudo* in the Doge's Palace takes its name from the coat of arms of the reigning Doge, which was exhibited in this room where he granted audiences and received guests. The largest in the Doge's apartments, the room runs the entire width of this wing of the palace. Its decoration with large maps was designed to underline the prestige and significance of geographical knowledge and included areas of Venetian activity such as Greek waters. The two globes in the centre of the hall show the Earth and the Stars, a division also seen in Philip II's library in the Escorial near Madrid.

Malta

The Turkish fleet was not deployed offensively between 1561 and 1564, despite the advantage that the victory at Djerba had brought. However, in 1565, Süleyman the Magnificent sent a powerful expedition of 140 galleys and 50 large transports and about 40,000 troops to capture Malta. The heavily fortified harbour base of the Knights of St John, the Hospitallers, at Valletta served as the centre for an unremitting campaign against Turkish shipping, as well as against Venetian ships that were trading with the Turks. Malta was considered as a pirate base by both, and one of the contributory reasons for the attack was the seizure by the Knights of a large Turkish carrack returning from Venice to Constantinople and belonging to Kustir Aga, the chief eunuch of the seraglio (harem) of the Sultan. The Knights had made extensive preparations to receive an attack, and had been boosted by the gift from Cosimo I, Duke of Tuscany, of 200 barrels of the finest corned gunpowder, which proved a major advantage during the siege.

Naval power provided the power-projection capability, and it might have appeared that the campaign would be a second version of the successful siege of Rhodes in 1522. However, the Turkish forces were initially hampered by divided leadership, specifically the failure of the land and sea commanders to agree and implement a coordinated and effective command structure and plan. After an initial rebuff before the main defence lines at Birgu, the main Turkish attack was focused on the small fort of St Elmo, which commanded the entrance to the main harbour and to the important subsidiary harbour of Marsamuscetto, which the Turkish admiral Piali Pasha wanted to use as his fleet anchorage. The initial Turkish attack on St Elmo was poorly coordinated, and it was not until the arrival of Dragut that the attack made headway. Dragut had the reputation and ability to act as a successful intermediary between the land and sea commanders.

For long, the Turks could not prevail over the determined defence. Positions and fighting were at close quarters. Indeed, Francisco Balbi di Correggio, who was in the garrison, claimed, 'We were now so close to the enemy at every point, that we could have shaken hands with them.' The resistance, especially the extraordinary heroism of the defenders of the fort of St Elmo, which delayed the Turks for thirty-one days, was crucial as it exacerbated the logistical problems the attackers encountered, and also gave the Spaniards sufficient time to mount relief attempts. The Turks lost a quarter of their force during the attacks on St

Elmo, and Dragut was killed by a splinter of rock, thrown up by a cannonball. There is a modern monument in Istanbul that shows him with his hand resting on a globe. Turkish warships have also been named after him.

The ferocity of the fighting indicates the intensity of religious conflict. At its height, the bodies of three dead knights were decapitated and disembowelled, then nailed to wooden crosses that were floated across the harbour in order to discourage further reinforcements entering the fort. Most of the defenders of St Elmo died fighting. Only five badly wounded knights were captured, although none were ransomed. They were also nailed by the Turks on crosses that were floated across the harbour. Five Maltese defenders leapt into the harbour and swam across to safety.

After the fall of St Elmo, the defenders of Birgu and Senglea could only try to repel attacks: they were not strong enough to mount a sortie, although they were aided by sorties from the small garrison at Mdina in the centre of the island. The garrison received and guided into the main defensive position at Valletta a small force of 700 reinforcements from the Spanish territory of Sicily, who arrived six days after the fall of St Elmo. A larger relief force, 11,000 strong, attempted to sail from Sicily, but was twice forced back by bad weather. It eventually managed to land unopposed on 7 September, 112 days after the initial landings by the Turkish fleet.

Although the Turks attacked the relief force, they were demoralised and had been decimated by the severe fighting and by disease. Problems with the supply of drinking water in the summer heat were considerable, and there was also a lack of siege artillery and ammunition. The Turks were routed by the fresh troops of the relief force but, despite this, the discipline of the janissaries held, and they successfully covered the re-embarkation of the remnants of the Turkish army in St Paul's Bay. Effective resistance, combined with relief by sea from a nearby base, had saved Malta; and not a naval battle.

As an instance of public interest, the first printed and illustrated accounts of the siege appeared in Italy and Germany within a month of the Turkish withdrawal. In England, Shakespeare's rival, Christopher Marlowe, made reference to Malta in the title of his play *The Jew of Malta*, which was written in 1589 or 1590, and which presents the Turks as attacking Malta. The Mediterranean, indeed, provided drama for the rest of Europe, both contemporary and, with the Classics and Bible, historical. It was the setting of much of Europe's history and news.

The attack on Malta marked the high-water mark of westward Turkish maritime expansion, and created a de facto maritime boundary that ran from Corfu, through Messina, to Malta and Tunis. This boundary was consolidated when Cyprus was captured by the Turks in 1570, although Crete continued in Venetian hands until conquered in 1645–69.

The Turks never again attacked Malta. It was rebuilt after the siege and the fortifications were improved. The Hospitallers, a community of military men pledged to chastity, continued to rule the Maltese archipelago. This provided noble families from across Catholic Europe, mostly French, with an opportunity to place their youngers sons in an exemplary fashion. Chastity itself proved a bit much. The Grand Master's expulsion of prostitutes from Valletta in 1581 led to violent unrest and he was deposed.

Spain and the Religious Struggle

The strength of the Spanish response in 1565 reflected the major effort made by Philip II in the Mediterranean in the early 1560s. This owed much to Genoa, which provided about two-thirds of his loans. Philip's effort included operations on the coast of North Africa. Aside from the Djerba expedition in 1560, the Spaniards broke the blockade of Spanish-held Oran in 1563. The following year, Spain sent an expedition to gain the *Peñón de Vélez*, which it had earlier held from 1508 to 1522. This onetime island, from 1934 a peninsula joined by sand to Morocco, has since remained a Spanish possession. In 2012, Spain arrested Moroccan activists who planted flags there. The fortified territory, inhabited only by troops, is reached from Spain by helicopter.

Meanwhile in the sixteenth century, Spain, which had already expelled its Muslim population, carefully policed its *Moriscos*, the forced converts who had ostensibly converted to Christianity. There was no lasting room for compromise. Instead, in a vigilant oppression, customs held to betoken continued Muslim sympathy, such as eating couscous, speaking, writing and reading Arabic, and frequenting bathhouses, were all banned in 1567. A major uprising in Granada the following year was ruthlessly crushed in 1570, and the *Moriscos* were expelled in 1609, the last leaving in 1614. It may be convenient to argue that antagonism between Christianity and Islam has been exaggerated, as opposed to rivalries within them, but the expulsion was intended and perceived in the light of an existential antagonism.

The *Moriscos* could at least hope to look for support from the Turks. There was no comparison for the Jews, as they had no sponsor power. Nevertheless, they also suffered from the power and prejudice of Spain. Jews were persecuted and expelled, and their ghettos were destroyed. Thus, in 1492, Cagliari's Jews were expelled. The synagogue was replaced by the church of Santa Croce. The same happened in all the Spanish-ruled Italian territories. Tourists can visit such sites across much of the Mediterranean.

Such social and ideological hatred owed something to the broader environmental challenges of the period, notably the 'Little Ice Age' and the impact of colder temperatures on food production, as well as the pressures created by the rise in the population of the Mediterranean. Famines were increasingly common from 1569 and they affected politics, leaving even theoretically stable cities such as Venice affected by popular disorder.

Communities were joined by place, identity and the many-tiered nature of religious activism and piety, notably worship, charity, health and education. Yet, communities were also divided by family rivalries and social tensions, as well as the more apparent sectarian and ethnic imaging that sapped cosmopolitanism.

Cyprus

Cyprus was an easier target for Turkish conquest than Malta. It was closer to the centres of Turkish power and the Venetian rulers appeared less formidable. In 1570, Süleyman's successor, Selim II, sent 116 galleys and 50,000 troops, who, landing on 2–4 July, rapidly overran the island. The three leading Venetian towns on the island, Nicosia, Girne (Kyrenia), and Famagusta, had all had their fortifications expensively and extensively upgraded, especially Nicosia. However, Nicosia, which suffered from its position at the centre of the island, and thus was without any hope of relief from the sea, fell on 9 September, largely due to poor leadership. The commander of Girne surrendered shortly afterwards, once he had been presented with the heads of the commanders of the Nicosia garrison as a warning to accompany the offer of a safe evacuation of himself and his garrison. They left safely for Crete where, as a punishment for surrendering, the commander spent the rest of his life in prison.

A substantial garrison of about 8500 troops continued to hold Famagusta despite the request for surrender being accompanied by the head of Niccolò Dandolo, Lieutenant of Cyprus on behalf of Venice, who had been killed at Nicosia. Famagusta was an altogether tougher proposition than the other two fortresses. It was much larger than Girne and had sea access. Famagusta's defences, which the Venetians had spent much effort upgrading, were probably superior to those of Malta, and it contained one of the best ports in the eastern Mediterranean, as Richard I the Lionheart of England had been quick to spot in 1191 during the

Third Crusade. Moreover, both its civil and military commanders were of exceptional courage and ability.

Although gunpowder stores ran down, Venetian relief vessels did break through with supplies during the siege, and, in Venice, it was felt that there was good reason to believe that the city would hold out. Turkish cannon fire had failed to breach the land walls and the Turks had been forced to commence mining operations, which took time. Had the garrison realised that the Turks would not honour the terms of their surrender, it is unlikely that they would have surrendered, although the garrison was starving and running critically short of gunpowder. A relief force was only days away, and conceivably could have changed the outcome of the siege. The unusual refusal of the Turkish commander to honour the terms of the surrender owed much to his anger with the success of the small garrison in inflicting such heavy casualties during a siege of eleven months, although the same had been true of Rhodes in 1522, and the defenders there were treated leniently. At Famagusta, Marcantonio Bragadin, the brave commander, was flayed alive.

Lepanto

In response to the Ottoman attack on Cyprus, in a contemporary parallel with the Crusades, and in a militarised instance of the Catholic or Counter-Reformation, a Holy League of Spain, Venice, the Papacy, Genoa, Tuscany, Savoy and Malta was organised by Pope Pius V in May 1571. Fighting under a Papal banner, the Christian fleet, under Philip II's illegitimate half-brother, Don John of Austria, who had led the campaign against the *Moriscos* in Granada in 1569–70, found the Turkish fleet off the west coast of Greece, although, as with so many battles, not by the place from which it took its name: the battle took place 40 nautical miles (74 kilometres) west of Lepanto near the mouth of the Gulf of Patras, close to the Curzolaris islands; not too far from the waters in which the battle of Actium had been fought.

The Turks, under Müezzinzade Ali Pasha, had about the same number of ships (recent Turkish work has reduced the figure from 282 to about 230) to about 236 Christian ships, but fewer cannon, 750 to 1815. The Turkish fleet was suffering from disease and lacked some of its usual complement of janissaries, while Don John had made modifications to his ships to widen their field of fire. More than 100,000 men took part in the battle on 7 October, a reminder of the major manpower requirements of naval power when strength was a function of a large number of ships, certainly in comparison to the situation for sail and steam warships. In the latter cases, numbers of ships and of men were both still important, but not to the same degree.

At Lepanto, Don John relied on battering his way to victory, although he also benefited from having a reserve squadron, which permitted a response to the success of the Turkish offshore squadron. Superior Christian gunnery, both from cannon and handguns, the fighting qualities and firepower of the Spanish infantry, who served on both the Spanish and the Venetian ships, and the exhaustion of Turkish gunpowder, all helped to bring a crushing victory in four hours' fighting. Moreover, the Turkish fleet was exhausted because the campaign had begun in March, unusually early, while losses in the campaign, and the departure already of many soldiers for the winter, meant that there was undermanning.

The effective cannon of six Venetian galleasses played a particularly important role in disrupting the Turkish fleet. These galleasses were three-masted, lateen-rigged, converted merchant galleys, which were longer and heavier-gunned than ordinary galleys, and they carried firing platforms at poop and prow, and sometimes along their sides. Their height also gave them a powerful advantage as they could fire down on opponents. If they were able to crash into the side, or sweep away the oars, of an enemy galley, the impact of their weight was much larger than that of a normal galley. The deployment of galleasses to break the force of the Turkish assault represented a considerable tactical innovation, especially when it was combined with a reserve squadron.

The willingness of both sides to engage in an open sea battle was important and extremely unusual. The Turks could have pulled back under the guns of the fortress at Lepanto and forced the Christian forces into a risky amphibious assault. The Turks indeed were aware of the presence of the galleasses, but did not appreciate their potential, and their use during the battle probably came as a tactical surprise. Good morale and determined leadership characterised each of the sides, and this may have led to a riskier approach being taken by both commanders, as also with it being late in the year – 7 October – so that both sides needed to show that they had achieved something in that campaign. The normal caution of the galley commanders was overridden on the Christian side by the charismatic and determined leadership of Don John. Müezzinzade Ali Pasha was initially reluctant to join battle, but was persuaded by the aggressive orders from the Sultan, and by inaccurate intelligence reports.

Casualty figures vary greatly, and the limited extent of the Turkish sources is a serious problem, but all agree that the Turks lost far more men, possibly 30,000 dead (including the admiral) to maybe 9000 Christians, while the freeing of maybe 15,000 Christian galley slaves accentuated the serious disruption to Turkish naval manpower. Figures vary, but the Turks lost about 113 galleys sunk and most of the remainder captured, as well as their cannon and naval stores; whereas the victors lost only about 12 galleys. The Turks lost their pool of trained sailors and mariners, as the Spaniards had done at Djerba in 1560, and these were more difficult to replace than the galleys themselves. The use of gunpowder weaponry differentiated Lepanto from such Classical battles as Salamis and Actium; although the first provided

Christian Europe with a resonant historical image in terms of defending civilisation.

After Lepanto

The battle was applauded as a triumph throughout Christian Europe, a decisive victory over a feared foe, and was much celebrated in the arts, notably in paintings. Representations of the battle can be seen in art galleries across the Christian Mediterranean. The Turks were now less feared, and their despotism thereafter was increasingly associated with decay, although only notably so from the late 1680s when the Austrians conquered Hungary and the Venetians the Peloponnese.

However, Lepanto was also to serve as an important reminder of the complexities of naval power, particularly the extent to which, as on land, triumph in battle did not necessarily lead to success in war. Lepanto occurred late in the year, and could not be followed up by the recapture of Cyprus, let alone, as Don John hoped, by the capture of Constantinople or the liberation of Palestine, the Crusader goal. More modestly, an attempt to retake the port of Modon, a former Venetian base in southern Greece, failed in 1572. This was a major failure as this campaign represented much of the window of opportunity for the Holy League. Conversely, had the Turks succeeded at Lepanto, they might well, benefiting from subsequent Venetian, Papal and Spanish naval weakness, have captured Corfu and invaded southern Italy, and/or operated in force up the Adriatic.

In the event, the ably commanded Turks carefully avoided battle in 1572–3, and rapidly constructed a new navy, which included *mahones*, their impressive version of galleasses. As the result of a formidable effort, the Grand Vizier, Sokullu Mehmed, organised the building of about 150 new galleys, in just one season. By April 1572, about 250 galleys and 5 *mahones* were ready for action. In order to improve the firepower of the Turkish fleet, there was a stress on an ability to use handguns among those called on to serve in the fleet, which was a recognition of the loss at Lepanto of the skilled marine archers who had predominated in the Turkish fleet in 1571.

The role of alliance dynamics was also crucial, as so often in warfare. The outcome of Lepanto, although disappointing from the Christian viewpoint, was fatally undermined by the Venetian decision to sue for a unilateral peace with the Turks: in March 1573, Venice recognised the loss of Cyprus and agreed to pay an indemnity. By doing so, Venice, which feared the loss of Dalmatia, reopened trade with the Turkish Empire and obtained security in the Adriatic. Moreover, it was clear that Cyprus would not be reconquered.

Tunis, which had fallen to the Turks in 1570 and been regained by Spain in 1573, fell to the Turks the following year: they deployed 240 galleys, 15 *mahones* and 40,000 troops to that end. Under serious pressure, especially from the Dutch Revolt in the Low Countries, Philip II felt unable to respond, and, instead, Spain followed with a truce with the Turks. Murad III's decision in 1577 for a full-scale invasion of the Safavid Empire to the east similarly led the Turks to other commitments.

Lepanto was decisive more for what it prevented – a possible resumption of the Turkish advance in the Mediterranean and Adriatic – than for pushing the balance of military advantage towards the Christians. Malta (1565) and Lepanto (1571) were crucial in discouraging the pursuit of westward expansion. The end result was the de facto establishment of a maritime frontier between Spanish and Turkish spheres of influence in their respective halves of the Mediterranean. This extended to North Africa where Turkish authority in Algiers, Tunis and Tripoli declined. In 1600, Tangier, Ceuta, Melilla and Oran were all still under Spain. Thus, there was a parallel to the Austrian success in stopping the Turks, albeit in less dramatic fashion, in Hungary, which similarly led to the establishment of a new boundary.

The Moroccan success in smashing a Portuguese invasion in 1578 was not followed by a revival of Muslim activity across the Strait of Gibraltar, as had been the case with the Moroccan-based Almoravids, Almohads and Marinids from the eleventh to the fourteen centuries, albeit ultimately without success. Instead, Portugal, including Ceuta and Tangier, fell to the invading Philip II of Spain in 1580; while in 1591, the Moroccans, having sent an army across the Sahara, conquered the Songhay Empire in the Niger Valley. As with the Spanish commitment in Northern Europe in resisting the Dutch Revolt, intervening in the French Wars of Religion and opposing Elizabeth I of England, this was a Mediterranean power responding to its broader range of commitments and opportunities.

Large-scale naval warfare between Turkey and the Mediterranean Christian powers did not revive until the mid-seventeenth century. Although the Turks and the Austrians were at war in 1593–1606, Spain, at war with France until 1598, with England until 1604 and with the Dutch until 1609, did not use the opportunity to join Austria in attacking the Turks. An unsuccessful Spanish assault on Algiers was launched in 1601, but it did not foreshadow a major effort. Nor was the Neapolitan system of coastal fortifications maintained sufficiently to prevent much of it falling into decay. This absence of conflict can be seen as a sign of a more widespread stagnation of Mediterranean galley warfare. However, as always when discussing Mediterranean history, not least naval power, it is also necessary to give due weight to the other commitments of the combatants and the potential combatants.

In geopolitical terms, Turkish naval power was confined but, despite considerable Turkish interest in the Indian Ocean, it is inappropriate to think in later geopolitical terms of an attempt to break through to the oceans, as if the Turks were the Soviet Union during the Cold War. Instead, the geopolitics of galley warfare was very different. Carrying soldiers greatly increased galleys' consumption of food and water, both already high due to the number of rowers, and therefore affected their range. The range also reflected the difficulties galleys faced in confronting rough seas, which were serious in the winter, although not only then. Such seas challenged not only the manoeuvrability of galleys, but also their ability to remain seaworthy. For example, unable to find water on the island of Djerba in 1510, the unsuccessful Spanish attempt to capture it lost over 3000 dead. Few harbours and anchorages were able to support and shelter large fleets transporting substantial numbers of troops. The situation affected operational methods and strategic goals, as access to, or the seizure of, these nodal points was crucial.

This capability, in turn, provided a critical political dimension. Thus, as long as 'Barbarossa' had access to French ports through diplomatic efforts, the operational range of his fleet was greatly enhanced and he could play a more prominent role in the western Mediterranean. The bitter civil conflict of the French Wars of Religion from 1562 to 1598 therefore greatly lessened Turkish options.

Galley conflict was not unchanging and, although the requirements of galley operations posed formidable constraints, it is wrong to treat the galley as a conservative contrast to the progressive development of sailing ships. The emphasis on firepower in galley warfare had increased, with Venice redesigning galleys to carry large centreline cannon, an innovation rapidly adopted by Spain and France. These cannon were carried forward and supplemented the focus on forward axial attack already expressed by the presence of a metal spur in their bow. This spur might damage enemy oars and could be pressed into the hull of an enemy galley if a boarding was attempted. The strengthened and lengthened prow provided the access/boarding ramp onto an enemy ship. These spurs could not sink ships as the (underwater) ram was intended to do, but the latter was a weapon of the Classical period that had disappeared. Like spurs, cannon were intended to help to disable the opposing ship as a preparation for boarding.

Galleys became easier to row in the mid-sixteenth century, as one-man oars (with the typical galley having three men on a bench with one oar each) gave way to rowing *a scaloccio*, in which there was one large oar for each bench, and this oar was handled by three to five men. This change, which reflected the shift from skilled volunteer oarsmen to convicts and slaves, led to an increase in the number of rowers, and also made it possible to mix inexperienced with trained rowers without compromising effectiveness. Experts were long divided about the respective success of the two systems.

Maps and Navigation

The Mercator projection, presented in a world map published in 1569, offered a response to the problems of the depiction on a map, and thus in two dimensions, of the Earth, which is a sphere. The projection did so by providing negligible distortion on large-scale detailed maps of small areas. 'Gerardus Mercator' (Gerhard Kremer, 1512–94) looked back to Ptolemy in employing coordinate geometry as a guarantee and means of a mathematically consistent plan and logically uniform set of rules. The combination of the grid of latitude and longitude with perspective geometry proved a more effective way than portolan charts to locate places, and thus to adapt to the range of new information. Portolan charts, in contrast, had similar or identical chart symbols, but lacked common scales and units of measure, and were essentially directional guides based on analogue, rather than digital, methods. In turn, the emphasis on geometry ensured that mathematical proportionality was applied. Mercator's 1554 map of Europe covered most of the Mediterranean reasonably well, although there were errors in coastal alignment, notably for North Africa.

Venice was a major European centre for the production of early printed maps, as of books, and the most significant in the Mediterranean. It was also a key point for the accumulation of information that was of value in mapping.

The use of the compass encouraged the recording, systematisation and use of navigational information. Dead reckoning was no longer an adequate method. The printing of sailing directions became more frequent, as in England with *The Mariner's Mirrour* (1588). Meanwhile, the problem that a straight line on a plane chart was not a straight course because of the curvature of the Earth had been highlighted by Pedro Nunes in his 1537 *Tratato da Spherea* (Treatise of Spheres). In these and other respects, incremental improvements were important to a spread of more reliable navigational data.

Tourist Sites

The fortifications of the period have left splendid remains, notably in Cyprus and Malta. The latter are being made more accessible, particularly at St Elmo in Valletta, which was restored in 2009–15. For that and other reasons, those who last visited Malta many years ago should revisit it. Valletta was European Capital of Culture for 2018. In Cyprus, the major Venetian fortifications at Famagusta and Kyrenia receive few tourists because they are in Turkish North Cyprus. In contrast, the well-preserved Venetian walls of Nicosia are easier to visit. Less prominent sites are also worthy of visit, not least because of the views they can command. Thus, near Sarandë in Albania is the ruined castle in Lëkurës, which was built in 1537 by Süleyman the Magnificent in order to control the coastline and offset the Venetian fortress at Corfu.

6. The Seventeenth Century

In the seventeenth century, there was no repetition of the serious challenge to the Christian position in the Mediterranean mounted by the Turks and Algiers from the 1520s to the 1570s, let alone any recurrence of the Arab sway over much of the Mediterranean in the ninth century. This situation reflected the absence of Turkish action in the western and central sections of the sea. As with the Chinese in the Indian Ocean in the fifteenth century, the key element was not the response to the imperial power in question but, rather, its intentions and policies.

North Africa

In contrast to Turkish moves, raiders from the Barbary states – Tripoli, Tunis, Algiers and Morocco – harried the coastline of Mediterranean Europe and went further afield, including to the British Isles and Iceland. With North Africa producing little wealth, and certainly few goods that could earn money, the raiders sought loot and captives, both as slaves and for ransom. The last was always important to the economics of piracy, with ransom part of a complex system that encompassed prisoner exchange, while slavery proved the fate of those who were not ransomed. There were naval attempts by the Christian powers to constrain the raiders, through both attacks on Barbary bases and attempts to protect trade, but neither proved especially effective, the English fleet, despite a major effort including a bombardment of Algiers in 1622, being essentially ineffective in the 1620s.

France made more of an impact in the 1680s, heavily bombarding Algiers in 1682, 1683 and 1688, each attack producing a treaty; and bombarding Tripoli in 1685, leading to the return of all French captives and a large ransom. Under the threat of bombardment, Tunis in 1685 agreed to return all French captives. There was widespread redemption activity in Christian Europe, with religious efforts to collect money to this end encouraged by sermons and captivity accounts, although the *Pères trinitaires* only redeemed Catholics. Indeed, negative attitudes towards Islam in part reflected the Christian response to North Africa. There were, however, also captured Muslims used as galley slaves, by France, Spain and the Italian powers.

Although it proved possible to pay tribute to and/or intimidate the Barbary privateers into leaving the ships of particular powers alone, there was no long-term settlement to the issue until North Africa was conquered by the Western powers. Yet, the fragmented nature of the Barbary states, and their limited industrial and fiscal base, did not provide a foundation for their use of naval power in order to expand territorial strength or support commercial penetration. The powerful Moroccan state created in the late sixteenth century collapsed in the early seventeenth century, in the face of dynastic division, army revolts and the growing diffusion of gunpowder weaponry in Moroccan society, the latter permitting a successful challenge to state authority.

The Turks

The Turkish emphasis was on conflict on land, notably against Austria in 1593–1606, 1663–4 and 1683–99, and against Persia until 1639. In the first forty-five years of the seventeenth century, at a time when most of the *Kapudan Pashas*, admirals of the Mediterranean fleet, were landsmen, the prime Turkish naval task was defensive and small scale, aimed at protecting the Black Sea from Cossacks based on the Rivers Don and Dnieper. When at peace with Venice, the Turks, moreover, accepted that no war-ship should enter the Adriatic, which the Venetians called 'the Gulf of Venice'.

The situation changed in 1645 when the Turks invaded Crete, Venice's largest island colony. Sultan Ibrahim (r. 1640–8) assem-bled a massive force of 51,000 soldiers and 348 ships and, in 1645–6, much of the island was overrun. However, the siege of the capital, Candia (Heraklion), begun in 1647, lasted until 1669, becoming one of the epics of Mediterranean history, although lacking its Homer. The Venetians sent reinforcements, including 33,000 German mercenaries, while political divisions under-mined the Turkish war effort, which also faced serious logistical problems. Slaves and Cretan peasants alike were forced by the Turks to dig trenches to support the siege.

In order to block the Turkish supply links, Venice and its allies (the Papacy, Malta and Tuscany) sought to blockade the Dardanelles from 1647, leading, in 1648, to food shortages, and the overthrow and execution of the extravagant, mentally weak Sultan Ibrahim, and again from 1650. A Turkish fleet that evaded the blockade was defeated off Naxos in 1651, while in 1656, despite the Turks having galleons as well, the Venetians largely destroyed another fleet off the Dardanelles, one of the key mari-time choke points in Mediterranean naval history. This was the most serious Turkish naval defeat since Lepanto in 1571, and the challenge to Turkish naval power in the Aegean was greater than it had been in the sixteenth century.

Mehmed IV (r. 1648–87) came to the throne aged six. As a result, it was the vigorous Köprülü Mehmed, who became Grand Vizier in 1656 in the subsequent political crisis, who took the key role. He rapidly rebuilt the fleet as well as reorganising the army and seeking to lessen corruption, and, in 1657, the Turks were able to resupply their forces in Crete. His son and successor led a renewed effort to take Candia. The Venetians were greatly outnumbered at sea and unable to cut off the flow of Turkish reinforcements. In 1669, a quarrel between the Venetians and their European allies in the garrison led the latter to retire and forced the Venetians in the badly battered city to capitulate. All the churches in Candia were destroyed, bar four which were transformed into mosques, as the cathedral at Famagusta had been after the conquest of Cyprus. In addition, during the war, many islands in the Aegean were lost and retaken, while there was much fighting in Dalmatia.

This lengthy struggle made a great impact in Christian Europe, not least because of the major efforts to support Candia. Louis XIV of France (r. 1643–1715) had sent troops to help Candia in 1668–9, although, poorly commanded, they proved of no value. Louis was also Protector of the Order of Malta (the Knights of St John), a role he took seriously. The order had branches throughout Catholic Europe, especially in France. The Very Christian King of France was also the Protector of the Catholics in the Turkish Empire, a source of prestige.

A major consequence of the Candia war was the arrival of Dutch and English merchantmen in the eastern Mediterranean. They obtained from their East India Companies what had previously been easier to find in Venice and provided the Turks with these goods. In particular, the war marked a surge in the English presence in the eastern Mediterranean.

Slave Soldiers

Like other Islamic states, Turkish expansion heavily relied on slave soldiers. The treatment of the boys conscripted in the Turkish Empire from Christian households was described in *The Laws of the Janissaries*, which was written in the early seventeenth century. Boys were regarded as easier to train and subdue than men. The best-looking were allocated to the palace to serve the Sultan, but most were destined for the elite janissary corps. First, they were assigned to Turkish farmers in Anatolia in order to accustom them to hardship and physical labour, and to teach them some basics of Islam and, more significantly, Turkish, the language of the corps. Recalled, they were then trained in the barracks of the novices. Circumcision served to assert their Muslim future.

Naval Conflict

In August 1676, an English diplomatic agent in Holland reported: 'They are much alarmed at Amsterdam by news come thither of a great Turkish fleet of thirty men of war and fifty galleys besides many other vessels appearing between Sicily and Italy, who, some advices say, have already taken possession of Messina.' In reality, such speculations were of another age, and it was the Dutch, French and Spanish fleets that contested Sicilian waters in the 1670s. Composed of sailing ships, a French squadron that carried more cannon than the opposing Spanish galleys raised the Spanish siege of rebellious Messina in 1675, only for the Dutch, in response, to send a fleet of their own sailing ships. The Dutch had become a major presence as a result of their earlier war with Spain, destroying a Spanish fleet off Gibraltar in 1607. After the Messina rebellion was suppressed in 1678, Spain, between 1680 and 1686, built a more powerful citadel, protected from attack from the mainland by a moat. Much of it, however, was demolished in the twentieth century.

So also earlier in Italian waters further north: the importance of coastal shipping was linked to the building and maintenance of fortifications. Thus, on Elba in Porto Longone (Porto Azzurro), beginning in 1603, Spain built a large pentagon-shaped fortress (Fort San Giacomo), which was an important position supporting the movement northward of Spanish troops from Naples. Alongside Piombino, the fort fell to the French in 1646, being recaptured in 1650 when France was weakened by civil war. Fortresses from the period can also be seen in France, notably Fort Sainte-Marguerite on the Îles de Lérins off Cannes. Spain seized the islands in 1635–7, which led Louis XIV to extend the fortress. In Alexandre Dumas's novel *The Man in the Iron Mask*, the central character is imprisoned there.

France failed to exploit large-scale anti-Spanish rebellions in Naples and Sicily in 1647-8. The Neapolitan rising of 1647, led by Tommaso Aniello or Masaniello, was in large part a response to the fiscal demands of a Spanish government desperately short of funds for the war, notably a tax on fresh fruit. Divisions within Naples, which led to the killing of Masaniello, helped the Spaniards recapture the city in 1648. The episode became the setting for Daniel Auber's dramatic opera *La Muette de Portici* (1828), which also features an explosion of Vesuvius. As with Prosper Mérimée's novella *Carmen* (1845), later adapted into an exhilarating opera by George Bizet, *La Muette* contributed to a Northern European view of Southern Europe as violent, troubled and exotic.

Louis XIV was a frequent assailant of the Spanish system which included, in the western Mediterranean, Naples and Sicily. In 1684, this policy led to an attack on Spain's ally Genoa, the port through which Spanish troops were moved between Barcelona, Naples and Milan. Without any declaration of war, about 13,000 cannonballs were fired by the French fleet, although the attempt to land troops was repulsed. As a result of the attack, Genoa moved closer to France, the Doge going to see Louis at Versailles in 1685. Indeed, Genoa thereafter was generally part of the French system, although it remained an important component or support of the Spanish commercial world, including in trade between Spain and Spanish America.

Battle at sea, as opposed to smaller-scale clashes, was occasional. It generally required both sides to be willing to fight.

Given the difficulties of forcing battle on opponents who did not want to fight, planning was very much ad hoc. Reconnaissance of opposing forces was necessarily limited to eyesight, telescopes and visual recognition of ships and flags. The closest to over-the-horizon information was from observers in the rigging and the masthead as they could take advantage of the curvature of the Earth. Once cannon opened fire, the details of a battle generally became obscure, which reflected the extent to which cannon were using black powder, which produced copious quantities of smoke.

Incremental changes made shipping more robust. In place of the clinker method of shipbuilding, using overlapping planks, came carved building in which hull planks were fitted flush together over a frame. This contributed to the development of stronger and larger hulls, which were able to support more cannon and the impact of volley fire. Moreover, the sternpost rudder spread.

Improvements in armaments, rigging and sail patterns had helped to ensure that sailing ships (galleons), rather than galleys, became far more important in Mediterranean warfare, although galleys continued to have a role until 1814 when they were discarded by the navy of Piedmont/Sardinia. With their reduced demand for manpower and, thus, water and food, and their greater storage capacity, galleons were less dependent on local bases than galleys. The English and Dutch vessels that had introduced new methods into Mediterranean naval warfare were copied by the Mediterranean powers, including, first, the North African Barbary states, which adapted Atlantic naval technology in the late sixteenth century through the intermediary of English and Dutch privateers.

The Turks were not confronted by the example, challenge and threat of galleons until later, the key intermediary being Venice, which adopted galleon construction in response to the threat from the Western European and Barbary states, before using these ships against the Turks. In 1597, in response to the suspension of Venice's protectionist laws, Dutch ships carrying Baltic grain supplied the city, providing another example of this type of construction.

In response to the war with Venice over Crete, the Turks began to construct galleons, ten being built in 1650, but the galleon only became their standard warship in 1682. The limitations of the Turkish fleet helped explain the time taken to conquer Crete. Of the Italian powers, only Venice deployed what it termed the 'Big' or 'Heavy Squadron', that of large sailing vessels. The others – Naples, Tuscany, Genoa, the Papacy and Savoy-Piedmont, had galleys, but these were insufficient in number to protect the Italian coastline from privateers. This led these powers to a reliance on coastal fortifications, notably watchtowers, but also encouraged the depopulation of coastal regions and a preference for inland settlements and routes.

Venice and Genoa, city-state republics, continued to be widely applauded as models of good government and civic virtue, resonating with Classical values that were closely associated with republicanism. Public virtue was presented as a republican characteristic, the product of states with a 'balanced' constitution. This view was given historical resonance in the shape of republican Athens and Rome. More generally, there was in the Mediterranean world a continuity of the city as not only a setting for authority and power, but also, in real effect, their wielder whatever the formal nature of the political system.

Venice, as part of the Holy Alliance created by Pope Innocent XI, and including Austria, Poland and later Russia, resumed conflict with the Turks from 1684 to 1699. The Venetians in 1685–6 exploited an anti-Turkish revolt in the Morea (Peloponnese), seizing the key positions there. In 1687, they moved north to capture the towns of Lepanto, Patras and Athens, where the Turkish magazine in the Parthenon was blown up by a mortar shell, causing serious lasting damage. The Venetians, however, were unsuccessful in attacks on Euboea in 1689 and Crete in 1692.

They captured the island of Chios in 1694, but their unpopularity led to a rebellion and their expulsion in 1695. Landings on the Dalmatian coast, initially repelled in 1685–7, were subsequently more successful, leading to Venetian acquisitions there. Venice's wartime gains were retained in the Peace of Karlowitz of 1699. As with the contemporaneous Austrian conquest of most of Hungary, this appeared to be a significant shift in power politics, one with consequences across the Mediterranean. Venice's continued interest in the Greek world emphasised its difference to the rest of Italy, and notably now to Genoa.

In the seventeenth and eighteenth centuries, in response to amphibious attacks by Venice, Maltese privateers and assorted pirates, the Turks constructed and strengthened coastal fortifications, both in the Aegean islands and along the coasts of modern Lebanon and Israel. Many of them were improvements on older castles, including Venetian ones in the Peloponnese, as well as Seljuk, Byzantine and Crusader structures, but new defences were also constructed.

The Uskoks of Senj

Among the pirates the most prominent in the Mediterranean were the Uskoks of Senj, a town in modern Croatia. The Uskoks, Croatian irregulars who fought both the Turks and the Venetians, had initially been based on Klis, but this fell to the Turks in 1537, and they then based themselves at Senj. Using light, swift boats to operate in local waters, the Uskoks first fought the Turks, but then added Venice which sought to protect Adriatic shipping. Venetian attacks were ineffective, but a war between Austria and Venice in 1613–17 was followed, in 1618, by an agreement between them under which the Uskoks were expelled from Senj.

England and the Mediterranean

This new world was not to be dominated by Venice nor, indeed, any other Mediterranean naval power. They could not match the growing relative advantage of Northern European states. Instead, ushering in a situation that has lasted to the present, and one that was to accentuate the complexity of Mediterranean power politics, it was an outside naval power, England (from 1707 Britain), that was now to the fore.

England had acquired a western base for the Mediterranean, not Gibraltar, which was not captured until 1704, but Tangier. It was transferred from Portugal, in 1661, alongside Bombay (Mumbai), as part of the dowry of Catherine of Braganza when she married Charles II. English place names were introduced. Tangier had to be defended against Sultan Mawlay Ismai'il of Morocco (r. 1672–1727), notably in 1680. An extensive defensive system was prepared, as was the mole designed to protect the harbour. This was built in part by slaves captured in the Mediterranean from North African ships. The Sultan, who wished to be free of local political pressure, had developed a corps of black soldier slaves, who contributed greatly to the military pressure he brought to bear against English and Spanish bases. So also did the claim of *jihad*, which also helped affirm his role and legitimacy. English and Moroccan state and empire building interacted in a process made more complex by domestic pressures and alternative international commitments. Tangier was abandoned by the English in 1684. Charles II was then trying to rule without Parliament and could not afford the difficult struggle with the Sultan.

Further east, the English presence had long been under the control of merchants in the shape of the Levant Company, which essentially sought a commercial presence. The company chose and paid the Ambassador at Constantinople, to which the first envoy had been sent in 1583, although its role in the choice largely ceased from 1691. Among the papers of Sir William Trumbull,

Ambassador in 1687–91, there are copies of merchants' petitions, depositions and appeals. The Turkey trade was certainly important. In 1693, during the Nine Years War, over eighty merchantmen were lost when the Smyrna (İzmir) convoy bringing home goods from Turkey was intercepted by the French off Portugal, a blow that sparked a political crisis in England. The Turks did not decide to establish permanent embassies until 1793, preferring, instead, to send individual missions for particular purposes.

A Cityscape of Power

Marseille was enlarged by the French Crown in 1660, beginning its outward expansion from the organic street plan of the ancient Old Port area into the surrounding countryside where a more regular street plan was introduced. The harbour entrance was guarded by two forts, medieval St Jean, on the north side, and St Nicolas, built in 1660 on the south side and a demonstration to the city of the power of Louis XIV.

Maps and Travel Information

Increased travel to places of interest by a broader segment of the social élite meant more guidebooks and maps. Illustrative woodcuts of cities became more accurate and far less generic, so that viewers had a better idea of what individual cities looked like. Moreover, improved maps and globes ensured that knowledge of the Mediterranean was more widely disseminated.

So also with the development from the early seventeenth century of a large-scale newspaper press in Europe. This was eventually to become most active (and most free) in the Dutch Republic and (from the 1690s) England, but there were newspapers and manuscript newsletters in Mediterranean centres. Moreover, the Dutch press, which was the centre of the most far-reaching information system, took pains to acquire sources of information there. The most important, due to its commercial activity, for Dutch and English newspapers was Livorno. Merchants there provided information. The letters they wrote became the model for written newsletters which, in turn, were the basis for newspapers, as well as providing news for the latter. So also in particular with Genoa and Venice, the latter long the major source for information about the Adriatic, the Turkish Empire and the eastern Mediterranean.

Newspapers could offer background information on the Mediterranean to readers. On 31 August 1749, an item of news from Malta in the *Worcester Journal* was followed by a note giving a brief account of the island, its history and the Knights of St John. The outbreak of plague in the Ionian Islands led to their description in the *Flying Post*, a leading London newspaper, in its issue of 9 May 1728. Nevertheless, there were deficiencies in knowledge of the Mediterranean. In his *Geography Epitomised* (1784), Robert Davidson reported being told by the clergyman James Hervey that he did not know the location of Jerusalem, which had led him to buy an atlas.

7. The Eighteenth Century

Touring the Mediterranean

Chartering a captured French frigate armed with cannon to repel attack was a sensible step when James, 4th Viscount Charlemont (1728–99) sailed from Leghorn (Livorno) in April 1749. Succeeding to his father's title in 1734, he travelled both longer and further than most tourists of the age, setting off in 1746 and not returning to Dublin until 1755. Travelling with another Irish aristocrat, Francis Pierpoint Burton, they visited southern Italy, before joining forces in Sicily with two English tourists, Roger Kynaston and John Frederick, and the artist Richard Dalton. They sailed to Malta and then Constantinople, before visiting the islands of the eastern Aegean, and sailing south to Alexandria, whence Charlemont travelled to Cairo. Prevented by the weather from reaching Cyprus, Charlemont returned from Egypt, via the coast of southern Anatolia and the Cyclades islands, after which he explored some of the major Classical sites in the Peloponnese. The Aegean, however, provided him with both the hazard of storms and the irritation of being becalmed, while Turkish officials, as at Halicarnassus (Bodrum), were not always helpful. Dalton, who published engravings of monuments he had seen in Greece, Turkey and Egypt, later became Keeper of the Royal Pictures and purchased paintings in Venice for George III.

The cost of arranging one's own transport ensured that Mediterranean cruises were usually considered only by the very wealthy. Separately, travellers also found it easiest to obtain a passage there in a warship, as did the Reverend John Swinton, who sailed thereby to Livorno, and Henry, 10th Earl of Pembroke, an army officer who in Venice in 1768 allegedly eloped with a woman on the night of her wedding to someone else. The young John, 4th Earl of Sandwich, after whom the sandwich was later named, toured the Mediterranean in 1738–9, visiting Sicily, Greece, Turkey, Rhodes, Cyprus, Egypt and Malta. Turkey meant the coast. In 1741–2, John, Marquis of Granby, with his former Eton tutor John Ewer, toured the Aegean in a large Turkish boat called a *volique*. Granby explored Greece ancient and modern, the Classical accounts of Strabo and Pliny as present for him as the Greek dancing he enjoyed and about which Lord Byron was later to write. In 1763–4, Frederick, 6th Lord Baltimore visited Greece, Constantinople and the Balkans, observing 'what I saw in my travels recalled strongly to my remembrance the Classical erudition I was so happy as to receive at Eton College'. He died in 1771, leaving 'a whole *seraglio* [harem] of white, black etc to provide for'.

A committed traveller, whose connivance in his wife's affairs had hit his reputation as a result of a messy legal case, the wealthy Sir Richard Worsley left Rome for Athens in 1785, going on to tour Greece and visit Rhodes, Cairo, Constantinople and Troy, returning to Rome in 1787 with a large collection of statues, reliefs and gems. Willey Reveley went with him as an architectural draughtsman, producing views of the pyramids based on measurements. Later envoy in Venice, Worsley built up the most extensive collection of ancient Greek sculpture in Britain prior to the purchase of the Elgin Marbles. In Constantinople in 1785, Worsley met Lady Elizabeth Craven, whose adultery had led her to leave Britain, travelling to St Petersburg and then on across Russia and the Black Sea. From Constantinople, she toured the Aegean, leading to smutty sneers in the British press, while he visited Egypt.

Also in Constantinople in 1785 was Charles Sloane, later 1st Earl Cadogan of the second creation, who visited Sicily – being impressed by the 'magnificent remains of antiquity' at Agrigento – Egypt, Cyprus and Greece. It was not, however, always easy to find passage. Sloane wrote to his brother from Constantinople on 10 November 1785: 'opportunities cannot be found to go from here to Alexandria, as you can step into the Reading Dilly [coach] and go to Chelsea'; and again on 7 December: 'I have been detained here owing to the uncertainty of sea operations near double the time I intended to stay'. Another traveller of this period, John Hawkins, having gone overland from Vienna to Constantinople, went on to Cyprus, Crete, mainland Greece, Zante, a month's quarantine in Messina, and Naples.

Different purposes underlay the visit of the Oxford botanist John Sibthorp, who, in May 1786, sailed from Naples to Crete, spending much of the summer there. He then travelled extensively in the region, including to Cyprus and the coasts of Greece and Asia Minor; although a land journey through Greece was rendered impossible in 1787 by insurrection and plague. In 1794–5, Sibthorp revisited Constantinople and Greece, including the Ionian Islands, climbing Mount Olympus, visiting the site of Sparta, and being delayed at Mount Athos by nearby pirates. On his travels, he collected 3000 botanical species. Earlier, British tourists to such areas were so rare that their return merited a mention in the press, such as that of William Lethullier who returned from the Turkish Empire in 1723 with an Egyptian mummy.

Most travellers, going no further east than Italy, and, indeed, no further south there than the Naples region, were neither that adventurous nor that energetic. However, those who did found much of interest, Thomas Watkins writing of obtaining in Constantinople 'what I never tasted before I came here, *good* coffee, for you have it not in England, as it loses so much of its flavour upon the sea'. He added from Corfu in 1788: 'You will read it over a comfortable English breakfast, which is not however preferable to ours in the Greek Islands, of rich fruits, good bread, and excellent coffee.' There was, however, also an anti-Semitic riot there that year. His letters were published as *Travels Through Switzerland, Italy, Sicily, the Greek Islands to Constantinople Through Part of Greece, Ragusa* [Dubrovnik], *and the Dalmatian*

Isles (1794), and are worth reading. They provide an account of the region before it was engulfed by the spread of the French Revolutionary and Napoleonic Wars.

Dalmatia was an area of brigandage and piracy, for example from the Turkish position at Ulcinj, and, to a degree prefiguring the situation in the early stage of the Cold War, the Roman antiquities on the coast were not on the tourist itinerary. Indeed, Robert Adam, who went to Italy in 1754, chose to make a careful study of the ruins at Spalato (Split) because they had not been tackled hitherto. Returning to Britain in 1762, he published his *Ruins of the Palace of the Emperor Diocletian at Spalato in Dalmatia.* An indefatigable traveller, Frederick, 4th Earl of Bristol and Bishop of Derry, toured Dalmatia with the Venetian naturalist Alberto Fortis and investigated the subterranean rivers of Istria. Fortis's *Viaggio in Dalmazia* (1774) was published in London in an English translation in 1778, providing information on a region not hitherto well-known by British readers. In 1795, he was elected a Fellow of the Royal Society.

Visiting Marseille

'It is one of the most debauched towns in France. It is astonishing the quantity of whores. They are impudenter and bolder than in any other town.' So wrote a tourist, possibly Marmaduke William Constable-Maxwell, in 1784.

Claude-Joseph Vernet's painting *L'entrée du port de Marseille* (1754) offers an impressive sunlit vista. Travellers of course could have the less positive memory of experience. William Mildmay sailed to Genoa from Toulon in 1730, having visited Marseille:

This city is large and populous, they reckoning upwards of 100,000 souls in it, but the chiefest part of it being built with narrow streets upon the side of a hill, makes the passage through them very troublesome and inconvenient.

And what is still worse is that there are no aqueducts under them to convey away the filth and nastiness thrown out from all the houses, which have nowhere any conveniences belonging to them ... the perpetual stink in all these streets ... The harbour ... the galleys and ships are perpetually throwing out their nastiness ... the stench and colour of its water in hot and calm weather is like that of a stagnated lake or pond.

Marseille's broad streets met with greater approval, although, in 1754, a tourist thought the wine 'too strong and fiery' and the meat 'excessive bad'. In contrast, in 1785, Lady Craven ate the most excellent crayfish and trout she had ever tasted. As a reminder of the varied fates of tourists, the deaf William, Lord of Kilmaurs was involved in a duel in 1765 as a result of talking loudly in the theatre.

The French Revolution brought change. In 1792, Marseille, a centre of radicalism with a major Jacobin Club, used force to transfer administrative and judicial functions from Aix. Marseille's volunteers marched into Paris singing the war song now known as the 'Marseillaise'. The following year, an anti-revolutionary rising in Marseille was swiftly repressed.

Italy in 1710

Visiting in 1710, while Britain was at war with France, Richard Coffin had travelled, via Amsterdam and Germany, to Venice. He spent longer there than he wished because his servant fell ill. Then, via Verona, Mantua, Bologna, Loretto, Rome and Capua, he arrived at Naples, 'reflecting on Hannibal's fate' and enjoying 'a delicious country'. As he informed his cousin, Coffin was:

charmed with the situation of this city [Naples], no place I ever saw yet pleased me half so well. From the Carthusian Monastery (which stands upon a hill atop the town), you have a full view out; and if the beauty of a prospect is in the variety of objects, certainly this must be preferred before any. Just under you, you have a full view of one of the best cities in Europe, one side a calm sea, the island Capri makes a very fine bay and washes Naples on one side, on the other Campafelice, to the left Mount Vesuvius and the black dismal country about it, and over against Pozzolo and Baia, and the charming little creeks and bays the sea makes there.

Naples and *Così fan tutte*

Travel is a matter of routes, occasions and the imagination, as much as routes, occasions and experiences. On 26 January 1790, far from the Mediterranean, *Così fan tutte*, an opera by Mozart, was first performed at the Burgtheater in Vienna. The libretto, by the Venetian Lorenzo Da Ponte, a Jewish-born convert who became a priest, and was then banished from Venice for public concubinage, very much offered a seductive view of Naples, where the opera was set.

The lively sun-drenched harbour views that eighteenth-century tourists purchased from painters, especially those by Pietro Fabris and Claude-Joseph Vernet, captured the attraction of the city, which was generally presented as more fluid and sunlit than Venice. It was certainly the hottest city experienced by many British tourists, and, prior to air conditioning, this encouraged tourists to avoid it in the summer. In his *Travels through Italy* (1766), John Northall referred to 'the usual method of going to see Naples before the weather grew hot'. Norton Nicholls wrote in July 1772 of a city where 'the nights are so delightful and the days so hot' that no one slept at night: 'I am become a greater friend of the moon than the sun.' Winter visitors found the air delightful. The largest city in Italy, and the capital of a kingdom that ruled southern Italy and Sicily, Naples by 1800 was one of the nineteen cities of the world believed to have had a population of over 300,000, Naples came fourteenth in the world, and was the fourth in Europe, behind London, Constantinople and Paris. Its size was disproportionate to that of the kingdom of Naples and posed a major economic burden for the latter.

In 1790, when *Così fan tutte* appeared, Naples was ruled by Ferdinand IV (r. 1759–1825), a Bourbon. The city was receiving more visitors than in the earlier decades of the century as a result of growing interest in nearby Herculaneum and Pompeii, where excavations had been pressed on from mid-century. In the 1760s, the theatre and the Temple of Isis in Pompeii were unearthed, and became important tourist sites. The Greek remains at nearby Paestum, long abandoned in a depopulated area, were also attracting attention. They were the most accessible Greek remains in Western Europe and became a significant site from the 1770s, in part thanks to the fame brought by engravings by Piranesi.

Closer to Naples, Vesuvius became a potent tourist attraction. Without any equivalent in Northern Europe, as Iceland saw very few tourists, it was a natural phenomenon close to a city, and it was therefore possible to see it without making the special expedition that most such phenomena usually required. Margaret Grenville recorded: 'there was a magnificent eruption at Mount Vesuvius which created two streams of lava that winded down the hill a considerable length and from our windows at night it was really a glorious sight, and perfectly answered Mr Burke's idea of the Sublime'.

Indeed, the frequent images of Vesuvius presented the ability of Italy to validate the new Romantic sensibility as well as that of Neoclassicism. Its natural power appeared particularly potent when depicted on canvas as erupting by night. Picture collections frequently included such works, for example Giovanni Lusiere's *Mount Vesuvius by Moonlight: the Eruption of 1787* at Attingham Park. Mary, Lady Palmerston, who visited Naples with her husband in 1792–3, saw an eruption in 1793:

> The different tints and forms of the different lavas has a most picturesque appearance and looking into the mouths of these craters you see all the different colours which are formed by the sulphurous matter ... the view was superb. The mountain continually throwing out red hot stones which resemble the stars of a number of rockets and the stream of lava, which was considerably increased and fallen very low, illuminated great part of the side of the mountain and made the valley quite luminous, and all dispersed over the mountain you saw light which looked like stars, which were the torches of the different parties who were wandering about.

Travel was much about sex, which was also the librettist Da Ponte's theme in Mozart's opera *Don Giovanni* (1787). There was a public emphasis on chastity for women, but, in practice, this was a matter of premarital sex. Indeed, 'cicisbeism' was found across Italy. Horace Mann commented on how 'an English traveller frequently deranges the whole harmony of *"cicisbeship"*', by which a married woman had a male companion, a *'cavalier servente'*, who accompanied her to social gatherings, and was sometimes her lover. The system provided travellers with opportunities for a relationship that was in accordance with local customs. Thomas Pelham of Stanmer (1728–1805), later 1st Earl of Chichester, had a long affair in Florence in 1750 with the married Countess Acciaioli, who then took another British lover. Her married friend Maria Serristori had had a relationship with

Charles, 2nd Marquess of Rockingham in 1748–9, while Francis, 10th Earl of Huntingdon (1729–89) was, in 1755, reputed to be the lover of Marchesa Capponi, 'the flower of Florentine nobility and, as I've heard, lewdness'. Philip, 4th Earl of Chesterfield was clear of a value of travel for his illegitimate son, Philip Stanhope: 'The Princess Borghese [Agnese Colonna] was so kind as to put him a little upon his haunches, by putting him frequently upon her own. Nothing dresses a young fellow more than having been between such pillars, with an experienced mistress of that kind of manège.' Like Venice, Naples was noted for the number of its prostitutes.

In *Così fan tutte*, the two fiancées return in disguise as Albanians. Albania was in the news in 1790 because of Kara Mahmud, hereditary Pasha (Governor) for the Turkish Empire of the Sanjak of Scutari from 1775 to 1796. In the 1780s, he clashed with the pashas of southern Albania and with Montenegro, while his interest in becoming the independent King of Albania led to conflict with the Sultan, Selim III. The Albanian lands had an element of mysterious violence, as in 1788 when Kara beheaded a delegation from Austria and Russia that had sought to recruit his assistance in their war with Selim, and sent their heads as trophies to Selim. Albania was the furthest west of the actual and imaginary 'East'. Albanians were not the figures of menace they might have been earlier in the century. Nevertheless, they would have been a wild contrast to Neapolitan men, yet another reminder of differences within the Mediterranean.

Kara Mahmud's pursuit of independence led to an unsuccessful Turkish siege of Scutari, but he was killed fighting Montenegrin tribes in 1796. His brother, Ibrahim Pasha, then ruled Scutari until 1810, working closely with the Turks. In 1831, Scutari was successfully besieged when the following Pasha pursued a quest for independence. These struggles did great economic damage to the region and sustained its lawlessness.

Political Outline

In the age when the European empires rose to dominate the world, with Anglo-French forces eventually occupying Beijing in 1860, it is easy to overlook the Mediterranean, or at least to treat it as an inconsequential backwater. While Robert Clive blazed the trail for Britain's empire in India in the 1750s or Captain James Cook explored Europe's 'dark side of the Earth' in the 1770s, the Mediterranean no longer appeared to be the centre of what the historian Edward Gibbon called 'the world question'. Islam's advance had been stopped, Venice was sunk into decay, and the key routes of trade and cultural interchange no longer ran across, and around, the blue sea.

As with most commonly accepted historical interpretations, there is a measure of truth in this, and it would be foolish to pretend that the Mediterranean played as central a role as hitherto. Yet, there is also much that is misleading, if not wrong, about the standard neglect of the sea and its surrounds.

An epic battle serves to show the continued importance of events there. On 1 August 1798, a British fleet under Admiral Horatio Nelson found its French counterpart anchored in Aboukir Bay on Egypt's Mediterranean coast. At dusk, launching the Battle of the Nile, Nelson unexpectedly attacked, and did so on both sides of the French line: on the shallow inshore side of their line, where the French were not prepared to resist, as well as simultaneously on the other side, a manoeuvre that was not without risks: *Culloden* ran aground and was unable to take part. In a battle fought at night in which the British fired at very close range, the French lost eleven of their thirteen ships of the line present: the other two fled; though both were lost by the end of 1800.

The nature of the French position was such that Nelson had been able to achieve a battle of annihilation, first defeating the ships in the French van and then pressing on to attack those moored behind; the latter had been unable to provide assistance.

French gunnery proved inadequate, and the French were not only poorly deployed, but also failed to respond adequately to the British attack. The British navy worked as a well-integrated force: Nelson had ably prepared his captains to act vigorously and in cooperation in all possible eventualities, and had fully explained his tactics to them. Moreover, British seamanship was superior, and the well-drilled gun crews outshot the French.

This decisive battle changed not only the strategic situation in 1798, wrecking Napoleon's Egyptian campaign, but also the history of the Mediterranean. From then, until the post-1945 decline of British naval power, the Mediterranean was, if not a British lake, at least a sea dominated by their naval strength. This, indeed, was to be the pre-condition of British imperial strength in the Mediterranean and on the shores of the sea, both directly – in Malta, the Ionian Islands, Cyprus, Egypt and Palestine – and indirectly, for example in Greece. It was also the pre-condition of British economic power in the region.

But how did the British reach this situation of predominance, and why was it that in 1798 British and French forces were competing for control of Egyptian waters? This had not happened earlier. French and Spanish squadrons had fought off Italy during the war of 1635–59, and the French had fought Dutch–Spanish squadrons off Sicily in 1675–6, but there had been no penetration by these powers of the eastern basin of the Mediterranean equivalent to what was to happen in 1770 with Russia, and in 1798 with both France and Britain. To understand the dramatic shift, it is necessary to turn back to consider the decline of Islamic power and notably that of naval strength.

North Africa

The naval strength of the North African powers – Morocco, Algiers, Tunis and Tripoli – relied on galleys, although they also used galleons as well as the *chebeck*, a light sailing vessel with auxiliary oars. In line with the privateering economies of these territories, of which all bar independent Morocco were autonomous Turkish provinces, the warships were employed for commerce raiding, not fleet engagements, and sought to avoid clashes with other warships. Their privateering, however, played a major role in keeping alive in Christendom the idea of Islam as hostile.

In turn, Western powers sent warships to deter attack. Attacks on their ships led the Dutch to send men-of-war twice yearly to escort merchantmen to Italy and the Near East. Formal conflicts involving the Dutch included war with Algiers in 1716–26 and 1755–9. In 1770, in response to privateering, a French squadron attacked Tunisian targets and obtained a treaty. Venice, which acted repeatedly against Algiers and Tripoli between 1761 and 1778, did so successfully against Tunis in 1784, 1785, 1786 and 1787. Bizerta, Sfax and Sousse were among the towns bombarded. Completed in 1794, and held in the *Arsenale* armoury, the monument to Admiral Angelo Emo by Antonio Canova is a testimony to this final flourish of Venetian power. There was no reason at this stage, however, to believe that it would be a final flourish.

The presence of the Royal Navy at Gibraltar helped protect British trade, just as French warships operated from Toulon, Spanish ones from Cartagena, Maltese ones from Valletta, and so on with Livorno and Naples. In 1739, Rear-Admiral Haddock was ordered to Algiers to support the consul in demanding the release of enslaved British subjects, and in 1751 an agreement with Algiers was concluded.

Like other North African centres, Tunis compensated for the decline in its supply of Mediterranean slaves, as a consequence of successful European pressure against raiding, by increasingly tapping the trans-Saharan slave trade. In the 1790s, the *Souk el Berka*, the slave market of Tunis, sold as many as 6000 slaves a year from sub-Saharan Africa. However, conflict with the North

African states was generally fruitless other than in encouraging the latter to show restraint. Occasionally, privateering bases were attacked, but they usually proved difficult targets, not least because Western deep-draught warships risked running aground on uncharted rocks off their approaches. Alongside conflict, there were acceptable relations for much of the period, and particularly with Tunis.

The fate of Western bases in North Africa varied. Spanish-held Ceuta held off Moroccan sieges in 1694–1720, and Melilla another in 1774–5; while, lost in 1708, Oran was recaptured by Spain in 1732 in a major display of strength, only to be sold in 1792. In 1741, the Bey of Tunis seized the offshore island of Tabarka, which the French had purchased from the Genoese Lomellini family who had held it since 1540, defeated a counterattack by a small French force in 1742, and sacked the French Africa Company's base at Cape Negro, now a tourist resort.

Failure at Algiers

In 1775, in a pattern that looked back centuries, about 21,000 Spanish troops embarked at Cartagena and set sail in a convoy of 44 warships and about 350 transports. Delayed by bad weather and then because the Conde de O'Reilly could not decide exactly where to attack, the landings were characterised by great confusion, and the exposed Spaniards were pinned down on the beaches by heavy fire from Moorish coastal artillery, while their own artillery was delayed by the coastal sand. By mid-afternoon, the Spaniards had suffered 2400 casualties for no gains, and O'Reilly ordered re-embarkation. Complete panic ensued, with the loss of possibly 3000 troops as prisoners.

In 1784, a line of Algerian warships thwarted an attack on the city by a combined Spanish, Portuguese, Neapolitan and Maltese fleet. In turn, Algiers was able to send privateers to attack the shores of the northern Mediterranean, including the seas off Genoa, Nice and Sardinia in 1787.

Touring Italy in the mid-1750s, the painter George Stubbs made friends with a Moor and visited the Spanish base of Ceuta with him. From the walls, Stubbs saw a lion seize a white Barbary horse, and this powerful scene provided the subject of numerous of his paintings, including *A Lion Seizing a Horse* (1764) and *A Lion Devouring a Horse* (1770). Once engraved, these proved popular prints. Stubbs's skill as a painter of racehorses explains part of their attraction. Nevertheless, there was a sense, with these works, of observing the savagery of the non-European world that locates the focus of contemporary impact. This was a world in which animals were still powerful, and, apparently, many of the people were regarded as in some way akin to animals. Such racist attitudes suggested that Europeans were best placed to define and spread civilisation. Somewhat differently, Louis XVI of France, in the 1780s, used his consul in Algiers to obtain animals for his menagerie, including four ostriches.

The Turks

Although Turkish activity did not range as far as in the sixteenth century, the navy remained significant in the eastern Mediterranean, and notably because the traditional dependence on galleys had been replaced by new galleons that carried more cannon. This Turkish fleet was feared, with rumours circulating in Venice in 1708 that it would be sent to the Adriatic. In 1715, when, unlike in the mid- and late 1680s, the Turks benefited from not being at war with any other power, they were extremely

successful in using amphibious power to support the rapid reconquest of the Morea (Peloponnese) from the Venetians. The Turks
also profited in this conflict from taking the initiative, from
greater numbers (100,000 to 7000 troops), and from expertise
in siegecraft. The Venetian garrisons enjoyed scant support from
the predominantly Greek Orthodox population.

In 1716, the Turks went on to invade the island of Corfu, the
key protection for Venice's position in the Adriatic, but the fortifications of the main position there proved too strong. This might
seem a major failure, but the same had occurred for the Turks in
Corfu in 1538; while, in turn, Spanish failure at Algiers later in
the century is instructive. Victor Amadeus II of Savoy-Piedmont
was sufficiently concerned in 1716 to issue orders for the defence
against Turkish attack of his new territory of Sicily. Moreover, in
1718, off the island of Kythira, a major location on the maritime
route between the Aegean and the Mediterranean, the Turkish
fleet had the advantage over Christian opponents, principally
Venetian warships. However, then and later, the Turkish fleet did
not really move from Greek waters, and, from 1716, the Turks
were fully involved in a disastrous war with Austria that lasted
until 1718. Austrian forces captured Belgrade in 1717.

Peace from 1718 encouraged a reduction of the Venetian fleet
and, thereafter, it essentially served to protect trade from privateers,
and did not wage war. The Turks also reduced their navy, understandably so, as their major challenge in the 1720s, early 1730s and
1740s – as earlier, for example, in the early 1510s, 1580s and 1620s
– was that of Persia. As so often, Mediterranean power politics
were an interactive aspect of a wider world. In the 1720s, clerical
opposition to Sultan Ibrahim, which helped cause his overthrow in
the Constantinople uprising of 1730, arose largely from his failure
to carry out his divine mission to spread Islam, and, in particular,
from his 1724 treaty with Russia and his war with Persia.

The Turks were no longer mentioned as threatening or
potentially influencing Italian politics. In Henry Fielding's play

Rape upon Rage, later retitled *The Coffee-House Politician* (1730), 'Politic', a London tradesman, is a figure of fun when he repeatedly suggests that the Turkish fleet could attack England. He adds the Classical reference: 'Troy was taken in its sleep.' Separately, although there was still menace in Mozart's *The Flight from the Seraglio* (1782), the Singing Turk became a figure of fun or of weakness in operas. So also with Turkish puppet shows.

Nevertheless, despite Turkish weakness, good relationships with Turkey were sought by Naples and Venice, both in order to help trade and because, although Turkish authority declined markedly in Algiers, Tripoli and Tunis, they were part of the empire. In 1783, however, Algiers pursued direct negotiations with Western powers, Tunis following immediately. The Turks did not intervene when Western navies attacked them soon after, and the process of state-building developed in North Africa.

The Balkans

In the eighteenth century, in the Turkish-ruled Balkans, a new group of provincial rulers, commonly known as *ayan* (notables), emerged with a local power base. Effective local administration was frequently provided only by them. Powerful local families dominated Albania, central Greece and the Morea with the aid of private armies. The sale of state land to rich officials in much of the Turkish Empire did little to increase central authority. The weakness of the central government forced it to co-opt many of the *ayan* into the provincial administrative system and, particularly in periods of difficulty, they were granted official appointments. At other times, determined leaders sought to curb *ayan* power, the energetic Grand Vizier, Halid Hamid Pasha, launching one such attempt in 1785, but it was abandoned when war with Russia broke out in 1787.

In 1706, Robert Harley, one of the English Secretaries of State, thought that French influence in Constantinople could be countered 'when the Turks know we have so powerful a fleet in those seas, which can safely visit them'. In practice, the English, later British, deployed warships essentially in order to fight France and Spain, and that at this stage, unlike with the French in 1798, entailed the western Mediterranean. In 1713 and 1731, as part of diplomatic settlements that Britain had played a key role in negotiating, British warships escorted new rulers to Sicily and Tuscany respectively: Victor Amadeus II of Savoy-Piedmont, and Don Carlos, later Charles VII of Naples and Charles V of Sicily (r. 1734–59), and then Charles III of Spain (r. 1759–88). A century later, in 1833, it was to be to Greece to which British warships escorted a new ruler.

In contrast, during its war in with the Turks 1768–74, Russia sent, in 1769, a fleet from St Petersburg, via England and an overwintering in Livorno, to attack the Turks in the eastern Mediterranean in 1770. It did so at Çeşme off Chios on 5 July: the closely moored Turkish fleet, of twenty ships of the line and frigates, and at least thirteen galleys, was outmanoeuvred, and almost totally destroyed by fireships. About 11,000 Turks were killed. The Russians were then able to blockade the Dardanelles, as Venice had done in earlier conflicts. They also operated in the Aegean, for example establishing themselves in Milos, but attempts to capture Lemnos, Euboea and Rhodes were unsuccessful. Encouraged by assurances of assistance, the Greeks in the Morea rebelled, but the Russians failed to provide their promised support, and it was difficult to coordinate Greek action.

Indeed, the Russians proved less successful than the Venetians had done in the 1680s, although they lacked Venice's nearby bases, and also faced a greater range of military commitments, notably large-scale war with the Turks in the Balkans and the serious Pugachev's Rebellion within Russia. The Turks were able to suppress the revolt, but Russian naval power had a major economic effect on them.

Other Mediterranean powers were forced to consider the possible implications of Russia spreading its power. When its warships at Zante (Zakynthos) in the Ionian Islands disregarded Venetian quarantine and other regulations in 1773, observers wondered what military, political and commercial consequences might flow from Russian gains from the Turks, including a possible base in the eastern Mediterranean.

The subsequent threat from the French Revolution led to a total volte-face in 1799. In response to Napoleon's invasion of Egypt the previous year, Turkey and Russia (which had fought again in 1787–92) signed an alliance and sent a joint fleet that occupied the Ionian Islands, successfully besieging Corfu. France had occupied Venice in 1797 and seized the Ionian Islands, which were organised as three French *départments*. In 1800, as part of the more general process of redrawing Mediterranean borders and creating new states that was particularly significant in 1793–1815, the new conquerors established the Septinsular Republic, which lasted until 1807 when it was ceded by Russia to France by the Treaty of Tilsit. In addition, the French seizure of Malta from the Knights of St John in 1798 showed how traditional geopolitical alignments had been transformed by the French Revolutionary War.

The Mediterranean Islamic world was now, at least in part, dependent for its security on European assistance. Alliances between the Turks and Christian European states were not new, and, in the early sixteenth century, the Turks had cooperated with Francis I of France against Emperor Charles V; but these alliances changed in character in the eighteenth century to become increasingly defensive.

Again, the late eighteenth century was the crucial period. There had been earlier talk of driving the Turks from the Balkans, when Austrian or Russian forces had done, or seemed about to do, well, for example in the early 1690s, 1711 and 1770–1, but this talk became far more insistent from the 1780s. The easily-achieved Russian annexation of the Crimea in 1783 led to interest by others in equivalent gains. A memorandum of 1787 in the French foreign ministry archives claimed that, if France joined her ally Austria, as well as Russia, against Turkey, she herself could hope to acquire Crete and Egypt from the latter. The French occupation of Cyprus and Rhodes was also suggested and the need to prevent Britain occupying Egypt was emphasised. There was therefore a degree of continuity between pre-Revolutionary and Revolutionary times when, in 1798, French troops were to invade Egypt.

Nevertheless, the shift in the pattern of French policy was to have consequences for the Mediterranean. Hitherto, France had been the firmest Christian ally of Turkey: in the sixteenth and seventeenth centuries, because the French saw the Turks as their ally against the Habsburgs; and in the eighteenth, because they saw Russian power and expansion as a threat to their understanding of Europe. By the 1780s, France had achieved a dominant position in the foreign trade of the eastern Mediterranean. For both political and commercial reasons, she was the most influential foreign power in the Turkish Empire, and also supplied military assistance. The French were also increasingly aware of the strategic importance of Egypt. In 1785, they signed an agreement with the Mamluk beys, who wielded most influence in Egypt, opening the Red Sea route to India to trade over the Isthmus of Suez. Marseille merchants sought to exploit the route as they also wished to develop trade with the Black Sea.

The views of the French were of particular importance because France's position in the Mediterranean had been greatly strengthened earlier in the century as Spain came into the French alliance system from 1700 with the replacement of the childless last of the Spanish Habsburgs by Louis XIV's grandson, Philip V

(r. 1700–46) and, more consistently, from the alliance of the two powers in 1733. Spanish ministers were concerned about Russian expansionism in the Mediterranean.

French expansionism in the Islamic world did not yield territorial gains until 1830. However, it became a major theme in Mediterranean history. At the same time, there was also continuity between the opposition to Russian gains seen prior to the French Revolution and that at the time of the Crimean War (1854–6). In each case, cooperation with Britain was sought by France.

Printing in Constantinople

In Europe, the publishing of books was most limited in the Turkish Empire. Although there had been short-lived presses in Constantinople for the printing of Hebrew, Greek and Armenian, religious views had prevented the introduction of Turkish and Arabic printing, and it was not until 1729 that secular Turkish works began to appear. Ibrahim Müteferrika, a Hungarian by birth who had become a court steward, was permitted to publish seventeen works, historical, geographical and scientific, mostly in editions of five hundred. These publications were dependent on Western expertise: the second book, a geographical work, was seen through the press by an apostate Spanish monk, while the plates were engraved by a Viennese workman. After Ibrahim's death in 1745, no book appeared in Constantinople for fifteen years and no more than eight in the following forty. Publishing only revived seriously in the nineteenth century.

The Rise of British Power

English warships had been to the Mediterranean before 1694, especially under Robert Blake in 1655. Then, the refusal of the Bey of Tunis to provide compensation for attacks on English shipping led to the destruction of shore batteries and privateers at Porto Farina, which is now Ghar el-Melh. Thereafter, there had been other English missions to protect merchantmen against the Barbary privateers, protection that was necessary for trade with Italy and the Levant. From 1694, however, such naval deployment was more closely linked to strategic confrontations, as the interests of Austria, France and Spain in the western Mediterranean ensured that it was the cockpit of European diplomacy. This situation led to battles with the French (Malaga in 1704 and Minorca in 1756), Spain (Cape Passaro [also known as Capo Passero], Sicily's south-eastern promontory, in 1718) and a Franco-Spanish fleet (Toulon in 1744), battles which affected public assumptions about British naval capability.

Battle alone was not the issue. John Chetwynd, the envoy in Turin, commented in 1704 about the plan to send an English fleet to the Mediterranean, 'Unless there are 10,000 soldiers aboard the fleet it will not have that respect paid to it which it deserves.' During the War of the Spanish Succession, in which England/Britain was involved from 1702 to 1713, Barcelona was captured in an amphibious operation in 1705, followed by Alicante, Majorca and Ibiza in 1706, and Sardinia in 1708. In 1707, Toulon was attacked in a combined operation by British and Dutch warships with a siege by Austrian and Piedmontese forces. The siege was stopped when it became clear that the city would not fall speedily, but the destruction of the French fleet in harbour there meant that the strategic goal had been achieved. Force projection also led to the capture by Britain of what became colonies: Gibraltar in 1704 and Minorca in 1708. This imperial expansion in turn ensured the continuation of naval deployment in the region. Naval bases were developed at both.

The British were far less successful in their plans to intervene on France's Languedoc coast on behalf of a Protestant rising in the Cévennes mountains in the interior. Landings in 1707 and 1710 failed to sway the situation. The second led to the temporary capture of the port of Sète before re-embarkation in the face of a build-up of French forces.

Spain enjoyed a resurgence of power when Philip V's victory in the War of the Spanish Succession increased the effective authority of the Crown. New energy and resources were devoted to the build-up of a new fleet, but this was smashed by the British in 1718 at Cape Passaro, which resulted in the capture of ten ships of the line and the destruction of four more. This victory led to British euphoria about naval capabilities, the *Weekly Journal* claiming on 18 October: 'This single action renders the King of Great Britain as much master of the Mediterranean as he has always been acknowledged to be sovereign over the British seas'; although a 1718 pamphlet by Reeve Williams claimed that most Britons had no idea where Sicily and Sardinia were. The bold proposal in 1738, as Anglo-Spanish relations deteriorated, of James, 2nd Lord Tyrawley, the martial envoy in Lisbon, that the British conquer Majorca and also use the navy to back a Moroccan invasion of southern Spain, however, was not pursued, which was just as well as it was ridiculous.

In 1742, during the War of the Austrian Succession (1740–8), a British squadron entered the Mediterranean and was ordered to support Charles Emmanuel III, ruler of Savoy, Piedmont, Sardinia and Nice. As a result, the Spanish army destined for Italy marched via southern France rather than crossing the Mediterranean. The fleet landed marines who helped thwart the Spanish threat to Nice, but a repeat operation in 1743 failed to do so. In 1744, the British fleet provided supplies to the Austrian army operating south of Rome, while also preventing France and

Spain from sending troops by sea to Italy. In 1745, Genoa entered the war on the Franco-Spanish side, but, in 1746, with British naval support, the Austrians and Sardinians conquered Genoa, liberated Nice and invaded southern France. British warships also transported Sardinian troops to back a Corsican rebellion against Genoese rule and, when Genoa drove out its Austrian garrison, helped blockade the city.

In the Seven Years War (1756–63), Minorca fell to French attack in 1756, Admiral Byng being shot for failing to relieve it. Most of the British fleet was in home waters, prepared to resist a feared invasion of England. As a result, only a small squadron of ten ships of the line under Byng was sent to the Mediterranean. Reinforced by three ships from Gibraltar, Byng attacked a French fleet of comparable size under the Marquis de La Galissonière 30 miles south-east of Minorca on 20 May. Approaching the French line, Byng heaved to in order to dress (reorganise) his own, but there was a failure to concert operations between the parts of his force. The van, under Rear-Admiral Temple West, engaged with the French at close quarters but, approaching nearly head on, was badly pummelled by the heavy raking broadsides of their strongly gunned opponents. The rear, under Byng, failed to come within effective gunshot and, by the time it was ready to act, the van was in a bad way, and Byng decided not to renew the attack on the French, who remained on the defensive. Instead, Byng withdrew to Gibraltar and the besieged garrison at Fort St Philip surrendered.

Byng was convicted by court martial on the grounds that he had failed to do his utmost to destroy the French ships. Neglect carried a mandatory death penalty unless royal pardon was exercised, though the court martial had also recommended mercy. Mercy was not the view of George II, nor was it a popular position outside Parliament. Byng's execution in 1757, shot on the quarter-deck of his ship, fortified the subsequent determination by naval officers not to fall foul of a court martial.

Byng's failure affected Britain's Mediterranean trade, with consequences for employment in Britain. Minorca, however, was regained in 1763 at the subsequent peace. The fortifications were strengthened, but Minorca was lost anew in 1782 in the War of American Independence: a long siege without relief had let scurvy ravage the garrison.

In contrast, Gibraltar, which was easier both to defend and to relieve, survived Spanish sieges in 1704–5, 1727 and 1781–3. The remains of the *Línea de Contravalación* can still be seen north of Gibraltar where they were built by Spain in 1727–35 to threaten the position and prevent incursions. They consisted of a wall with an anchoring fort at each end – Forts Santa Barbara and San Felipe. In 1779, when Spain and Britain went to war, a blockade began, a formal siege following in 1781. On 13 September 1782, a major attack was made with floating batteries, but most were sunk by British fire and, thereafter, the siege became a less intense blockade and bombardment. The British ability to relieve the position by sea was crucial, although it depleted naval strength elsewhere.

France, Spain and Austria

Britain might be the leading power in Mediterranean waters, and notably so after defeating its rivals in battle in 1704, 1747, 1759 and 1798. However, the Mediterranean, both sea and, even more, shores, also had a role for other powers. Indeed, in large part, British naval moves arose from the interaction of these others. Thus, in the late 1710s, the key element for Britain and France was that of resisting Spanish expansionism. This interaction took a physical form in naval warships and infrastructure. Moreover, the significance of Atlantic concerns for Spain and France meant major naval facilities on the Atlantic, notably Cádiz, Corunna and Brest, but that did not mean the lack of a Mediterranean role.

Competition between the powers took many forms, notably supporting protégés in lesser states. In particular, the Italian territories were a focus for competition, as they had been for centuries. Indeed, this had been a central theme of Italian history and Mediterranean power politics since the fall of the Roman Empire. Competition took many forms, including intervention in Papal conclaves (elections), a practice that had become again more common from the 1590s. The recruiting of Italian aristocrats for service in the armies of the major powers was another aspect of this competition.

The Fate of Corsica

In 1768, the French government announced the union of Corsica with France. In the face of the Genoese practice of considering Corsica a colony and of refusing to treat its major families as noblemen, much of the Corsican population had long been rebellious, notably in 1729–32 and 1734–9. In 1729–30, the rebels sought to open the major posts in the administration, army, church and judiciary to Corsicans: they were reserved for Genoese. The rebellion took the form of a struggle between the countryside and the towns (where many Genoese lived and where their troops were based), both competing for the control of the fertile alluvial plains. The towns were seen as the domain of Genoese, usurers and merchants. However, while the poor of the town of Bastia, when it was attacked by the rebels, did not support them, fearing pillage and preferring communal solidarity, the clan structure of Corsican society divided the rural interest. The Corsicans were increasingly interested in independence and sought to obtain it in the 1730s and 1740s, but France backed Genoa.

A failure to control the island encouraged Genoa to agree in 1764 to sell it to France. The French, however, were perceived as enemies and French occupation was resisted: initially, Corsican resolve, knowledge of the terrain and fighting qualities, combined with French overconfidence and poor planning, led to Corsican successes. However, in 1769–70, larger French forces, better tactics, and the use of devastation, terror and road construction so as to move troops, led to eventual victory, notably as a result of the battle of Ponte Novu in 1769. Corsica was incorporated into France, making a French subject of Napoleone di Buonaparte, who was born in 1769 (he later changed his name to the French spelling Napoleon Bonaparte). French administrators produced the *Plan terrier*, a blueprint for the social and economic development of the island. The conquest was criticised by, among others, Voltaire and Rousseau, who felt that the French government should concentrate on domestic problems rather than foreign adventurism, and who, like James Boswell, romanticised the Corsicans, but the French benefited from the absence of foreign governmental support for the Corsicans. French rule was not to be universally popular in Corsica, the forcible enlistment of men for the military leading many to flee to Italy.

Economic Change

Change can be seen clearly with one set of economic statistics. Whereas in 1660 Marseille imported only 19,000 quintaux (100 kilograms to a quintal) of coffee, of Yemeni origin from Egypt, in 1785 it imported 143,310 quintaux, of which 142,500 came from the West Indies. The Europeans had taken over the bulk of world trade in coffee. Introduced to Martinique and Guadeloupe in 1725, and to Saint-Domingue in 1730, French West Indian coffee was more popular than that produced by the Dutch in the East Indies, and it swiftly became the principal global source. In 1770, 350,000 quintaux were produced, and in 1790 over 950,000. Most went to France and much was then re-exported, from Marseille principally to the Turkish Empire, reversing the trade flow of 1660: the westward flow across the Mediterranean had been replaced by an eastward one.

The Mediterranean still had goods to sell to those at a distance. Primary products were matched by manufactured goods and by services. Salt, notably from Cagliari in Sardinia, Alicante and Ibiza in Spain, and Trapani in Sicily, was recorded in the Sound Tolls as moving into the Baltic. Salt in the 1780s was the foremost Swedish import from Iberia and the Mediterranean, linking Sweden and Denmark to the island of Sardinia, whose leading export it was. Used for gunpowder, sulphur was Sicily's leading export until the end of the nineteenth century. A very different export was currants from the Ionian Islands. By value, 78.7 per cent of Piedmont's exports in 1752 was silk. Culture was one of the principal exports from Italy, with pictures, statues and musical performers all earning money.

Such exports helped to bring money into the Mediterranean, but they could not compete with the value of the transoceanic goods brought to Atlantic Europe: tea from China, cotton cloth from India, sugar, coffee and tobacco from the New World, gold from Brazil. Nor did the Mediterranean produce the industrial goods that were of increasing value from the late eighteenth century: the products of forges and steam-driven equipment that were starting to come from Britain.

As a consequence, trade was increasingly a matter of the penetration of the Mediterranean by foreign goods and by foreign merchants seeking raw materials for exploitation. Thus, in 1722, Jewish and French merchants competed for Thessaloniki's trade. The French were particularly active in the Turkish Empire, developing their presence greatly in the 1720s and 1730s. The French replaced the British as the leading foreign traders at the foremost port in the empire, Smyrna, and acquired a monopoly of Palestine's external maritime trade, while the Venetians were hard-pressed commercially in the Peloponnese and the Ionian Islands, and the Dutch faced French competition at Thessaloniki. French trading privileges in the Turkish Empire were renewed in 1740 after the successful mediation the previous year of a peace treaty between Austria and Turkey.

Attempts to introduce free trade in Mediterranean states did not greatly help local economies. Livorno's prominence as a trading centre owed much to its designation as a free port in 1675, with no tariffs on exports or imports, and with an effort to counter religious tensions. Other Italian rulers sought to emulate this achievement. Messina became a free port in 1728 and Ancona in 1732. When, in 1719, Austria wished to boost her Adriatic commerce, Trieste and Fiume (Rijeka) were given this status. In 1748, free internal trade in the Papal States was introduced. With Papal support, Ancona was made a free port and a large mole built to protect the harbour.

Diplomats devoted many pages of their dispatches to trade issues. In July 1776, Clermont d'Amboise, the French envoy in Naples, complained that, whereas the British were allowed to sell prohibited goods, the French were not, and that their ships were searched despite their privileges to the contrary. He added that French vice-consuls alone were threatened with the loss of the privilege of putting up their ruler's arms. The following month, Clermont d'Amboise complained about the more favourable treatment of the Genoese in the Calabrian oil trade, while, in September, the Neapolitans protested that a French ship had given a murderer refuge. The year 1777 brought renewed disputes over the customs, the respect allegedly not paid to the French flag and the debts owed to Marseille grain merchants. The French were concerned about the willingness of Neapolitan consuls to allow

Genoese and Tuscan smugglers to use their flag, while Clermont d'Amboise suggested that if the orders to visit Neapolitan ships in Marseille were revoked, this would help French traders in Naples. In 1778, he pressed Naples to allow grain exports to France and to stop the imprisonment of French sailors seized for smuggling.

Such complaints interacted with the determination of the lesser trading powers, such as Naples, to improve their economy, to resist their major counterparts, such as France, and to derive greater benefit from trade. Somewhat differently in 1777, Clermont d'Amboise paid court to the Queen's chamber woman, whom he believed influential, while, in 1778, both he and the Austrian envoy sought to have compatriots appointed to teach the heir to the throne.

There were also frequent tensions between diplomats and merchants. French envoys in Constantinople, such as Villeneuve in the 1730s, criticised the Marseille Chamber of Commerce over its prominent role in the organisation of the Turkey trade. There were attempts by other French economic interests, for example in Amiens, Rouen and Languedoc in the 1730s, to open up this trade, possibly via Dutch merchants. The envoys, however, preferred a regulated trade, rather than liberty of commerce. French consuls also clashed with merchants in Cairo, Sidon, Thessaloniki and Tripoli (Lebanon).

Commercial policy could not transform the economy. Livorno was not to lead to a Tuscan industrial revolution. There was no particular Mediterranean 'reason' for this situation. Elsewhere in Europe, successful ports, such as La Rochelle and Cádiz, also led to enclave economies rather than economic transformation. Similarly, Marseille in the second half of the eighteenth century contained cloth, sugar, glass, porcelain and soap factories. So also with Trieste, where Austria established a company to develop trade with Turkey.

Since most of Europe did not experience industrialisation and significant economic transformation until the twentieth century, it is not helpful to think in terms of failure. Moreover, the criteria adopted to define economic progress fail to give due weight to the variety of economic activity in this period. Research on a number of areas not generally seen in terms of economic development, for example the Veneto at the close of the seventeenth century, or Spain in the eighteenth and nineteenth centuries, has indicated a considerable degree of resilience and adaptability that suggests that an economic geography of Europe portraying the Mediterranean as backwards is unhelpful. There was no fundamental restructuring of societies and economies, but the continuation of a mixed economy, rather than one based on specialisation. This situation reflected a sensible avoidance of risk and over-commitment, as the nature of comparative advantage had not yet driven out of profitability most of the other sources of income, and did not yet encourage such specialisation in both production and employment.

Allowing for this point, and remarks about backwardness have to be handled with care, the tide of revisionism has not yet managed to portray a Balkan industrial revolution in the late eighteenth century, nor a Sicilian counterpart as a backdrop for Garibaldi's invasion in 1860. Indeed, it is no accident that one of the major exports from Sicily and Naples was to be people, who were seeking economic advantage and opportunities for a better life in the New World. The same, of course, was true of Scotland, where there very much was an industrial revolution, but all the economic indicators suggest a major difference between the two.

It was not only industry that was different. The same was true in agriculture. In Sicily, increases in wheat production could be achieved only by extending the area of land under cultivation, and crop sizes were maintained only by sowing on tilled fallow. The tilling was done by hoes that barely scratched the surface of the soil. There were significant agricultural improvements in Lombardy and Venetia but, in general, the Italian position was bleaker, substantially a matter of traditional methods and extensive cultivation, rather than agricultural changes and intensive methods. The mixed farming of the Lombard plain, with animals providing manure and milk, made little progress elsewhere, and efforts to encourage the cultivation of the potato in order to provide inexpensive food had little impact.

The principal problems there and across the Mediterranean – harsh terrain, denuded soil, poor water supplies, inadequate communications and a lack of investment – still dominated Italy in 1800, and the major cause of increased production was the expansion, particularly from mid-century, of the cultivated area. Official figures for Italy showed that the standard production of grain per hectare (2.5 acres) remained 10 metric tons in 1860 and had only risen to 10.1 by 1909–10. Subsequently, due to the use of improved strains and to Mussolini's 'Battle for Wheat', it was 16.1 in 1938. Now, depending on the soil, it is 65–90 tons.

Commercial farming certainly spread in most of Italy in the second half of the century, and common lands were enclosed. Distant and local markets were served. Genoa exported lemons and olives, while, in southern France, Languedoc wine production developed thanks to the growth of the provincial market. Nevertheless, subsistence agriculture was still the norm in most of Italy and across much of the Mediterranean. This was particularly so in the Balkans and in North-West Africa.

Transhumance, the seasonal movement of livestock often over very long distances, which had long been a crucial aspect of agricultural activity throughout Europe, was still also the norm. Indeed, man's domination of upland pasture zones, and their link to the Mediterranean coastline, was only seasonal. Thus, the cattle left the Savoyard mountains for the valleys every year on 10 October. At about the same time, the sheep of the Mesta, the Spanish wool monopoly, set off on their march from their open summer grazing lands in central Spain to the lowlands, the largest annual migration of animals in Europe. Pasture was the principal benefit derived from mountainous zones, and transhumance linked regions: the Apennines to the Emilian plain, the Abruzzi mountains to the plains of the Capitanata near Foggia, and so on, to create the complex patterns that made up the Mediterranean economy. Sheep were driven from Roussillon to Barcelona, and cattle from Piedmont to Genoa.

There were some transport improvements in the period, but few major ones before the coming of the train. The opening of the Col de Tende pass at the southern end of the Alps to wheeled traffic reflected hopes in Piedmont that wine could be exported to England via Nice, but they were cut short by the outbreak of the French Revolutionary War in 1792.

Meanwhile, the Balkans were affected by significant epidemics of plague in the 1710s, 1720s, 1730s, 1740s, 1770s and 1780s. The epidemics could spread westward, in 1743 killing about 48,000 in Messina. However, the 1720 Marseille outbreak, which was limited by isolating the city, was the last in France, and that of 1743 both the last in Italy and not on the scale of the major plague there in 1629–31. Malaria was a significant and more regular problem in parts of the Mediterranean. Famine was an issue, leading variously to riots, as in Istria in 1716, and the building of public granaries, as in Marseille.

The Crisis of the 1790s

Interest in preserving the Turkish Empire reflected shifts in the Mediterranean world, and in wider geopolitics. In the latter case, it was in a new departure, a concern of the British in the late eighteenth century. Anxiety about the possibility of Russian expansion towards the Mediterranean at the expense of the Turks led in 1791 to the Ochakov Crisis, in which the British nearly went to war with Russia and contemplated for the first time the dispatch of a fleet to the Black Sea. A trade treaty with the Turks was considered. It was also rumoured in 1791, although without cause, that the Turks would cede Cyprus, and thus provide Britain with a major commercial base in the eastern Mediterranean.

The crisis led to the dispatch of British military observers who, prefiguring commentators in the nineteenth century, argued that there was need for a total reform of the Turkish system. George Koehler, a German in the British artillery, spent six months in 1791–2 studying the situation. He claimed that 'a complete revolution in their government, finances, national character, mechanical arts etc. must be accomplished ... this indifference which reigns through every branch of their government both civil and military is perhaps the greatest of all their obstacles to improvement.' George Monro added in 1793: 'It appears to me a perfect impossibility that the Turks can keep possession of Turkey in Europe much longer; without the assistance of some of the European powers: or unless they made such an universal change in every department: as would occasion a thorough revolution in the Ottoman constitution.'

Such comments marked the new attitude towards Oriental civilisations, with the fear and awed respect of the fifteenth, sixteenth and seventeenth centuries replaced by contempt and a sense of superiority that ignored the inherent strengths of other cultures and that have continued to the present. Such comments also looked forward to the great crisis of the Mediterranean world in 1797–9. Already in 1794, Robert Liston, British envoy in Constantinople, had been instructed to win the support of the Turks in order to resist a barbarism within Europe reinvented with the French Revolution:

In all your conferences with the Ottoman ministers you cannot too strongly impress upon their minds the dangerous tendency of the avowed principles of the present French government if the most absolute anarchy can be so called, where the miserable people, deluded by the specious pretence of liberty, groan under the most despotic tyranny. Your Excellency will explain to them that those principles aim at nothing less than the subversion of all the established religions and forms of government in the whole world, by means the most atrocious which the mind of man will ever conceive.

A year earlier, as the triumph of the Revolutionaries was resisted within France, the British sent a fleet to Toulon to help the Royalists there, but it was driven out by the young Napoleon's deployment of artillery, albeit with the destruction of much of the naval dockyard. The British fleet rescued 15,000 Royalists. Those who stayed were killed by the Revolutionaries. British bases were also established on Corsica (1794) and Elba (1796), but only briefly; while Genoa was successfully blockaded in 1800.

Other Mediterraneans: Anglo-Corsican Kingdom

Turning against France, the Corsicans requested British protection in 1793. A fleet arrived the following year, and the French troops on the island were defeated, although Nelson lost an eye in the siege of Calvi. A democratic constitution was established with an elected Parliament and a British viceroy. There was talk of Britain being offered the crown of Corsica. However, Spain moving to join France, and thereby altering the naval situation, led the British to withdraw from the Mediterranean and, in 1796, the French reconquered the island. Under Napoleon, the capital was moved from Bastia to his birthplace, Ajaccio. There are several statues of the Emperor in the city, including a large equestrian one commissioned by Napoleon III in 1865, as well as the *Maison Bonaparte*, the *Musée Fesch* and the *Chapelle Impériale*.

The French challenge to the old order was a double one: conquest and the encouragement of rebellion, for example that in Sardinia in 1794–6.

In 1797, Venice, a long-lasting fulcrum of Mediterranean culture and trade, and, for much of the previous millennium, power, lost its independence. Napoleon, one of the leading generals of the Directory government of France, had marched on in 1796 from his triumphs over Sardinian/Piedmontese and Austrian forces in north Italy to occupy Venetian territories up to the River Adige. In April 1797, he proposed that Austria gain Venice, with the exception of the city itself which was to retain independence. In his intimidation of defenceless Venice, Napoleon declared war, while the cities of the Veneto rejected Venetian authority. Venice rapidly capitulated. Napoleon not only seized Venice, but also took antiquities, such as the Horses of Saint Mark, from there to France. This was part of a comprehensive process of cultural pillage that was designed to exalt France, and that hit Italy hard.

The Austrians were then forced, in the Treaty of Campo Formio in October 1797, to accept a new settlement of Italy, which left France with the Ionian Islands, Venetian Albania and Mantua, and much of northern Italy under a French client state, the Cisalpine Republic, while Venice and the Veneto were ceded to Austria. In 1798, the Roman Republic was proclaimed: the French assumed that they had brought the Papacy to an end.

Trade was part of the struggle. Thus, in 1795, a British squadron entered the Aegean to protect trade against French frigates based in Smyrna. In contrast, Napoleon's occupation of Livorno successfully closed this major port to the British.

After conquering northern Italy in 1797, Napoleon planned to invade Britain, but, having decided that such an invasion would fail, he pressed, instead, the case for an invasion of Egypt, in order both to retain his own military position and for France to be better able to challenge the British in India. The last French force sent to Egypt had been a Crusader army.

Mounted in 1798, this was a major independent initiative on the part of Napoleon. It revealed a characteristic absence of

the sense of mutual understanding that is crucial to the successful operation of the international system. Focusing on war
with Britain, and not on conquest from the Turks, Napoleon
wrongly presumed that the Turks, the imperial overlords of
effectively autonomous Egypt, could be intimidated or bribed
into accepting French action, which indeed followed a whole
series of provocative acts. These assumptions were coupled
with a contempt for Turkey as a military force: 'In Egypt, I
found myself freed from the obstacles of an irksome civilisation. I was full of dreams . . . I saw myself founding a religion,
marching into Asia, riding an elephant, a turban on my head
and in my hand the new Koran that I would have composed to
suit my needs. In my undertakings I would have combined the
experiences of the two worlds, exploiting for my own profit the
theatre of all history.'

Having first easily overrun vulnerable Malta in June 1798,
which angered Tsar Paul I, the Protector of the Order of Malta,
Napoleon's army landed in Egypt on 1 July. After capturing
Alexandria, he defeated the Mamluks at Shubra Khit (13 July) and
Embabeh, the battle of the Pyramids (21 July), victories for defensive firepower over shock tactics. French rifles were described as
'like a boiling pot on a fierce fire'.

Cairo fell, but Nelson's naval victory at the Battle of the
Nile completely stranded the French. In the face of a hostile
population, which mounted a brutally suppressed rising in
Cairo, Napoleon consolidated his position, sending General
Louis Desaix up the Nile to control Upper Egypt. Napoleon and
most of his army invaded Palestine, then ruled by the Turks. El
Arish, Gaza, Jaffa and Haifa were taken, Jaffa with a slaughter
of many of those who surrendered. Acre, however, successfully
resisted, helped by British naval gunners. Napoleon's siege
train had been captured by British warships, he had underesti-
mated his opponents, and successive French assaults on Acre
all failed.

Napoleon fell back on Egypt where, on 25 July 1799, he defeated a newly landed Turkish army at Aboukir, storming the earthworks with a cavalry charge. This was of scant benefit to him. In the face of British naval power, the French were still isolated. On 24 August, Napoleon abandoned his army and fled back to France by sea, seizing power there on 9 November.

Égyptomanie

The scholars who accompanied Napoleon greatly advanced knowledge of ancient Egypt. He hoped they would also fulfil his wish to establish a benevolent and progressive administration. Organised in the *Institut d'Égypte*, the scholars made little impact on Egyptian culture, but they helped to increase and satisfy European interest in Egypt. The *Voyage dans la Basse et la Haute Égypte* by Baron Denon was reprinted in over forty editions and translated into English, German and other languages. The *Description de l'Égypte* that resulted from the expedition appeared in twenty-one volumes from 1809 to 1822.

Egypt fused the widening interest in Antiquity with the interest in the East, and was to be a rich source of cultural and intellectual inspiration. However, as with British concern about Italy, this was an interest in Egypt past. The *Description* presented Egypt as having declined since Antiquity, the Egyptians as timid, passive and indifferent, and their rulers as barbaric and superstitious. Clearly, it would benefit from French rule.

'Jewels', such as obelisks, could be plucked from such a decayed civilisation and used to enhance European cityscapes. In 1820, Mehmed Ali, who was compared with the Pharaohs in works such as Thomas Waghorn's *Egypt as it is in 1837* (1837), presented an obelisk, now known as Cleopatra's Needle, to George IV. Transported to London half a century later from Egypt, inside a great floating cast-iron cylinder nicknamed *The Cleopatra*, the obelisk was erected atop the recently completed Victoria

Embankment on the north bank of the Thames in 1878. Modern empires were keen to associate themselves with ancient counterparts. Erected by Thutmose III, the obelisk had nothing whatever to do with Cleopatra, but Paris had acquired one in 1833, which the French dubbed *L'Aiguille de Cléopâtre*.

8. The Nineteenth Century

> Thirty years ago, Marseilles lay burning in the sun one day. A blazing sun upon a fierce August day was no greater rarity in southern France then than at any other time, before or since. Everything in Marseilles, and about Marseilles, had stared at the fervid sky, and been stared at in return ... Boats without awnings were too hot to touch; ships blistered at their moorings; the stones of the quays had not cooled, night or day, for months ... A sea too intensely blue to be looked at.

Marseille in 1825 is the opening setting for Charles Dickens's novel *Little Dorrit*, which appeared in serial form from 1855 to 1857. Two contrasting milieux are introduced. The villainous cosmopolitan murderer Rigaud tells his cellmate how he killed his wife, while Arthur Clennam, a British trader from China, meets other travellers while doing quarantine. The vivid juxtapositions of a Mediterranean port-city emerge clearly at a time before regular steamship services and the Suez Canal were to transform travel to, in, and from, it. Built in 1524–31, the grim Château d'If off Marseille was the place of imprisonment in Alexandre Dumas's *The Count of Monte Cristo* (1844–6), a novel in which, among much else, Mediterranean smuggling and slavery also played a role. The château can be visited today by boat from Marseille.

The Napoleonic Struggle

Napoleon's complete victory over Austrian and Russian forces at Austerlitz in the modern Czech Republic in 1805 brought Venice, the Veneto and Venetian Dalmatia from Austria as additions to

his kingdom of Italy: the fate of the Mediterranean was being set-
tled a long way from its shores. Napoleon had become King of
Italy in 1805 and had crowned himself with the Iron Crown of
Lombardy. In 1808, the kingdom was expanded with the seizure
of Ancona and its surrounding area from the Papal States, while
France itself directly gained Tuscany in 1807, the Papal States in
1809 and Austrian Dalmatia (Trieste, Fiume and Croatia) in 1809.
The Ionian Islands were handed over to France by Russia in 1807.

The Mediterranean basin was now a zone of conflict between
the alliance systems of two rival clashing empires, but, unlike
the clash between Rome and Carthage, this was not a struggle
controlled by Mediterranean powers. Instead, it was one in which
the Mediterranean was understood in terms of geopolitical axes
envisaged by foreign commentators and devised by strategists
in distant capitals, and its resources were used to support their
strategies. Thus, Venice became a French naval base while many
Italians served in Napoleon's armies across Europe, including in
the invasion of Russia in 1812.

The role of these distant capitals helps to explain the French
invasion of Spain in 1808, and the British counter-intervention
there, as well as the campaigning of both powers in southern
Italy and in the Adriatic. A British force briefly landed in Calabria
in July 1806 and attacked the French, who had successfully
invaded the kingdom of Naples after Austerlitz. This was the only
British invasion of southern Italy prior to that in 1943 during the
Second World War. To the British troops who defeated the French
at Maida in 1806, this must have seemed as distant as the Roman
legionaries had found Britannia. After their victory, they speedily
returned to Sicily.

Yet not all rivalries and issues could be fitted into the Anglo-
French struggle, and nor could the mighty forces of these
empires necessarily overawe other powers. The British were
given a clear demonstration of this in 1807 in Egypt. Six years
earlier, a British army had totally defeated the French there and

forced their capitulation. In 1807, however, the British discovered the dangers of pressing on with inadequate knowledge in the face of hostile local forces. In order to prevent the French from establishing a presence there when Britain began hostilities with the Turks, 6000 troops were sent to besiege Alexandria. It fell rapidly, but misleading information about the need to expand the area of control in order to ensure supplies led to an attempt to gain control of Rosetta, a crucial point for trade on the Nile. The assault was a disaster, with the centre column, attacked from all sides by snipers taking advantage of the narrow streets and tall houses, suffering heavy casualties. A second attempt was also unsuccessful. The Egyptians then blockaded Alexandria by land. The intractable nature of the conflict led the British to abandon their presence, not to return until 1882.

Also in 1807, the limitations of British power at sea were seen when Vice-Admiral Sir John Duckworth failed in his attempt to obtain the surrender of the Turkish fleet at Constantinople. His fleet took damage from Turkish cannon in the Dardanelles. This failure is less famous than that at Gallipoli in 1915, but is similarly notable.

Further west, bitter resistance to brutal French occupation in Calabria and Spain demonstrated the determination of Mediterranean peoples to fight on even when their state structure had collapsed. The French had to commit 48,000 men to suppress the Calabrian rising that began in 1806. Alongside considerable brutality, the French attacked the rebels' food sources. Far greater French efforts were unsuccessful in Spain in 1808–13 in part because of the inherent difficulties of the task but also due to British intervention on the side of the Spaniards.

Britain to the Fore

The French Revolutionary and Napoleonic Wars were a long slog for the British with very difficult passages, but they emerged triumphant. The return of Minorca to Spain in 1802 under the Peace of Amiens with France made the new base at Malta even more important. The British refusal to surrender it, as obliged to do under the peace terms, helped lead to the resumption of war the following year. French interest in the reconquest of Egypt did not improve relations. Thereafter, crucially thanks to victory outside the Mediterranean at Trafalgar in 1805, victory over a Franco-Spanish fleet then en route from Cádiz to Naples, the British dominated the Mediterranean albeit at the cost of an onerous blockade of Toulon. This blockade was the first line of defence for British and allied interests, such as the protection of Sicily and Sardinia, and to complement more offensive steps, including military intervention in Spain. The prevailing winds could drive warships blockading Toulon off station, as in 1798 (helping Napoleon sail to Malta and Egypt); but there was no retreat from the Mediterranean, as there had been in 1796–7. Malta, however, was a very distant base for the blockade, which led to a reliance on Sardinia, described in 1804 by Nelson as 'an invaluable possession in every respect. It is the Ceylon of the Mediterranean.' A French sortie from Toulon was turned back in 1812.

The naval presence resulted in the spread of British influence. In 1810, a later Prime Minister, George, 4th Earl of Aberdeen, who had spent much time in Greece, argued that there was considerable interest in independence there, adding 'a French connection, from the absence of naval intercourse and protection, is much less desired than the friendship of this country'.

The sound of British guns rang out over much of the Mediterranean. In 1809, after a victory over a French fleet, Cephalonia, Ithaca and Santa Maura in the Ionian Islands were captured, although Corfu held out until 1814, albeit blockaded by a British squadron. On 13 March 1811, off the Dalmatian island of Lissa (Vis) – a British raiding base seized in 1807 that the French were trying to gain – Captain William Hoste, one of Nelson's protégés, hoisted the signal 'remember Nelson' to the cheers of his crew before his four frigates, with their superior seamanship and gunnery, defeated six French and Italian frigates, with the latter losing three. These waters were to see a raiding Austrian fleet defeat an Italian one in 1866. On 29 November 1811, a smaller French Adriatic force was destroyed, while the Apulian coast was raided and Ancona blockaded. In 1813–14, Rear-Admiral Thomas Freemantle, a friend of Nelson, went on to help drive the French from much of the Dalmatian coast, assisting in the capture of Fiume, Trieste and Zara in 1813, and Dubrovnik in 1814. Only Corfu held out. This was very much Hornblower before his time.

In 1815, when war was resumed after Napoleon regained control of France, a squadron of British frigates entered the Bay of Naples and threatened to bombard the city unless the pro-Napoleonic navy surrendered within forty-eight hours. It did, mirroring a successful British naval intimidation of Naples in 1742. Also in 1815, there were amphibious occupations of Marseille and Toulon in conjunction with local Royalists.

The Congress of Vienna (1814–15) left Britain with the Ionian Islands as well as Malta; although Minorca was not regained and has remained ever since with Spain, albeit with a few echoes of British rule such as sash windows and gin. British naval interests were also helped by the wider territorial settlement, with shipbuilding ports that had been a threat in French hands put in those of British allies: Trieste and Venice with Austria, and Genoa with Piedmont/Sardinia. The latter state was built up as a barrier against French expansion into Italy. To that end, Britain supported the Piedmontese acquisition of Genoa, which was an event much resented there.

The British navy continued to play a major role in the Mediterranean. The bombardment of Algiers by a largely British fleet (with Dutch support) in 1816 led to an agreement to end the taking of Christian slaves, the background to Rossini's opera *The*

Italian Girl in Algiers (1813). The attack also reflected the capacity of the British industrial system. The British squadron alone fired 40,000 round shots and shells.

Thanks largely to superior British gunnery at close quarters, an Anglo-French-Russian fleet under Sir Edward Codrington destroyed the Turkish and Egyptian fleets at the battle of Navarino Bay on 20 October 1827, the last great battle of the Age of Fighting Sail, and one in which the Western fatalities were far lower than those of their opponents: 177 to about 17,000. There was concern in Britain about the responsibility for starting the battle, and the result exacerbated governmental anxiety about Russian expansionism. The Russians themselves emphasised their support for the Greeks, a fellow Orthodox people. Whatever the governmental concerns, the British public responded with pleasure. The Greek insurrection had broken out in 1821, but the intervention on the Turkish side of Mehmed Ali, Viceroy of Egypt from 1805 to 1848, changed the situation. His forces crushed the rising on Crete in 1824 and had an initial success when they landed in southern Greece the following year. The Greeks were reliant on irregulars, many of whom were brigands, while the Turkish army was weak and divided. The Egyptians were more effective, but the defeat of their fleet at Navarino Bay undercut their position. It was crucial to the failure of the Turkish attempt to suppress the Greek struggle for independence, which was recognised in 1830. Thus, foreign intervention helped the liberal national cause to victory in Greece, whereas in the shape of Austrian and French intervention respectively, it brought to an end the cause in Naples (1821) and Spain (1823).

The Royal Navy did not act at Navarino Bay to end the slave trade, but the effect of its actions was to help stop it, and part of the reason for philhellenism in Britain, a philhellenism particularly associated with George, Lord Byron, was the depiction of the Turks as slavers. *The Slave Market, Constantinople*, a painting that caused a great impression when it was exhibited in London in 1838, depicted a black Egyptian slave merchant selling a Greek slave girl to a Turkish pasha, and was a scene of distress and pathos. William Allan supposedly based it on what he saw in 1829–30 when he accompanied the British diplomats to Constantinople, who negotiated the independence treaty. Memorabilia from the War of Independence, including Byron's helmet and sword, can be seen in the National Historical Museum in the old Parliament building in Athens.

Byron's Mediterranean

Byron, born in 1788, spent all his life from 1816 abroad. From that winter, he was in Italy mostly in Venice, Ravenna, Pisa and Genoa. In 1823, Byron chartered the brig *Hercules* in order to help the Greeks, and sailed to Cephalonia, reaching Missolonghi on the mainland in January 1824. He died of fever in April having given generously to the Greek cause. Earlier, Byron had written in favour of the Armenians. Much of Byron's poetry related to the Mediterranean. Thus, *The Corsair* (1814), about pirates, began:

O'er the glad waters of the dark blue sea,
Our thoughts as boundless, and our souls as free,
Far as the breeze can bear, the billows foam,
Survey our empire, and behold our home!

Byron's *The Giaour* (1813) was allegedly a fragment of a Turkish tale, while *The Book of Abydos* (1813), with its 'night of stormy water,' was described as a Turkish tale. *The Two Foscari* (1821) was set in Venice, as was *Beppo* (1818) in which the carnival is depicted:

And there are dresses splendid, but fantastical,
Masks of all times and nations, Turks and Jews,
And harlequins and clowns, with feats gymnastical.

Don Juan (1819–24) had shipwreck, piracy, slaving, a witty
parody in part of the *Odyssey* and an idealisation of Greece:

And further on a group of Grecian girls,
The first and tallest her white kerchief waving,
Were strung together like a row of pearls,
Link'd hand in hand, and dancing.

Britain's role was a matter not only of power, but also of influence. In 1833, Prince Otto of Bavaria, the newly chosen King of Greece, was escorted from Trieste to Athens by HMS *Madagascar*. His palace in Athens is now part of the City of Athens Museum. Greece proved a difficult responsibility for Otto and, in 1843, a revolution led to the introduction of constitutional monarchy.

Alongside shows of power, the surveying of Mediterranean waters was important to British and non-British commerce, as was the negotiation by Britain of free-trade agreements, for example with Turkey in 1838 and Egypt in 1841. Surveying reflected the range of British naval activity. Sir Francis Beaufort, later Hydrographer to the Navy, was active in 1810–12 in Turkish waters as a frigate captain, suppressing piracy (being badly wounded), and surveying the coast, producing, as a result, *Karamania, Or a Brief Description of the South Coast of Asia Minor* (1817). Another naval officer, William Smyth, published *The Hydrography of Sicily, Malta, and the adjacent islands* (1823) and also surveyed the Adriatic and the North African coast.

Technology was focused by British achievements, notably in shipbuilding. In 1824, when the threat of naval bombardment led the Dey of Algiers to capitulate anew to British demands, this expedition including HMS *Lightning*, a steam-powered paddle-ship equipped with three cannon launched at Deptford in 1822, the first operational deployment of a British steamship. Four British-built paddle steamers were used for the new Greek fleet from 1827.

By the 1840s, the steam-mounted screw propeller offered a clearly better alternative to the paddle wheel by making it possible to carry a full broadside armament. The new naval capability, enhanced by the shell guns that replaced solid shot with exploding shells, was demonstrated in 1840 when a British fleet bombarded Acre: steamers showed their ability to operate inshore, while a shell caused the explosion of the fortress's main magazine. The garrison was forced out, a decisive blow in the expulsion of Egyptian forces from Syria. In addition, the British used warships and marines to storm Sidon in an operation led by steamships; as well as blockading the Egyptian fleet in Alexandria. The linkage between the situation in Egyptian waters and that in Syrian ones had been seen in earlier episodes, and notably during the Crusades.

The British, concerned about Egyptian expansionism and supporting French ambitions, had intervened to maintain Turkish rule in the area. Mehmed Ali, already autonomous, had successfully rebelled against Turkish rule over Egypt, which was never re-imposed. However, his eventual failure in Syria ensured that the Egyptian sphere of influence did not extend in that direction as it did into Sudan until the successful rebellion by the Mahdi, a *jihadi* leader, in the 1880s.

In turn, in the Crimean War of 1854–6, the British intervened in the Black Sea to preserve Turkey, and the British-dominated route to India, from Russian expansionism. Alliance with France and Piedmont provided Britain with total control over the Mediterranean route during this conflict. Unlike in 1769–70, when faced only by the Turks, Russia was in no position to contest this control.

The importance of the region was accentuated by the opening of the Suez Canal in 1869 and, six years later, the Egyptian government's shares in the Suez Canal Company were purchased by Britain. Already, in 1836, British concern about French ambitions had led to the mapping of the Suez isthmus. In 1878, in response to the movement of Russian forces overland to near Constantinople, a British fleet was sent there, despite the fear of the Admiralty that it would not be able to force the Dardanelles, a key focus of the relationship between land and sea power. In the event, the Russians backed down. The terms 'jingoes' and 'jingoism' were coined that year in Britain as a result of a music-hall song by 'the Great MacDermott', the chorus of which stated, 'We don't want to fight, but by jingo if we do, we've got the ships, we've got the men, we've got the money too.'

Part of the price for British support for Turkey in 1878 was the conclusion of a convention prohibiting the import and export of slaves into Turkish territories. It was concluded in 1880, although not ratified until 1883. Also with Turkish permission, Cyprus became a British protectorate in 1878, although it was not annexed until 1914. Malta acted as a key base during the 1878 crisis. In contrast, in the aftermath of a rebellion in 1848, and in light of pressure for union with Greece, the less strategically significant Ionian Islands had been ceded to Greece in 1864 as a way to help the new pro-British king, George I. He had replaced Otto after a crisis that involved a British naval deployment. Cyprus was better placed than the Ionian Islands to support Britain's interest in the Suez Canal and any action in Egypt.

In 1882, the British government was initially unwilling to intervene in response to nationalist agitation in Egypt, but the murder of fifty of Alexandria's European residents led to a more active stance. The navy joined in an international mission to evacuate the city's foreigners, and was ordered to stop any strengthening of the city's defences. The British duly entered the harbour and bombarded its defences. This bombardment deployed far more power than that on Algiers in 1816, while the defences were shoddy from poor management and lacked the support of mines and torpedoes. The naval bombardment, including the fire from the four 16-inch guns on HMS *Inflexible*, drove terrified, half-trained gunners from their posts on land, but did not do enormous damage. It was landing parties that did the real work in the attack. Soon after, the navy landed 15,000 troops who, at Tel el Kebir on 13 September, routed the Egyptian army. This was the most important battle in Mediterranean history until El Alamein in 1942. Hospital ships and the sea-based desalination of drinking water were important in this campaign.

Although the Khedivate of Egypt remained an autonomous province of the Turkish Empire until 1914, a British quasi-protectorate over Egypt was established. This position was seen as important in thwarting French plans in the Mediterranean, as well as in securing Britain's position on the route to India via the Suez Canal, and thus protecting South-West Asia from Russian expansion. The Suez Canal gave Britain dominance over a crucial sea lane, one that could be more readily controlled than the routes that passed Cape Town, Singapore and the Falkland Islands. The route had become more significant with the British annexation in 1839 of Aden at the other end of the Red Sea.

To strengthen Britain's position in the Mediterranean, and to make it easier to handle larger ships, notably the newly begun *Majestic*-class battleships, work started in Gibraltar in 1895 on a mole and an extension of the dockyard. Moreover, concern about the Mediterranean axis caused the deepening of the Suez Canal in 1898. That year, competing interests in Sudan led, in the Fashoda Crisis, to the risk of war with France, and, as a result, there was a major display of British naval power in the Mediterranean. The *Majestic* class had been begun because of the 1892 Franco-Russian alliance, and the risk of supporting French action in the Mediterranean in the event of a Russian attack on the Turkish Empire. In 1894, Lord Rosebery, the Prime Minister, told the Austrian Foreign Minister that a British fleet could no longer be deployed to defend Constantinople as in 1878 for fear of French naval action in the western and central Mediterranean. Two years later, the Director of Naval Intelligence expressed the fear that the Russian Black Sea fleet would therefore be able to sortie into the eastern Mediterranean, and thus threaten the Suez Canal. In the event, British intimidation successfully resolved the crisis in 1898.

Evelyn Baring, later 1st Earl of Cromer, who had been appointed British commissioner for the finances of Egypt in 1877, ran the Egyptian government from 1883 until 1907, as Consul General and Adviser to the Khedive. Britain imposed bans on the slave trade, while Egypt became the base for British intervention in the Sudan, which was eventually successful in 1895–9: total victory at Omdurman outside Khartoum in 1898 over the Mahdists was a product of Britain's Mediterranean position and control of Egypt. British racial stereotypes about Arabs affected their stance in Egypt, which was seen as akin to India in some respects, but without the 'martial races' of the latter. Cromer himself regarded Islam as a medieval religion that held Egypt back.

The French Mediterranean

France was a more serious challenge to Britain because of the major expansion of the French Mediterranean. For most of the eighteenth century, this expansion had largely been a matter of gaining territories for junior branches of France's ruling Bourbon dynasty: Spain in 1700; and Naples and Sicily in 1734. Corsica had been purchased from Genoa in 1768, and a rebellion there suppressed. However, despite rumours of French ambitions in the eastern Mediterranean, nothing was attempted until after the Bourbons were overthrown.

In 1796–8, the French Revolutionaries swept all before them, conquering mainland Italy and Egypt. This expansion was undone;

but, under Napoleon from 1800, the French returned anew, to conquer mainland Italy and to add Spain for the Emperor's brother, Joseph, in 1808, thus launching a short-lived dynasty. Piedmont and Elba were annexed to France in 1802, Tuscany in 1807 and Rome in 1808. This territorial order fell victim to Napoleon's failure in 1812–15.

Napoleon on Elba, 1814–15

In 1814, Napoleon was exiled by the victorious powers to Elba, but given sovereignty over it, as well as a revenue of 2 million francs from the French government which, in the event, proved unwilling to pay up. He used the opportunity to improve the situation of the inhabitants, including by roadbuilding and educational reforms. However, this was no long-term solution for Napoleon, but, instead, a frustrating lesson in impotence that mocked his greatly inflated sense of his own dignity. On 26 February 1815, Napoleon escaped, evading two patrolling French ships and one British one. He landed near Antibes on 1 March, launching an eventually disastrous bid to regain power in France. Napoleon's residence at the Villa San Martino has been transformed into a museum.

The French rapidly resumed Mediterranean activity, invading Spain in force to help their earlier opponent, Ferdinand VII of Spain (r. 1808, 1813–33), to overthrow the liberal government in 1823, and occupying Algiers in 1830. The latter was intended to win popularity for Charles X of France (r. 1824–30), to show that he could succeed where previous Christian attempts had failed, and to end piracy from Algiers. Although the Archbishop of Paris called on the King to lead a crusade, this occupation was not intended to serve as the basis for a widespread French empire. In the event, sending his loyal troops to Algeria left Charles fatally weaker in the face of the July Revolution that overthrew him.

Yet, the general process by which commitments expanded in the face of opposition was also at play in Algeria. The new ruler continued Charles's commitment. Initially, the French were successful, seizing coastal enclaves, especially Oran in 1831 and Bône in 1833. However, from 1835, they encountered strong resistance led by Abd al-Qādir who created an emirate. The French, indeed, faced political as well as military problems. The most effective imperial method, incorporation, in which existing power structures were adapted and accommodated by the imperial state, was made far more difficult in Algeria by the seizure of land for French settlement. This greatly affected the situation in the localities and added a non-negotiable character to the invasion, but, as with other imperial powers, France won support, or at least acceptance, as a result of divisions within Algerian society. Moreover, by 1846, France had 108,000 troops there. Al-Qādir surrendered the following year, and Algeria was annexed in 1848. That did not mean that local people had no 'agency' or role. Instead, the new order depended greatly on local intermediaries, and notably so in political and economic terms.

Meanwhile, pressure was applied elsewhere in North-West Africa. Morocco was successfully attacked by France in 1844, although this intervention was not pushed forward at this stage. Two years later, Ahmed Bey of Tunis (r. 1837–55) made a state visit to France, the first by a ruling Muslim prince to Europe. Returning home, he sought to incorporate what he had seen in France and, in pursuing a protective reputation as an enlightened ruler, abolished the slave trade and closed the slave markets. This was very much the southern shores of the Mediterranean accepting the values of the northern.

France was subsequently to conquer not only the rest of what became Algeria, but also to take control of Tunisia, and to begin a presence that ultimately left them with all of Morocco apart from a Spanish section in its north. When Tunisia was made a protectorate in 1881, a French force invaded from Algeria, while other units were landed at Bône and Bizerta. The navy subsequently shelled Sfax, which had rejected French control, and covered a successful landing there.

The French set out to transform their conquests. In particular, French authorities carried out extensive town building in North Africa, producing, as part of a project of modernisation, the institutions of French civilian government, military power and cultural engagement, notably schools. So also with churches. Thus, at Hippo, the Basilica of St Augustine was built in 1883 to house a fragment of one of St Augustine's arm bones. More generally, North Africa became part of the French imagination, as with the impact of the Roman amphitheatre at El Djem on André Gide's protagonist in his novel *L'Immoraliste* (*The Immoralist*, 1902). Gide had travelled in North Africa from 1893. The French justification of their position drew on Christian and Orientalist themes, and saw France as the successor to the Roman Empire, a theme that was also to be adopted by Italy, as it justified empire.

France, however, lost out in the eastern Mediterranean to Britain. French influence in Egypt rose in the 1830s, while the Suez Canal began as a Franco-Turkish project in 1859. Yet, weakened after defeat by Germany in 1870–1, France was not in a position to defy Britain over Egypt in the 1880s.

Nevertheless, acceptance of British success in Egypt won British backing for French claims in Morocco. In 1912, the Moroccan Sultan was deposed. French power was presented in terms of a Protectorate of Morocco, which was a different goal to that represented by the conquest of Algeria, and notably without the comparable European settlement. Important to the French plan was the consolidation of control over the areas of Morocco where the Sultan had wielded only limited power. Moreover, the modernisation of Morocco was important to French intentions and their exposition.

The central significance of Marseille for French North Africa made that city the gateway to the French Empire, replacing the role that Bordeaux, La Rochelle and Nantes had had when France was a leading Atlantic power. This had consequences both for Marseille and for the French image of the city as uniquely cosmopolitan. Other ports had links with North Africa, for example Port-Vendres in Roussillon, but none were of even close to comparable scale.

American Power into the Mediterranean

After its independence from Britain, America's Mediterranean trade was no longer protected from Barbary privateers by the Royal Navy, and attacks began in 1784, with the captured sailors enslaved. In 1793, work on three frigates began in America in order to end this situation, but, under treaties signed in 1795–8, annual payments of tribute to the Barbary states were made in order to prevent their privateering attacks. Nevertheless, after a warlike confrontation by the United States with France was brought to a close in 1800, it was felt that paying tribute was humiliating and expensive, that operations in the Mediterranean would help train the navy, and that these operations would cost little more than retaining the fleet in home waters, which was a mistaken conviction.

In 1801, without consulting Congress, which had the right to declare war, President Thomas Jefferson sent Richard Dale with three frigates and a schooner to the Mediterranean, while the Bashaw of Tripoli declared war. A blockade of Tripoli, however, was made more difficult by the inappropriateness of deep-draught ships for shallow coastal waters, and was abandoned in 1802. Dale's successor, Richard Morris, instead sailed in search of privateers, an unauthorised policy that lacked the merit of success. He was recalled in 1803. Morris's replacement, Edward Preble, was able to intimidate Suleiman, the Sultan of Morocco, into settling his dispute with America. However, the frigate *Philadelphia* ran aground on a reef off Tripoli and was captured, the crew being paraded through the streets of the city.

In 1804, Stephen Decatur led a raid on Tripoli in which the *Philadelphia* was seized and burned, thus removing a powerful image of American failure. Nelson called this 'the most bold and daring act of the age'. Later on that year, fireship attacks were made on Tripolitan ships off their base. In 1805, commanded by William Eaton, a force of marines, Arabs and mercenaries aligned with the Bashaw's exiled brother, marched overland from Alexandria and captured the town of Derna. Peace with Tripoli followed, with no annual tribute stipulated, but with a $60,000 ransom for the crew of the *Philadelphia*.

The Americans continued to be vigilant. In 1815, after the War of 1812 with Britain was brought to an end, a force of ten warships under Decatur blockaded Algiers to force the return of American sailors. This achievement was followed by successful demonstrations by the squadron off Tunis and Tripoli.

While trading with the Mediterranean, the Americans, however, remained a minor military presence there. There was no equivalent to the highly demonstrative use of American naval power in Japanese or Latin American waters. Indeed, in 1867, the British Ambassador was told by the American Secretary of State that reports that America was seeking an island or base in the Mediterranean were untrue, although there had been interest in a base in Italy earlier in the century and there was a small supply and ordnance base near La Spezia from 1848 to 1867. In 1867, there was a proposal among the insurgents in Crete against Turkish rule to place the island under American protection, but it did not lead to anything.

Power Politics

The pattern set in the nineteenth century was to continue into the 1930s. The old order, of a mighty empire in the eastern Mediterranean, and a more fragmented pattern of sovereignty further west, had gone. The whole sea had been opened up to outside interests. The world of Islam was in retreat, and British naval power dominated the Mediterranean. In so far as Mediterranean Christian elements were able to gain advantage, it was as parts of nation states, and not as autonomous forces. Thus, it was a case of France, Spain and, eventually, Italy, pursuing advantages, not Marseille/Provence, Barcelona/Catalonia or Genoa/Venice/Tuscany/Naples. This was an important shift in European politics, one dramatised when the forces of Philip V of Spain successfully besieged Barcelona in 1714 and brought to an end Catalan liberties; again in 1821, when Austrian regulars defeated untrained and poorly disciplined Neapolitan *Carbonari* at Rieti, and went on to occupy Naples; and also in 1849, when starvation and cholera led a rebellious Venice to surrender to blockading Austrians.

The two last episodes were part of the world of revolution and counter-revolution that was so important in Europe in the decades after the Napoleonic Wars, one that focused on two years of (many) revolutions, 1830 and 1848. In many respects, the rivalry between revolutionaries and counter-revolutionaries took forward earlier tensions and divisions that had been power-charged by the legacy of violence in 1792–1815. Great-power assertiveness and competition were intertwined now with the world of revolution and counter-revolution, as with French support for opposition to Austria in Italy. In turn, the struggle for Italian unification was also linked to local and regional struggles, albeit with different contexts. Thus, there was fighting in southern Italy in 1815 linked to Napoleon's return, and in 1820 revolution in Palermo. This owed much to opposition to the Neapolitan Bourbons, whom it was even claimed in 1835–8 and 1854 had sent agents to Sicily in order to spread cholera and thus dominate the island. In 1816, the Neapolitan Bourbons took away Sicily's ancient autonomy, which launched not only the 1820 revolution and another in the city in 1848. The relationship between such a particularist cause and that of Italian unification, which eventually succeeded, was, however, precarious.

The number of states in the western Mediterranean declined between 1815 and 1900, with Italian unification and French expansion in North Africa. This unification, a long process, was an important development in the central Mediterranean, one that was hard fought, for example in Sicily in 1848–9 and 1860, with the intervention, sailing from Genoa, of Giuseppe Garibaldi and his 1000 red-shirted volunteers proving crucial in the last. The British connived in Garibaldi's success in 1860, not only by not using the Royal Navy to try to stop the expedition, or the advance later in 1860 from Sicily to the mainland, but also by interposing warships between Garibaldi's steamers and Neapolitan ships, which made it impossible to attack the steamers.

In 1866, the Veneto was gained by Italy as a result of participation in Prussia's war with Austria: Prussian success outweighed Italian failure. The easy occupation of Rome in 1870 brought Italian unification to an end. Italy was now a would-be great power, keen on acquiring overseas territories.

Meanwhile, the territorial situation in the Balkans remained unsettled. In 1877–8, at the same time as a broader Balkan conflict, the Greeks sent irregulars into Thessaly, Epirus and Macedonia (all then still part of the Turkish Empire) to attack the Turks. Rebelliousness increased in Albania from the 1870s, with a jockeying for position among the Albanian clans, as they manoeuvred in a situation of increased Turkish weakness and the apparently imminent departure of the Turks. In 1897, the Turks beat Greece in a limited war but, in 1911, there was a successful rebellion in Albania that launched the end of Turkey's European empire.

Unsettled Crete

Tourists today see Minoan sites and will be told about the German airborne invasion in 1941. In the nineteenth century, Crete was in the news due to a series of risings against Turkish rule. Those in 1821 and 1841 did not win independence, and in 1866 a large-scale rebellion broke out in an island divided between Christian and Muslim inhabitants and where there was particular dissension over religious conversions and the status of monasteries. In the war, the explosion by the last defendants of the powder barrels in the monastery of Arkadi as the Turks stormed it became an iconic act of resistance. The struggle was an international cause, with Victor Hugo supporting the rebels. In the end, the rebellion was ended in 1869, by military action and concessions to the Christians. Other unsuccessful rebellions in 1878 and 1889 were followed in 1897 by intervention by an international squadron and the establishment in 1898 of an autonomous Crete under Prince George of Greece, although with the Sultan still the suzerain. In 1908, Crete declared union with Greece, which was recognised internationally in 1913.

Change

The Mediterranean was affected by the changes seen elsewhere in Europe, although there were particular problems. Thus, the spread of train routes had to cope with the difficult terrain of much of the Mediterranean littoral, especially with mountains running down to the coast. Moreover, the poor shape of the economy also limited the appeal to investors. Thus, per square mile, there were far fewer railways in the Balkans, southern

Italy or Spain, than in Germany, the Low Countries or England. Nevertheless, each line that was built made a difference. So also with modern roads, bridges and tunnels, for example on Corsica the road around Cap Corse, thanks to which Napoleon III ended its remoteness.

Similarly, steamships greatly affected sailing times and predictability in the Mediterranean. Launched in Naples in 1818 with a British steam engine, the *Ferdinando I* was that year the first steamship to reach Marseille. Launched at Genoa in 1820, the *Eridano* followed, but was intended to travel the River Po. The first steamship to pass the Strait of Gibraltar was the British *Mercury* in 1828, while British steam engines equipped the first steamships launched in Marseille, the *Henri IV* and the *Sully*, both launched in 1831.

Sailing vessels remained important, as in François Barry's 1855 painting of the entry into Marseille's old port. Nevertheless, thanks to steamships, the impact of wind and tide diminished. Steamship lines became of greater significance in the Mediterranean, including the dominant British Peninsular and Oriental Steam Navigation Company (P&O) and the Royal Mail Orient Line, as well as such French lines as Valéry and Touache, Italian lines such as Navigazione Generale, Rubattino and Veloce, the Egyptian Khedivial Mail, the German Hamburg Amerika and Norddeutscher Lloyd, the Spanish Ybarra and the Austrian Lloyd Austriaco. Thanks to such lines, postal services became more predictable and large-scale, as delays and costs fell. This had major consequences for economic activity, and for the maintenance of diaspora and other links.

Steamships needed coal, and their requirements and capacity led to a focus of trade and transport on a small number of ports with the necessary facilities, such as Alexandria, Algiers, Athens, Barcelona, Genoa, Marseille, Naples and Tunis, while a large number of ports became very much second level. Major ports had new facilities in order to cope with large ships, not least the necessary coaling facilities. This process was accentuated by the role of steamship–train transhipment at particular ports. Whereas, in the 1850s, the journey from Beirut to Damascus took four days, over what James Farley, an Irish banker, described as a 'wretched mule path', the opening, thanks to French enterprise, of a railway line in 1895 reduced the time to nine hours, encouraged merchants and tourists, and assisted wine exports. Wine production in Lebanon had been important under the Phoenicians, declined under the Caliphate, and was revived from the mid-nineteenth century.

Demand from Europe's growing and more affluent population helped to drive agricultural, industrial and mineral production across the Mediterranean. Thus, in Bastia, the *Nouveau Port*, established in 1862, exported Corsican food, including wine, to France and Italy. In the nineteenth century, this rise in production extended to the Balkans, affecting in particular cotton and tobacco production. There was a colonial aspect to much of such production in the shape of an export chain of low value-added goods; as well as serious environmental consequences, for example deforestation on Sardinia and elsewhere. In Egypt, Mehmed Ali advocated a change from the cultivation of wheat to that of cotton for Europe's factories. This was linked to a proletarianisation of much of the agricultural workforce who performed compulsory labour on large rural estates.

At the same time, much activity across the Mediterranean remained subsistence in character or was only for the local economy. This was true of both agriculture and industry, and of relevant organisational systems such as guilds, and greatly affected the collective psychology of the population. Yet, such activity was put under growing competitive pressure as a result of new production and organisational processes, both in the shape of imports and due to changes in local economies.

Sorolla and the Traditional Economy

Born in Valencia, Joaquín Sorolla (1863–1923) captured on canvas the intensity of hot sunlight. After training in Rome and Paris, he returned to Valencia in 1888 before moving to Madrid. Much of his painting presented Spain's Mediterranean shores, whether for holiday, including the difficult *Sad Inheritance* (1899), which shows crippled children bathing on the shore at Valencia, or work, as in his first major success, *The Return from Fishing* (1894), which displays an ox bringing a laden boat ashore at Valencia, and *Sewing the Sail* (1896), which depicts a family sewing a sail for a fishing boat. The world of work was captured in *And They Still Say Fish is Expensive* (1894), which showed a wounded young fisherman in the hold of a ship. A different type of work was captured in *The Smugglers* (1919), a scene from above of three men climbing sheer cliffs on Ibiza, and one that presented the extent of opposition to the world of order. Cigarettes in particular were smuggled into Spain, as they still are today.

The immediate area, not the distant state, was the source of identity, interest and loyalty, and this was linked to an identity in which resistance to outsiders was important to concepts of liberty and justice. This was clearly seen in southern Italy after unification with the north in 1860, with resistance in Naples and Sicily to the new Italian regime, which was widely regarded as alien and a product of the overcoming of the *patria*. However, local feeling had not led earlier to much support for the Neapolitan Bourbons. The regime, both new and old, was fairly weak, especially in Sicily, much of which was close to ungovernable as a result of widespread brigandage. In Naples, the brigands were joined in 1860 by many former soldiers. However, from 1864, there was a reaction against the brigands. They became isolated and were reduced to small bands, which were destroyed by 1867 depending on the area in question. In Sicily, brigands were connected to the Mafia and paid by them to act as their armed side. The brigands were supported by the rural population who feared them. The army fought the brigands until the late 1870s, after which the situation improved, although some bands of brigands remained.

In Spain, support for the rebellious Carlists in the nineteenth century drew on local loyalties, especially in Navarre and upland Catalonia. During the Third Carlist War (1868–76), there was also a republican and anti-centralist rising at Cartagena in 1873–4.

Localism had also been strong within the Turkish-ruled Balkans, and there were connections between the decentralised power that characterised the eighteenth century and weak government in the nineteenth. Alongside the apparently clear-cut themes of outside dominance, economic backwardness and the rise of nation states, can be set a more varied reality. All the three points just noted were correct but, at the same time, there was also the diversity that is to be expected from such a varied and complex region and that helps to make the history of the Mediterranean so fascinating.

Resistance to change was strong and drew on deep-rooted ideological, political and social attitudes and structures, as well as on the role of ethnic and religious differences. This resistance could be overcome, as in 1836–43 when the feudal system was abolished in Sardinia, and in 1826, with the eventual success of the suppression of the janissaries as part of a shift toward a more modern Turkish army. Subsequently, Abdul Mejid I, Turkey's Sultan from 1839 to 1861, sought strength through Westernisation. Western influence indeed grew in many coastal cities of the Turkish Empire, including Beirut, Jaffa and Smyrna

(İzmir). Meanwhile, conscription and provincial reorganisation were designed to increase the control of the centre and were aspects of a policy of imperial reform. The basis, however, was fragile, and resistance to development proved stronger in Turkey than in the key countries of economic change. Western-style reform was replaced in the late nineteenth century by an anti-Westernism, of which the most unattractive facet was the massacre of Armenians in Constantinople in 1896.

Emigration was a major response to the problems posed by both change and continuity. Southern Italy was the leading source of emigration from the Mediterranean and helped ensure that cities such as New York and Rio de Janeiro became part of its history. Greatly assisted by the availability of large transoceanic steamships, emigration rose dramatically from the 1860s. Emigration was also internal, and notably so from the difficult areas of traditional agriculture, such as the Pyrenean mountains of Roussillon. They were affected by the goods, such as wheat and lamb, brought into Europe by the transoceanic steamships. Urban growth was a marked feature of the latter decades of the century.

Imagining the Mediterranean

The authority of Christianity and the Classics meant that the Mediterranean was regarded as the source of Western culture as it could not be seen for the world of Islam, for which the Hejaz (Mecca and Medina) and Baghdad offered more significant historical roots. This element of historical authority became more important in the nineteenth century as the older view of the *translation imperii*, in which the transfer of rule kept the dream of Rome alive, was increasingly presented in terms of modern empires as the apogee for a historical process looking back to Classical Greece and Rome. This was very much the case in Britain, where the élite idealised their perception of ancient

Greece. Two Prime Ministers, Edward, 14th Earl of Derby and William Gladstone, translated Homer.

This interest extended to popular fiction. Thus novels, such as Bulwer Lytton's hugely popular *Last Days of Pompeii* (1834), were set in the Classical past. A different view of volcanoes was offered in Jules Verne's novel *Journey to the Centre of the Earth* (1864) as the explorers escape through Stromboli's crater.

There were, however, interesting variations in the reach to the Classical world. It was easier for militaristic societies, such as Germany, to look back to Macedon and Sparta than it was for Britain, which was frequently happier with republican Athens and Rome. Separately, set in Carthage, Gustave Flaubert's bestselling exotic novel *Salammbô* (1862) offered a violence and sensuality not generally seen in novels set in Greece or even Rome.

Tourism

In 1844, P&O gave the major novelist William Makepeace Thackeray a free passage during which he visited Athens, Constantinople, Jerusalem and Cairo. He wrote this up in *Notes of a Journey from Cornhill* [London] *to Grand Cairo* (1846), which was intended to reassure potential British visitors that the region was safe.

Ships as the means to visit were soon supplemented by cruises. In 1857, the P&O ship *Ceylon* made the first sightseeing cruise, to the Mediterranean. Six years later, its ship *Carnatic* introduced the more efficient compound steam engine to the Mediterranean. Railway and steamship companies devoted great effort to taking travellers to the Mediterranean. Steamships ensured that contrary winds could be overcome, and also the calms in the Mediterranean. Replacing the prints produced in the past, posters proclaimed the wonders of what could be seen, at the same time that they sought to make money. Thus, in 1900, the Riviera Express Service of the Hamburg Amerika Line advertised sailings from Genoa via San Remo and Monaco to Nice thrice weekly, and in reverse order, also thrice weekly. British tourists were clearly the prime market as that information was only provided in English.

Trains sped tourists to the Mediterranean, the train reaching Monaco in 1868. Specific routes for tourists developed, as in the Dutch rail service from Amsterdam and The Hague via Paris to Marseille, Nice and Monte Carlo. This service was advertised in a 1913 poster by Jan Willem Sluiter in terms of a man and woman exchanging a warm greeting at the side of the sea. Combined train and steamship tickets were offered, as for the sailings between Marseille, Tunis and Palermo by the French company Touache in 1905.

Tourists in other countries also went to the shores of the Mediterranean. Thus, at Portorož in Istria in modern Slovenia, the Kempinski Palace Hotel dates to 1910 when it was in the Austro-Hungarian Empire. Nearby Trieste, the major Austrian port (now in Italy), enjoyed considerable economic growth at the expense of Venice, and also attracted visitors to the Adriatic. Hotels from the period survive in Trieste, as in the *Grand Hotel Duchi d'Aosta*, the *Hotel Savoia Excelsior Palace*, and the Hotel Victoria (where James Joyce stayed), as well as houses that have found new uses, such as the *Museo Revoltella*. With its grand square (now the *Piazza dell'Unità d'Italia*), its food and its café culture, it is surprising that Trieste does not attract more visitors, by ship or other means.

Tourism continued the pattern already familiar with the response to Italy during the Grand Tour. There was a view of the current inhabitants as unworthy successors to their illustrious predecessors, and, indeed, as a potential bar to tourists responding to the latter. Thus, in 1806, Augustin Creuzé de Lesser, a French traveller, observed 'Europe ends at Naples and ends there quite badly.' This view of what came to be termed 'the South' influenced the perception of southern Italy in particular, including by Italians, as when Luigi Carlo Farini wrote in 1860 'This is not Italy! This is Africa!' This attitude was also taken onwards from Italians to Greeks, the Balkans, Turks and Arabs. Thus, Palestine was seen in terms of biblical significance, with the Arab population, in contrast, widely regarded in a critical light. These racist attitudes were employed, then and subsequently, to justify rule from outside.

The Riviera

'A trifling little town but its environs are charming and it has a beautiful terrace which is raised on the sea shore and commands the most delightful view of the sea I ever beheld.' Not quite how Nice strikes us today, but William Theed, visiting at the start of the 1790s, was not going to a major resort. However, there was already a British community of invalids, who, as William Bennet noted in 1785, had moved from Montpellier to Nice 'where their health is at least equally benefited, and their accommodations infinitely better'. Menton became popular as a tuberculosis destination from the 1860s.

The activities of tourists long varied. Henry Fox spent much time in Nice with his older protector, Susanna Strangeways Horner. Wintering for his health, Charles, 6th Earl of Drogheda, a heavy gambler, lost £200 at faro, a popular card game.

This destination was to be transformed by railways and steamships. Going to the Riviera for the winter became easy for the affluent. With train services from Paris from the 1860s, Nice became the major holiday destination of those taking the train south across France. The palm-lined *Promenade des Anglais* was the setting for major hotels such as the *Hôtel Negresco* (1912) and the *Palais de la Méditerranée* (1929). The history of tourism in Nice can be followed in the *Musée Masséna* which is located in a 1898 villa. Churches also catered for the tourists, notably the Russian Orthodox cathedral built in 1902–12.

The light, vivid colours, exciting allure and difference from skies and scenes further north attracted painters such as Renoir, a resident in Cagnes from 1907 to his death in 1919, and Monet, who painted many landscapes in Antibes. The fishing village of St-Tropez was shown to a wider public by Paul Signac, who built a house there, notably in his paintings *Sailing Boats in St Tropez Harbour* (1893) and *The Quay* (1899). Henri Matisse followed. The *Musée de l'Annonciade* in St-Tropez, housed in a former chapel, contains many Signacs. So also with painters from other countries, such as the Australian impressionist John Russell who visited Antibes in 1890–1 and the Belgian pointillist Théo van Rysselberghe who began to visit the Riviera in 1892. To the west, in 1876, Paul Cézanne had stayed in L'Estaque, a fishing village near Marseille, capturing the impact of the strong Mediterranean light in scenes painted out of doors.

A destination in its own right, Nice also acted as the pivot of the Riviera, as resorts such as Cannes, Menton, Monte Carlo and St-Tropez gathered their particular enthusiasts. Hotels today date from this great age of tourism, for example the *Hôtel Splendid* (1871) and *Le Cavendish* at Cannes. So also with gardens such as the Val Rahmeh Botanical Gardens in Menton, established by Sir Percy Radcliffe in 1905.

'The Riviera' became a lifestyle and a phrase, just as the Côte d'Azur was invented as a term in 1887 by the writer Stéphen Liégeard. The British were an important tourist market, their visits given greater respectability in 1882 when Queen Victoria first visited. They were joined by the wealthy from across Europe and North America, and many of the villas of the period, such as the Villa Kérylos (1902–8) in Beaulieu, and the nearby rose-coloured Villa Ephrussi (1905–12), can be visited by modern tourists. Built in Italian palazzo style, the latter is surrounded by splendid gardens. Gambling was to the fore at Monte Carlo where the casino was opened in 1863 with the dramatic *Salon Europe* added in 1865. A Romanesque-Byzantine-style cathedral followed in 1875. 'The Man Who Broke the Bank at Monte Carlo', a music-hall song written by Fred Gilbert in 1891 or 1892, was inspired by the success of the British fraudster Charles Wells in 1891. There were other casinos as at Juan-les-Pins and Menton. Prominent intellectuals who lived on the Riviera included Nietzsche and Wagner. The Italian Riviera to the east also attracted tourists, but most of the Mediterranean did not, including France's unappetising Languedoc coast. Most of that of Spain was left to fishermen.

Travelling in Italy

Experience is individual: visiting Rome in 1847–8, Florence Nightingale wrote:

> Could not sleep for knowing myself in the Eternal City and towards dawn I got up . . . and I almost ran till I came to St Peter's . . . No event in my life, except my death, can ever be greater than that first entrance into St Peter's.

In contrast, Frances Elliot, visiting in 1870, in an account published in the *Diary of an Idle Woman in Italy* (1871), found:

> Imperial Rome only a third-rate modern city! . . . It presents a strange medley of the grand, the beautiful, the rich, the great, with dirt, ugliness, squalor, and vulgarity. I have seen St Peter's, and, truth to say, am sorely disappointed! To arrive there, I passed through some of the vilest streets I ever traversed. The dirt, the filthy population, the crowds of soldiers, the street-side kitchens, where fish, flesh, fowl, and fruit are all frying in the open air, form so disgusting an ensemble, that one feels almost ashamed of being seen on foot in such a bear-garden.

At the same time, Italian coastal resorts developed an international reputation. Thus, Ravello, where Scott Neville Reid created an entrancing garden at the Villa Rufolo in 1853, attracted D. H.

Lawrence, Richard Wagner and Virginia Woolf. Taormina and Ischia also entranced writers, artists and others.

Attracted by the Italian Riviera and the Sorrento peninsula, British travellers were troubled by the poverty they saw in southern Italy. In 1845, visiting Naples, Charles Dickens wrote, 'The condition of the common people here is abject and shocking.' Six years later, H. G. Wreford, a newspaper correspondent, remarked: 'Seeking health here in Naples, and meddling not at all with European politics, I find it impossible to walk with an impassive mind among the scenes that are daily presented to my notice.'

Guidebooks

Travelling on the continent in 1829, John Murray III was disappointed by the existing guides and gathered private notes, which his company began to publish in 1836. *The East*, which covered Greece, Turkey and Malta, was published in 1840, and was followed by *Northern Italy* (1842) and *Central Italy* (1843).

Barcelona

In the eighteenth century, the city eased overpopulation on its dense medieval site by reclaiming marshland and creating a housing development called La Barceloneta, a triangular spit of land in the old harbour. The industrial age added greatly to pressures on space, with the walls demolished in 1859 to enable the city to expand. In his scheme for Eixample Garden City, Ildefons Cerdà provided for both public transportation networks and open spaces by using a geometric grid pattern. The area is readily identifiable today, being bordered to the north by the long thoroughfare of Calle Barcelona, now Avenida Diagonal. It was in this modern showcase area that Catalan Art Nouveau architects, such as the innovative Antoni Gaudí (1852–1926), were able to realise their designs, although many of the envisaged green spaces were not created. Catalonia was the most industrialised region of the Mediterranean, notably with the expansion of the cotton industry there. The impact of industrialisation that tourists can see includes the Casamarona textile factory (1911).

In contrast, despite the importance of the shipyards, notably in Genoa, the focus of industrialisation in Italy was not on the Mediterranean, being, instead, in Milan and Turin. In France, the focus was on coal and iron-based areas in the north-east. Elsewhere in the Mediterranean, although Thessaloniki had a significant industrial base, there were no areas comparable to Catalonia, and no similar build-up of urban working-class radicalism.

9. The World Wars, 1914–45

Freeman Wills Crofts's *Found Floating* (1937), a leisurely British detective story set on a Mediterranean cruise aboard the *Patricia*, captured the 'moving cosmos' of a liner:

> The officer of the watch, looking out into the night from the bridge; the helmsman, his hand on the wheel, his eye on the lubber's line; the captain, dressing for dinner, his immediate anxieties over; the lookout man in the crow's-nest half way up the foremast, keeping his eyes skinned and fighting his natural enemy, sleep; the radio operator with his earphones; the engineers in their steel cavern of sound, watchful, concentrating on the one great task of keeping the revolution of the propellers to the required speed; the cooks, sweating over their pots and pans, almost ready for the coming dinner; the dining-room stewards, the cabin stewards, the deck steward putting away his chairs and the library steward his books; the stewardesses, the doctor, the nurse, the photographer; deck hands; clerical staff; the band, tuning their instruments; the laundry women, knocking off work for the day; all these, and many more, functioning that *Patricia* should continue her advance across the sea, so that the holiday makers she carried should eat meals and see sights and grow strong and wise above their fellows.

The change from coal to oil-power was noted by Croft who had an engineering background:

Instead of a dozen or more half naked firemen, sweating in an inferno of heat and flame, there were only two or three cool efficient-looking men. They swung no great shovelfuls of coal into the white hot maws of the furnaces, but calmly took readings and with delicacy adjusted wheel valves.

A prefatory Author's Note, however, brought a different reality: 'This book was written before the Spanish War broke out', a reference to the Spanish Civil War of 1936–9. The novel was also serialised in the *Daily Mail*.

In contrast, Eric Ambler's novel *Journey into Fear* was not an account of an attractive Mediterranean cruise, but it was one appropriate for its wartime year of publication, 1940. In this gripping story, a British engineer who has helped in British cooperation with Turkey escapes German assassination in Istanbul, travelling west on an Italian ship for Marseille, only to discover that a hired killer is also on the boat. The food was no more cruise quality than the company. The book was filmed in 1943.

Before the First World War

Angry about Tunisia, the part of Africa closest to Italy, going to France in 1881, Italy looked elsewhere for the empire it thought should follow unification. Initially, Italian expansionism focused on Eritrea, Somalia and Ethiopia. At first, this was successful, leading to the conquest of Eritrea and much of Somalia; but the Italians were heavily defeated by the Ethiopians at Adua in 1896. In response, in 1911, encouraged by the problems of the Turkish Empire, Italy invaded Turkish-ruled Tripolitania and Cyrenaica. The Italians called their conquest 'Libya', restoring an ancient name for the region, and drawing on the idea that they were the modern heirs to the Roman Empire. However, despite the first

wartime use of aircraft, the Italians found their conquest difficult. The use of aircraft had little impact on operations. Instead,
strong Arab resistance kept the Italians to a few coastal enclaves.
The Italians were more successful in capturing the Dodecanese,
Turkish islands in the south-eastern Aegean, notably Rhodes, as
well as in operating off Lebanon and in the Adriatic. Comparable
naval power was the key tool that the Turks lacked. In addition,
they had no ally to provide it.

In 1912, Rear-Admiral Ernest Troubridge, the Chief of the
War Staff of the British Admiralty, in a memorandum on the
Italian occupation of some of these Aegean islands, noted of
British policy:

> A cardinal factor has naturally been that no strong naval
> power should be in effective permanent occupation of any
> territory or harbour east of Malta, if such harbour be capa-
> ble of transformation into a fortified naval base. None can
> foresee the developments of material in warfare, and the
> occupation of the apparently most useless island should be
> resisted equally with the occupation of the best. The geo-
> graphical situation of these islands enable the sovereign
> power, if enjoying the possession of a navy, to exercise a
> control over the Levant and Black Sea trade and to threaten
> our position in Egypt.

Any threat to Egypt entailed also threatening the route to
India via the Suez Canal. The Italians were not alone in using
naval strength to expand. Attacking Turkey in the First Balkan
War of 1912-13, the Greek navy, which had been developed from
the 1880s with French expertise, loans and warships, cut Turkish
communications in the Aegean Sea and conducted amphibious attacks there that resulted in the capture and annexation
of Lemnos, Chios and Samos. In this war, Bulgaria, Greece,
Montenegro and Serbia overran and annexed the Turkish

positions on the Balkan mainland, with the exception of a small area round Constantinople. Bulgaria overran Thrace, while Greece (which had fought Turkey far less successfully in 1897) captured Thessaloniki. Montenegro seized Scutari, which it was made to transfer to Albania.

An independent Albania was carved out of the Turkish Empire in 1913, albeit with Greece and Serbia only withdrawing their forces with considerable reluctance. In one of the many largely forgotten episodes of Mediterranean history that in practice have been very important in settling its frontiers, moulding identities and leaving grievances, Italy made Greece cede Northern Epirus to Albania, leading the local Greeks to set up the Autonomous Republic of Northern Epirus in 1914. Subsequent instability there was settled by Italian pressure in favour of Albania in 1921. Greece abandoned its claims in 1925.

Meanwhile, in the Second Balkan War (1913), which stemmed from the former allies falling out, Bulgaria was defeated by Greece, Romania, Serbia, Turkey and Montenegro. Bulgaria's Aegean port of Kavala was annexed by Greece, although the port of Dedeağaç and the region of Western Thrace was returned to Bulgaria. Greece did not gain them until 1919–20, after the First World War, in which Bulgaria had backed the Central Powers in 1915–18. In the Second Balkan War, Turkey regained Edirne (Adrianople), and it has held it since.

The challenge to imperial stability was not only in the Turkish Empire. The Austrian Empire faced nationalist pressure in the Balkans, especially in Bosnia, pressure notably encouraged by Russia's ally Serbia. In North Africa, there was uncertainty in both the British and French empires. In 1904, the British Director of Military Operations warned that in Egypt 'our whole position depends entirely on prestige', and referred to 'the small, and from a military point of view inadequate, British force' there. The French faced resistance in Morocco, while, in Algeria, it was unclear how best to respond to the assimilationist aspirations of the Young Algerian movement of Arabs. Ambivalent about Islam, France did not provide a welcoming response to these aspirations, although the situation was sufficiently easy to prevent significant disruption during the First World War.

Prior to the First World War, the Mediterranean naval powers built warships in a competitive race. Austro-Hungary (Austria for short), with its coastline in modern Croatia, Slovenia and Italy (at Trieste), built battleships, touching off a naval race with Italy and encouraging France, which was already in a race with Italy. With Britain focusing on a confrontation with Germany in the North Sea, France was concerned to safeguard its Algiers–Marseille route against Germany's allies, which apparently would be Austria and Italy. In the event of war, this was the route by which France would receive reinforcements from North Africa. Mediterranean power politics therefore were already in the shadow of what was to be the First World War.

Communications meanwhile speeded up in the Mediterranean. More powerful ships' engines were introduced in 1907 with the French packet boat *Charles-Roux* on the Algiers–Marseille route. Aircraft added different links. In 1913, Roland Garros flew alone from Fréjus on the Riviera to Bizerta in Tunisia, creating another link within the French world.

The First World War

At sea, the First World War focused on the North Sea and on maritime routes to Britain with Germany supplementing its surface ships with submarines. That challenge, however, did not make the Mediterranean irrelevant. Far from it, not least because Germany's failure to knock France out on land in offensives in 1914 and 1916, and, correspondingly, those of France and Britain to break the impasse on the Western Front in 1915–17, encouraged the competing alliances to seek success around the Mediterranean.

On 6 August 1914, Britain and France signed a naval convention under which the French navy was responsible for much of the Mediterranean, and the British for the remainder of the world. Although, as a result, there were no French warships in the North Sea, the alliance helped provide the Royal Navy with a sufficient margin of power there over the Germans to survive losses. In the Mediterranean, with British as well as French warships present, German and Austrian naval power was outnumbered and outclassed. This situation enabled France safely to move troops from North Africa to France, and also greatly affected the military and political options for Italy. In August 1914, the small German squadron in the Mediterranean, the battle cruiser *Goeben* and the light cruiser *Breslau*, shelled the ports of Philippeville and Bône in Algeria, evaded British attempts to intercept them, and took shelter with the Turks.

Italy's decision to abandon its allies Germany and Austria, with which it had agreed to a naval convention as recently as 1913, and, instead, to join Britain and France in May 1915 ensured that the Mediterranean was controlled by this alliance. The Italian-ruled Dodecanese became a significant naval base for Britain and France, and was used to support the Gallipoli operation against Turkey. In addition, a French squadron at Corfu and most of the Italian fleet at Taranto, supported by British and Australian warships, confined Austrian surface ships to the Adriatic and sought to stop submarines from there getting into the Mediterranean. However, Austria's position on the eastern seaboard of the Adriatic was strengthened by the defeat of Serbia in 1915 and the capture of Scutari the following year. Under the terms of the Treaty of London, by which Italy had joined the Allies, it was promised northern Dalmatia, Zadar (Zara) and most of the Dalmatian islands. Joining the other side in 1915, Bulgaria was promised Macedonia and most of Thrace by Germany and Austria. The continuation of pre-war territorial ambitions was clear.

Turkey had joined Germany and Austria in October 1914; and in 1915, reflecting the ease with which the Allies could send an expedition across the Mediterranean, an Anglo-French fleet was sent to force open the Dardanelles, en route to threatening Constantinople itself. This poorly planned attempt was stopped by minefields, shore batteries and an unwillingness, in the face of the loss of ships to mines, to accept the rise of further naval operations. There had been a misplaced belief that naval power alone could force a passage through the Dardanelles, and that despite a pre-war British naval mission that had provided valuable advice to the Turks on mine laying.

In turn, in the developing Gallipoli operation, there was an attempt to take control of the eastern side of the Dardanelles. However, the amphibious capability revealed was not matched by success on the part of the troops once landed against strongly defended Turkish positions. The failure was in part to overestimate what a landing by an Allied force of that size, a force of Australian, British, French, Indian and New Zealand units, could expect to accomplish once ashore. That the force then moved slowly was not the key issue, but it exacerbated the situation, as did the promptness of the Turkish response. The Allies found themselves blocked and on the exposed lower ground. Their sole success was eventually to evacuate their positions successfully.

The Allies, nevertheless, continued to dominate the Mediterranean. The Strait of Otranto at the entrance to the Adriatic was sealed by a massive minefield. In late 1916, in accordance with a British request, four Japanese warships were sent to the Mediterranean. Based in Malta, they added to the escort capacity against German and Austrian submarines. So also with American warships based in Gibraltar from 1917.

Naval dominance was also seen in the landing of an Allied expeditionary force at Thessaloniki in November 1915. This force was designed to save Serbia from conquest, but was too late to do so and was thwarted by successful Bulgarian resistance. Greece was divided between the pro-Allied Prime Minister, Eleftherios Venizelos, and Constantine I, who dismissed him in late 1915.

In turn, Constantine was deposed with Allied support in June 1917 and, now again under Venizelos, Greece declared war on the Central Powers. As a reward, it was to win territorial gains from Turkey in the subsequent peace treaty.

Attention on the war focuses on the Western Front in France and Belgium, but the shores of the Mediterranean were also an important area of activity. The Germans had hoped that bringing the Turks into the war would challenge their opponents. Indeed, *jihad* was declared on behalf of the Caliph, the Turkish ruler, but most of the Muslim world did not respond. In part this was because of Arab hostility to Turkish rule, hostility that had been enhanced by the recent emphasis by the Young Turks on a Turkish character to the empire. In Egypt, German promises of independence from Britain required Turkish troops to make them real: there was no supporting rising in Egypt. However, the Turkish attack on the Suez Canal in February 1915 was repelled by Anglo-French forces, including Indian troops. Similarly, German and Turkish attempts to use opposition to Italy in Libya to wider effect failed. Moreover, in 1916, France suppressed a revolt in Tunisia that had broken out the previous year, while Algeria remained quiet despite the movement of French troops to the Western Front. There were fewer problems there than those faced by the British in Ireland.

The British commitment to the defence of the Suez Canal was eventually translated from successful defensive preparations to a forward defence in which forces moved into the Sinai peninsula. However, there was no significant pressure on the Turks in Palestine until 1917, as the British first focused on creating the necessary transport and logistical infrastructure. After initial failures in attacks near Gaza in the spring of 1917 on well-prepared and ably defended Turkish defences, the British were successful later that year, attacking further east and, having broken through, capturing Jerusalem on 9 December. Indeed, General Edmund Allenby was lauded in Britain as a latterday Richard the

Lionheart. On 20 September 1918, Allenby launched his final offensive, swiftly defeating the Turks and capturing Haifa and Acre, before pressing on to take Tyre, Sidon, Damascus, Beirut and Aleppo.

Earlier, the Italians had taken very heavy casualties in 1915–17 in a series of offensives focused on the River Isonzo before, in late 1917, being heavily defeated and pushed back in the battle of Caporetto. The line was then stabilised on the River Piave, and, after a major victory at Vittorio Veneto in November 1918, their forces advanced. The heavy casualties in the war, about half as much again as in the Second World War, helped ensure Italian determination to benefit from the peace, and led to anger when they failed to do so.

The Interwar Period

There was no clean break between the First World War and an interwar period. Instead, conflict continued in new forms. In the Mediterranean, this was particularly seen in the Greek intervention in Turkey, which went down in total failure. British, French, Italian and Greek spheres of influence had been allocated in Turkey as part of the peace settlement. The Greeks were the most ambitious and, as so often with the powers of the period, looked to the past for validation. In attempting to gain control of western Anatolia, the Greeks made frequent reference, for both foreign and domestic audiences, to the integral role of Ionia in the Classical Greek world. While these arguments persuaded Greek opinion, and won support from Britain, they were destroyed by the total character of Turkish military success in 1921–2. This success led to an end of Ionia in the shape of the hybrid culture on the Turkish side of the Aegean. The fall to the Turks of the major city, Smyrna (İzmir), in 1922 was followed by it being extensively burned down, a fate recorded in photographs, and with many of the Greek men there killed.

In the Chanak Crisis of September 1922, Britain backed down in its confrontation with the nationalists in Turkey led by Mustafa Kemal Pasha, Kemal Atatürk. The Turks were threatening war over the Allied-occupied territory, particularly Constantinople and the Dardanelles. The bulk of the cabinet rejected the willingness of David Lloyd George, the Prime Minister, and Winston Churchill to risk war, the Minister of Agriculture remarking, 'I don't believe the country cares anything about Thrace.' Canada, France and Italy were also unwilling to fight the Turks. A rival of Greece, Italy, indeed, was ready to cooperate with the Turks.

The Treaty of Lausanne, the following year, saw an abandonment of the terms of the Treaty of Sèvres of 1920 and, instead, a peace that was more favourable to Turkish views. An exchange of Greeks and Turks from the newly settled states was part of the end to Greek hopes of gains on the eastern shores of the Aegean. Alongside the Greek sense of loss, Turks who had been settled for centuries, for example in Crete, were moved to Turkey.

This exchange was a major aspect of the move toward monoglot societies that was to be such an important feature of the Mediterranean over the century. Nationalism was cause, means and consequence of this change. The transition in the Turkish Empire was especially important. What had been a polyglot empire, with multiple ethnicities, intercommunality and cosmopolitanism, was moving in a different direction before the First World War under the impact of the Young Turks movement. As a result, minorities were treated as enemies. This process was accelerated during the war with the large-scale massacre of Armenians and with the 'Arab Revolt' against Turkish rule. The harshness toward Greeks was part of the pattern. A clearly proclaimed ethnic identity was to the fore. More generally, the move toward monoglot societies encouraged the flight of refugees. Armenians, Greeks and Kurds left Turkey as part of a wider and more complex process.

In 1923, Turkey became a republic, with Kemal Atatürk the President until 1938. The caliphate was abolished the following year and, in 1925, the beginning of a rebellion in eastern Anatolia led to the declaration of martial law and the suppression of political opposition. This pattern was to be a longstanding one in Turkey. Democratic practice had a limited purchase given the tendency of the state to see enemies within. Atatürk's system looked back to that of the pre-war Young Turks.

The war dramatically extended the power of Britain and France around the shores of the Mediterranean. In 1914, Egypt was made a British protectorate while Cyprus was annexed. In addition, the partitioning of the Turkish Empire led, in 1920, to League of Nations' mandates that entailed British rule over Palestine, Transjordan and Iraq, and French rule over Syria and Lebanon. These mandates were presented as a means to prepare for self-determination, but were experienced as imperialism. This is a contrast that is more widely useful for questions of rule and influence.

American pressure in the Versailles peace settlement on behalf of national self-determination thwarted Italian expectations of the cession of northern Dalmatia, which, instead, went to Yugoslavia, fuelling an Italian sense of having been cheated by the peace. Gabriele D'Annunzio, an extreme Italian nationalist and flamboyant novelist, entered the town of Fiume in September 1919 as a reaction to the negotiations at Versailles. which aimed not to award Fiume to Italy despite a plebiscite held there on 30 October 1918. He established a free state called the Regency of Carnaro. Then, under the Treaty of Rapallo in 1920, Italy and Yugoslavia agreed that Italy would make some gains, notably Istria, Trieste and Zadar. However, D'Annunzio rejected the treaty and at the end of 1920 his Regency was swept out by Italian troops acting as an Allied force to implement the Versailles and Rapallo treaties. After D'Annunzio had left, an independent Free State of Fiume was established. In turn, this was seized by Italy in 1924 after another Italian–Yugoslav treaty was signed that year.

The war, however, did not only leave a highly contentious legacy in Italy. In the long term, this legacy was particularly the case in what from 1948 became Israel. In October 1915, Sir Henry McMahon, the British High Commissioner in Cairo, informed Hussein ibn Ali, ruler of the Hejaz (in modern Saudi Arabia), whose support against the Turks was being sought, that Britain was 'prepared to recognize and support the independence of the Arabs', but that districts to the west of Aleppo, Homs and Damascus should be excluded from a proposed independent Arab state on the grounds that they were not purely Arab. Zionists seized on this argument that Palestine therefore was not included in the state, and hence could be settled by Jews. However, in a dispute that continues to the present, their interpretation was hotly disputed by Arab leaders, who argued that the wording referred to Lebanon alone, where there was already a substantial Christian population.

Following the decision of the British War Cabinet of 31 October 1917, in which the Foreign Secretary, Arthur Balfour, had emphasised the favourable potential impact on pro-Zionist Jews in Russia and America, the Balfour Declaration, issued on 2 November, expressed support for a Jewish national home in Palestine, while leaving its borders unclear. The following May, Balfour, referring to an Arab kingdom in the Hejaz, an Arab state in Iraq and a 'Jewish "home"' in Palestine, argued that 'they will certainly give increased protection to British interests, both in Egypt and in India . . . "buffer states"'.

The Arab sense of betrayal extended to Syria, where France in 1920 thwarted the attempt at replacing the Turks by Arab rule. In part, France wanted to protect the Christian population of Lebanon, then part of Syria. There was also a concern, as with German territories in Africa, to match British gains.

From the outset, the new imperial order faced resistance. There were rebellions in Egypt and Iraq and, more successfully,

Turkish success in overcoming the original post-war settlement. The suppression of the rebellion in Egypt in 1919 indicated the resources of the British Empire, with warships sent to Alexandria and the Suez Canal. However, Britain did not want to face a long insurrection, and granted Egypt independence in 1922 while retaining military control of it. France was more determined, suppressing a Druze rebellion in Syria in 1925–6. France also created Lebanon as a Christian haven in a mostly Muslim Syria.

Underlying these issues were the problems of defining political communities in the aftermath of Turkish rule. Territories had to be defined and institutions created, and the difficult process of state formation was made much more complex by having to respond to new, non-Muslim, imperial masters. Religion and nationalism were in part shaped in this context as cultural and religious responses. That, in turn, highlighted the status and future of those defined as minorities, and their relationship with the imperial power. The inherently transient nature of the mandatory regime, with that of the British in Iraq ending in 1932, put a degree of pressure on the other mandates, and led to discussions over autonomy, if not independence, as in the Franco-Syrian treaty of 1936.

In the 1930s, Britain was to be challenged by nationalists in Cyprus and Malta, and by the Arab Rising in Palestine in 1937–9. The threat to the Islamic world from Western expansion was linked in the Middle East to sectarian tensions relating to Jews, Christians and Druzes. As a result of this response, the new imperial structures created after the First World War did not work well and had to be maintained by force.

In the case of Britain and Palestine, contradictory assumptions and promises that owed much to the exigencies of the world war Britain had recently nearly lost (a point usually forgotten today) greatly complicated the situation. Britain, moreover, sought to deal with competing Arab and Jewish claims in Palestine by compromise. That did not work. Following murderous Arab sectarian rioting in 1929, Arab disorder gathered renewed force in 1937 after the Peel Commission, established to tackle the linked issues of Jewish immigration and the violently hostile Arab response, recommended the partition of Palestine between Arab and Jewish states. The report was rejected by the Arabs and led to the Arab Rising against British rule. As is only to be expected, ethnic and religious groupings and identities, in turn, were riven by other alignments and by differences in collective and individual responses. Thus, among Jews there were differences between the long-established communities, who had largely adapted to their circumstances, and recent immigrants from Europe who tended to be Ashkenazi Jews and Zionists.

British concern about Palestine was accentuated by Benito Mussolini's attempts to exploit Arab nationalism, notably in Egypt and Palestine, as an aspect of the Italian drive for Mediterranean hegemony, a drive that entailed the overthrow of the British and French positions. However, although the Arabs were the majority, their opposition in Palestine lacked overall leadership and was divided, in particular between clans. Moreover, the British used collective punishment to weaken Arab support for the guerrillas, benefited from a measure of Palestinian support including a supportive militia, and sent significant reinforcements to regain and maintain control.

The situation in Libya was very different. This was straightforward imperialism. The Italians had recognised Libyan self-government in 1919, but Benito Mussolini, the Fascist leader who gained power in 1922, was not prepared to accept this. Employing great brutality against civilians, of whom over 50,000 were probably killed, the Italians subdued the colony in 1928–32. They benefited from the lack of foreign support for the Libyans.

So also with the brutal Spanish suppression of resistance in Spanish Morocco, where they had been heavily defeated at Annual in 1921. This Rif Rebellion was finally overcome in

1925–6 thanks to French intervention on behalf of Spain. The Spaniards made the first use of tanks in Africa.

In North Africa, France faced growing nationalism and popular political pressure, for example from the Algerian People's Party. The nationalist movements were divided over compositions, goals and methods, particularly on ethnic and sectarian grounds, and with reference to the attraction of assimilation, autonomy and independence. Nevertheless, a lack of stability and certainty were part of the equation of imperial authority and power, not least because separate political identities, activities and initiatives on the part of the local population were now obvious.

In the event, across their range of territories, whatever their status, the challenges to the British and French were overcome or, at least, contained. Indeed, imperialism continued to operate with a fair margin of consent, however grudging and dependent on intermediaries, and however much that consent is ignored today. This was particularly so in Algeria where the French presence had been strengthened by large-scale settlement by the *colons* (colonists), who were later to be called *Pied-Noirs*. Many were French, but Italians, Spaniards and Maltese were also important. About 10 per cent of the total Algerian population were of European descent and, by 1940, they owned about a quarter of the arable land. In 1930, France celebrated the centenary of the colonisation of Algeria as a civilising step with a monument erected at Sidi-Ferruch.

Concern focused on other imperial powers, rather than on rebellion. France was more worried about Italy than Arab nationalism, and understandably so in light of developments in the 1930s and early 1940s. In the 1920s, and again in the late 1930s, there was also anxiety about cooperation between Italy and Spain against France. This concern encouraged France to build coastal fortifications and to improve its navy.

The First World War had wrecked many existing commercial relationships. Indeed, 'Mr Eugenides, the Smyrna merchant' in

T. S. Eliot's poem *The Waste Land* (1922), is a reference to a trade that is gone, as well as capturing a dislike of the Mediterranean, as he is described as a propositioning homosexual, as well as unshaven. Yet, trade had continued, that in currants being a basis of the plot in Graham Greene's novel *Stamboul Train* (1932), the train being the Orient Express; and peace brought renewed profit to many port-cities.

The leading Mediterranean maritime routes – Gibraltar via Malta to Alexandria and the Suez Canal for the British, and Marseille to Algiers for the French – were supplemented by new ones thanks to the expansion of the British and French empires. Thus, British ships called at Haifa, the major port for Palestine and Transjordan, and their French counterparts at Beirut, the same for Lebanon and Syria. The Italians developed their maritime links from Italy to Tripoli and Benghazi in Libya, to Rhodes, and, via the Suez Canal, to Italian East Africa.

Alongside the extension of maritime links, there were also new goods to be transported, notably oil. This trade was linked to the significance of refining. Thus, the Mediterranean added a new system of trade and transhipment, with oil being moved in tankers and pipelines. France built a large refinery on the Mediterranean coast, while at Haifa, at the end of a pipeline from the oilfields near Kirkuk in Iraq, construction of what became a very large refinery was begun in 1938. This was part of the infrastructure of British power. Much capacity, however, came later, for example, with the Rome refinery built near the port of Fiumicino in 1965. The largest refinery in Spain, at San Roque, was commissioned in 1967, while a second in Israel followed at Ashdod in 1973. Oil was necessary in part for shipping, as Freeman Wills Crofts noted in *Found Floating*, although coal-powered vessels remained significant.

The end of the First World War saw both pre-war liners brought back into service and the building of new passenger ships. The Italians proved particularly active, building the *Augustus*, *Saturnia* and *Conte Grande* in the 1920s, and the *Rex* and *Conte di Savoia* in the 1930s, among others. Fincantieri was to become the world's leading builder of cruise ships. These and other ships focused on the runs from Europe to New York, with the Italian ships especially important for the Mediterranean as they sailed from Genoa, which was well-linked by train to Milan and Turin. There was large-scale emigration from southern Italy and Sicily, with Naples as the key port and, therefore, the last sight of Italy. The flow of migrants to the United States was cut by immigration legislation there in the early 1920s, but large numbers of Italians went to Argentina and Brazil. There was no comparable flow from Greece, Spain or, even more, Turkey, or, indeed, from countries with an Arab population.

The Mediterranean was a major cruise destination, and literature and maps were produced accordingly. Rolland Jenkins's *The Mediterranean Cruise* (1925) offered a simple outline map of the sea, but also detailed maps of Mediterranean ports, the Riviera, Palestine and Egypt, all crucial British cruise destinations. Agatha Christie's stories show her detective Hercule Poirot engaging with the Middle East alongside British tourists. This was particularly the case in *Murder on the Orient Express* (1934), *Death on the Nile* (1937) and *Appointment with Death* (1938), as well as the short stories 'The Adventure of the Egyptian Tomb' (1923), which involves a four-day crossing from Marseille to Alexandria, 'Problem at Sea' (1935), which is largely based on a cruise ship docked at Alexandria, and 'Triangle at Rhodes' (1936), which is set when the island is under Italian rule. A luxurious liner 'sweeping its lighted decks through waters floored with stars' was, as John Dickson Carr noted in *The Blind Barber* (1934), frequently the background in novels. So also in films. If the Atlantic crossing dominated such attention, as in *The Blind Barber*, the Mediterranean benefited from the general appeal of liner travel and from the specific attraction of the stops.

The wealthy could make private arrangements to travel, a process encouraged by the availability of steam-powered 'yachts'. That of Bendor, Duke of Westminster, a habitué of the Riviera, had a crew of forty. In 1921, Sir Horace and Lady Rumbold visited Gallipoli by yacht. Travel to the eastern Mediterranean (and to North Africa) was more exotic than to destinations further west. Staying with his wife Violet in Constantinople in 1921, Harold Farmer managed to secure a suite of rooms in the *Isma'il Pasha Khiosk* on the shores of the Bosphorus: 'Our rooms had windows on the water. Spaces were vast. The sitting room, 180 feet by 90 feet, covered with a scarlet carpet woven in one piece. Large gilt mirrors on the walls. Tables of white marble set in gilt – all the furniture of gilt, gold and scarlet. Our bedroom was on the level of the water.'

Howard Carter's excavations in Egypt, notably his discovery in 1922, in the Valley of the Kings, of the intact tomb of the 18th Dynasty Pharaoh, Tutankhamun, encouraged tourism there, as well as speculation about ancient Egypt. The latter was reflected in fiction and film.

The Mediterranean was also very important as a thorough-fare en route to the Indian Ocean, providing a quicker and less storm-tossed route than that via Cape Town. As such, it was an aspect of the British Empire, and of the development of the empire as a system, an important part of which centred on the Indian Ocean and the routes to and from it, notably the links with Australasia and the Far East. As a consequence, strategic impe-rialism focused on the Mediterranean and its protection. The advertising posters of the Empire Marketing Board established in 1926 emphasised mutual dependence and stressed maritime lines of communication. MacDonald Gill's poster *Highways of Empire* (1927) concentrated on maritime links. Charles Pears's series *The Empire's Highway to India* (1928) depicted Gibraltar, Malta, the Suez Canal, Aden and Bombay, and had a military theme, with the Gibraltar poster showing a warship, while its Malta counterpart had a RAF plane flying over a merchantman leaving Valletta. Photographs and postcards of similar scenes helped reiterate such images.

The development of long-range air routes by means of flying boats did not alter the situation as most people continued to go by the less expensive ships, which could also carry far more baggage. Founded in 1924, Imperial Airways traversed the Mediterranean. The outward route to South Africa in 1925 went from London via Marseille, Pisa, Taranto, Athens, Sollum [Egypt] and Cairo. The London to Karachi service, launched in 1929, included a flight to Basle, a train to Genoa and a flying boat to Alexandria. The 1933 London to Australia survey route went via Paris, Lyon, Rome, Brindisi, Athens and Alexandria. The Short Empire flying boats introduced by Britain in 1937 provided an enhanced service. Meanwhile, regular air services began across the Mediterranean, including, in 1938, from both Marseille and Rome to Tripoli, in Libya, which was the first part of a French route going on via Benghazi to Damascus.

The Riviera

The French Riviera continued its popularity, with the addition of particularly fashionable resorts, such as Juan-les-Pins, and the growing number of expatriates. In *The Blind Barber* (1934), John Dickson Carr, referring to 'international crooks', went on to mention 'The Prince or Princess Somebody kind, who always hang out at Monte Carlo.' Among the visitors of the 1930s to the Riviera were the Fitzgeralds (F. Scott and Zelda), the Duke of Windsor and W. Somerset Maugham. His lifestyle supported by thirteen servants, he referred to Monte Carlo as 'a sunny place for shady people'. Winston Churchill was often there. The great social question of 1938 was whether or not to curtsey to the Duchess of Windsor. There was much group socialising, including balls, firework parties and open-air concerts.

Images of the Riviera were most commonly present through the illustrated magazines increasingly popular in these years. Photography made the Riviera seem immediate as well as fashionable. The prominent, for example film stars, were pictured at ease and with each other. Cars were a major adjunct of their lifestyle and featured in the photographs.

Another set of visual images came from the depiction of the Riviera by an increasing number of painters, including Henri Matisse (from 1916), Pablo Picasso, Pierre Bonnard, Marc Chagall, Max Beckmann, Fernand Léger and Francis Picabia. Sites and paintings from this period can be readily found, for example the *Musée Matisse* at Cimiez in Nice. Matisse's work can also be seen in the *Chapelle du Rosaire* in Vence. There is a Renoir memorial museum in Cagnes, a Picasso one at Antibes and a Léger one in Biot. The walled village of St-Paul-de-Vence, with the Fondation Maeght collection, is a major 'arty' tourist attraction now. The Modernist architecture of Le Corbusier is another focus of interest. Tourists can also visit gardens from the period such as the Serre de la Madone in Menton, which was designed in the 1920s by Lawrence Johnston.

Crises from 1929

This world was challenged by the great recession that followed the Wall Street Crash of 1929. This recession hit the Mediterranean hard: employment, trade and liquidity declined. The fall in exports greatly affected primary producers. Their political systems buckled, which put pressure on existing political arrangements. Thus, Albania's economic difficulties led Italy to increase its control of the country.

Paradoxically, the recession also increased the percentage of trade within empires. The British took 49 per cent of exports in 1935–9, compared with 42 per cent a decade earlier. So also with the French imperial economy. The economic benefits stemming from empire helped justify imperial strategic commitments. For both Britain and France these, however, were challenged by the risk of another major war. Mussolini greatly expanded Italy's navy in rivalry with France, and in order to challenge the British position in the Mediterranean. Yet, he was less interested in naval affairs than in the situation on land. It was possible to talk of unlocking the gates of the Mediterranean at Gibraltar and Suez, but, as the Italian naval staff noted, there was really only hope of Italy controlling the central Mediterranean. A lack of carrier air cover and a battle fleet that could not match those of France, and notably of Britain, rendered other schemes futile.

This was part of the clash between aspiration and reality, the former compounded of bombast and vainglory, that was so important to Mussolini's rule. Despite its pretensions to modernity, not least supporting heavy industry, including shipbuilding, Mussolini's regime was characterised by a degree of factionalism and a major role for patronage that encouraged incompetence or, at least, timeserving. Indeed, alongside the weakness of the opposition in Italy, the Fascist regime was already exhausted prior to the Second World War, and this increased its dependence on propaganda and surveillance. Yet there was also improvement. In Sicily, brigandage had worsened after the First World War thanks to wartime experience as soldiers and then unemployment. However, the situation improved under Mussolini due to determined state action.

Britain and Italy came close to conflict as a result of the Italian invasion of Ethiopia in 1935–6, a step condemned by the League of Nations. In 1933, the British Chiefs of Staff Sub-Committee of the Committee of Imperial Defence warned 'our defensive arrangements in the Mediterranean are in many respects obsolete and have not been adjusted to the development of the French and Italian navies, and the increasing range and strength of French and Italian military aircraft.' However, in 1935–6, despite weaknesses, as well as concerns about Italian submarines based at Leros, the Royal Navy was confident of success. Britain considered oil sanctions and closing the Suez Canal, but did not wish to provoke war and was greatly affected by France's reluctance to join in action against Italy.

Similarly, the Spanish Civil War of 1936–9 did not lead to a wider crisis. The British navy protected trade routes threatened by Italian submarines acting on behalf of Franco's nationalists, but without any real clash. Instead, crisis focused in 1938–9 on Eastern Europe, first Czechoslovakia and then Poland. Indeed, in 1939, when the Second World War broke out, most of the Mediterranean remained neutral: Spain, Italy (and therefore its Albanian and Libyan territories), Yugoslavia, Greece and Turkey. Of the Mediterranean states, only the British and French empires went to war in 1939. At this stage, France was the only real democracy on the Mediterranean, although not in Algeria where the native population had no representation in the French National Assembly and enjoyed scant power in local government. Yugoslavia had become a royal dictatorship in 1929, and Greece was another from 1935.

Turkey had been ceded by France the Hatay area, including Alexandretta (Iskenderum), which initially became an independent state in 1938–9. Its Turkish minority wanted to join Turkey, the alliance of which France sought (while Turkey was concerned about Italian expansionism) and in 1939, following a referendum, Hatay joined Turkey. The Arab and Armenian population fled. The area is marked on Syrian maps as still part of the latter, but other states present it as Turkish.

Albania under Zog

Unstable in the aftermath of the expulsion of Turkish power, Albania, for long the forgotten Mediterranean country, saw coups, rebellions and foreign intervention after the First World War. From 1913 to 1925, Albania was a principality. Prince Wilhelm of Wied reigned briefly in 1914, before going into exile; although the country was not declared a republic until 1925. In

1924, Ahmet Zogu (Zog), the young Interior Minister, who came from a family of landowners, seized power in Albania with the backing of Yugoslav troops and White (anti-Communist) Russian mercenaries. Becoming President in 1925, and making himself King in 1928, he used force to overcome revolts by Catholic and Muslim tribesmen. Zog relied on his own retainers and loyal clans, the leaders of which he made colonels and paid. His limitation on the right to carry weapons was not extended to tribes on which he depended. Zog had close links to the Egyptian royal family. In 1939, he fled when the Italians successfully invaded with overwhelming force.

The Second World War, 1939–45

The world war rapidly escalated with Germany's success leading in June 1940 to Italy entering the war against both Britain and France, as well as to the surrender soon after of defeated France. The Germans occupied much of it, but most of the rest was left under the control of a government based in Vichy. Italy got little, in part due to Hitler's concern to bolster Vichy, but even more because Italian attacks had been held by the French in the Alps.

Vichy was essentially a Mediterranean empire, with Vichy controlling southern France as well as French North Africa, Lebanon, and Syria. Further afield, Vichy also controlled French colonies in West Africa, South-East Asia and Madagascar. Moreover, Vichy had a powerful fleet, based in Toulon and North Africa.

The war in the Mediterranean became very complex as a result of Italy's entry and Vichy's role. British concern about relations between Vichy and Germany led to the attack on a Vichy squadron at Mers el Kébir near Oran in Algeria on 3 July 1940, in which one battleship was sunk and two were damaged. This was followed, in June–July 1941, by the conquest of Lebanon and Syria in the face of opposition by Vichy troops. The attack at Mers el Kébir demonstrated Britain's continued resolve and naval strength, but also made it easier for Vichy to cooperate with Germany and compromised support for its opponent, Charles de Gaulle, the leader of the Free French.

Italy launched a series of attacks, including on British-ruled Egypt from 9 September 1940 and on Greece from 28 October 1940. Each was crushed by well-executed counterattacks, leading to invasions of Libya and Albania by Britain and Greece respectively. Seeking to overcome a threat that had affected war planning and defence policy in the 1930s, the British also hit the Italian fleet hard. Short of oil and confidence, and lacking an effective naval air arm, the Italians repeatedly lost the initiative to the British. The battle of Calabria on 9 July 1940 was indecisive, but British carriers hit Italian targets in North Africa, notably Tobruk harbour. The successful night attack by twenty-one torpedo bombers on Italian battleships moored, without radar support, in Taranto on 11 November 1940, badly damaged four of them, and encouraged the Japanese attack on Pearl Harbor just over a year later. In terms both of the damage inflicted and the number of attacking aircraft, the Taranto attack was more effective, not least because the Italians lacked sufficient shipbuilding capacity to create a replacement navy.

The long-term effect on the Italian navy was also different to that on Pearl Harbor. It withdrew units northwards, and thus lessened the vulnerability of British maritime routes and naval forces in the Mediterranean, notably by increasing the problems of concentrating Italian naval forces and maintaining secrecy. In addition to the senior commanders understanding the limitations of their ships and industrial base, Italian admirals were also averse to taking risks because they believed the war would be won or lost by Germany and that, in a post-war world, the navy would be Italy's most important military asset. On 27–8 March 1941, in the battle of Cape Matapan, the British, using carrier-borne torpedo bombers and radar-directed battleship fire, sank three of the best Italian cruisers and damaged a modern battleship, ending really meaningful Italian fleet operations.

The Germans responded by sending help to the Italians. In Libya, this came in the shape of the *Afrika Korps*, which drove the British back into Egypt. Moreover, on 6 April 1941, the Germans, with allied, including Italian, support, attacked Greece, as well as Yugoslavia, which had defied German wishes. The British sent an expeditionary force to help the Greeks, but it was pushed back. Using captured ships, the Germans also seized the Aegean islands.

The campaign culminated with the conquest of Crete by German parachute, glider-borne and air-transported troops. This risky attack gained the initiative from a poorly directed resistance. In contrast, British naval superiority, which had already enabled the evacuation of 43,000 troops from mainland Greece, led to the failure of the Germans to support their Crete operation by moving troops by sea: convoys doing so were successfully intercepted. Nevertheless, German air attacks hit the British attempt to reinforce, supply and eventually evacuate Crete by sea: three cruisers and six destroyers were sunk and some troops were left behind and captured.

This conquest took the Germans forward into the eastern Mediterranean, leading to British concerns, not least for the security of Cyprus. However, the possibility of Germany exploiting this success, moving on into the Middle East, was greatly lessened by continual British naval strength, and by the conquest of Lebanon and Syria from Vichy forces in a rapid, but hard-fought, campaign. This British success subsequently appeared more significant because the German attack on the Soviet Union in June 1941, the overrunning of Ukraine that year and the advance into the Caucasus in 1942 led to concern about the Germans moving south into the Middle East.

Germany focused its Mediterranean naval activity on aircraft, dispatched to Sicily from January 1941, and on submarines, both to deadly effect as far as the British were concerned. In January 1941, German dive bombers sank the cruiser *Southampton* and crippled the carrier *Illustrious*. On 11 August 1942, a British officer on another warship commented on the sinking by a German submarine of the *Eagle*: 'It was a terrible sight to see such a big ship do down so quickly. The great patch of oil and debris was full of heads, there were hundreds swimming and choking in the water.' One hundred and thirty-one lives were lost, although 929 men were rescued. The previous year, the battleship *Barham* was torpedoed with the loss of 869 lives.

Owing to German air power, British plans for amphibious attacks on Italian positions in the Mediterranean – Pantelleria or the Dodecanese – now seemed redundant, and the British were unable to prevent the transport of German troops to Libya. In addition, many Greek warships were destroyed by German bombers in April 1941. However, the Mediterranean was not closed to British shipping.

Malta

The British base in the central Mediterranean threatened maritime and air links between Italy and North Africa. There was no invasion of the island. Instead, only a blockade combined with an air assault was to be attempted. German and Italian air attacks on Malta's harbour and airfields, and highly damaging air and submarine attacks on British convoys supplying Malta in 1941–2, especially on the convoy codenamed 'Pedestal' in 1942, were central to a sustained, but unsuccessful, attempt to starve it into surrender. One of Malta's modern pilot boats is named *Ohio* after the famous tanker in this convoy. Spitfires delivered by carrier in March and, even more, May 1942 ensured that the air war over Malta was won by the British. Nevertheless, the Italians were able to keep the rate of loss on the Libyan convoy route low.

Allied Attacks, 1942–5

Naval strength in the Mediterranean was crucial to a series of Allied invasions. Operation Torch, the largely American invasion of Vichy-ruled Algeria and Morocco on 8 November 1942, was rapidly successful. The American landings at Oran and Algiers did not face the Atlantic surf seen with the landing at Casablanca. Despite Allied concerns, Spain did not intervene; nor did the Italian surface fleet, which was seriously short of oil. Thanks in large part to a careful cultivation of the French military leaders in North Africa, resistance by the far more numerous Vichy forces was rapidly overcome, although some units, especially of the navy, resisted firmly.

The Germans reacted swiftly, taking over Vichy France. In a dramatic episode, most of the Vichy navy, 250,000 tonnes of warships, was scuttled by the French when German forces attacked the great naval dockyard at Toulon. Having fought their way in, they reached the quaysides as the explosives in the ships were detonated. Much-battered, Toulon lacks any real charm and is not a tourist destination. Beaten to Marseille and Toulon by the Germans, the Italians took control of Corsica and part of south-east France up to the River Rhône, in particular of Nice and Savoy, each of which had been ceded to Napoleon III in 1860. Mussolini wanted the eventual incorporation of these areas into the Italian Empire.

Understandable in light of the risk of Axis air attack, the refusal of American commanders to include eastern Algeria and Tunisia among the landing zones was followed by the German–Italian occupation of Vichy-run Tunisia by troops moved from Italy by air and sea. Due to the acquiescence of Admiral Jean-Pierre Estéva, the Resident-General of Tunisia, there was no opposition. Nevertheless, British and American forces, attacking from Libya and Algeria respectively, conquered Tunisia the following spring, after strong initial resistance. The Allies forced large numbers of German and Italian troops to surrender.

Anglo-American invasions in the Mediterranean were successfully launched against Sicily in July 1943, mainland Italy that September, notably in Salerno, and again in January 1944 at Anzio, Elba (on a far smaller scale) that June, and southern France (Operation Dragoon) that August. The Italian armistice in September 1943 was followed by the surrender of much of the Italian navy to the Allies, with the fleet sailing from the port of La Spezia to Malta, although it was damaged by German glider bombs. Nevertheless, the conquest of Italy proved far harder than anticipated.

In response to this armistice, the fast-moving Germans took over much of Italy, as well as the Italian occupation zones in Mediterranean Europe, producing a new geography of occupation. When Italy was an ally, this had included Italian occupation zones in former Greece, Yugoslavia and France, for example the Ionian Islands, much of Dalmatia and Slovenia, and Montenegro. German control was violently imposed in 1943, with many Italian troops killed (as on Cephalonia) or imprisoned before being deported to work in Germany. In Italy, a more radical Fascist regime was established at Salò under Mussolini, who had been rescued by the Germans. There was in effect a civil war in northern Italy, with the resistance fighting both Salò and its German backers. Anglo-American forces had conquered Sicily and much of southern Italy in 1943, but the Germans were not driven from central Italy until the summer of 1944, and from northern Italy until the closing weeks of the war.

The German occupation of the French Riviera in November 1942 subsequently became more harsh as a shortage of resources affected occupiers and the local population. Food shortages led to riots. Resistance activities there became more intense, albeit being affected by the large-scale deportation of men for forced labour and by the harshness of German repression, which also benefited from support by collaborators.

Operation Dragoon in August 1944 was very much an American project, and reflected opposition to Britain's Mediterranean strategy. Dragoon was seen as a way to gain Marseille, aiding Allied logistics in France, and to cut off German forces in south and south-west France. The scale of the Allied naval support for successive landings was impressive. Five aircraft carriers were present for the Salerno landings in September 1943. For Operation Dragoon, 887 warships, including 9 carriers, 5 battleships and 21 cruisers, supported the 1370 landing craft. There was also overwhelming Allied air superiority. Once ashore, the largely American force rapidly overcame resistance. French forces also played an important role, liberating Toulon and Marseille, which were strongly defended by the Germans. Visitors can see bullet marks and shrapnel scars on the northern side of the *Basilique Notre-Dame de la Garde* in Marseille.

Allied naval dominance also provided the background for consideration of an invasion of South-East Europe. Strongly supported by Churchill, as a means to challenge Soviet influence and a way to bring Turkey into the war, this would have been difficult for logistical reasons and was blocked by American opposition. The exception, a British amphibious campaign in the Aegean in late 1943, was heavily defeated by German land-based air power. Suspicious of the Soviet Union and fearing German attack, Turkey did not declare war on Germany until 1 March 1945 and, in the meantime, provided it with crucial chrome.

In 1944, the Soviet advance further north in the Balkans led to the German evacuation of Greece, Albania and much of Yugoslavia. In Italy, Anglo-American forces broke through the German defences in northern Italy in early 1945 and, aided by the Italian resistance, overthrew the Salò Republic.

The eventual peace settlement saw major changes to the territorial boundaries of 1942–3, but far fewer compared to those after France's defeat in 1940. Italy lost its overseas Mediterranean empire, including Albania (independent), Libya (eventually independent), the Dodecanese (to Greece) and Istria (to Yugoslavia).

There was to be no real revanchist desire to regain an empire. Totally defeated in the recent war, Italy ceased to follow an ambitious, let alone expansionist, foreign policy. Instead, Italy was to pursue influence in its former African colonies, while finding Albania and Yugoslavia hostile.

The major recastings of the Mediterranean world occurred in 1918–23, and with decolonisation after the Second World War; and not in 1945 itself. There was an ethnic dimension, however, to the peace settlement. Italians were driven from the new Yugoslavia (about 300,000) and many were killed in Istria, with large numbers being thrown to their death into the *foibe*, limestone chasms. Others were driven from Corsica, Libya (about 95,000) and the Dodecanese (about 15,000).

The Holocaust

The German genocide of the Jews reached the Mediterranean with terrible effect, and most prominently at Thessaloniki where there was a large community of about 43,000. They were slaughtered at the extermination camp of Auschwitz in 1943 after a long train journey. This was a fundamental blow to Thessaloniki as a multi-ethnic community, a character that had helped give it a particular vibrancy and cultural importance. The former Jewish quarter there remains somewhat spectral, and the heat of the day does not stir the quiet.

The 1800 Jews from Corfu were another Greek community slaughtered in Auschwitz. The Germans delayed their withdrawal from Greece until after they had removed as many Jews as possible for slaughter, including nearly 2000 from Rhodes. Out of a pre-war population of 72,000, close to 60,000 Jews were moved from Greece to the extermination camps, including about 4200 in 1943 from Bulgarian-occupied western Thrace. Jews from elsewhere in Mediterranean Europe were also slaughtered.

There was active cooperation in this process in Croatia, Vichy

France and the Salò Republic in Italy, and a widespread failure after the war to face up to the degree of cooperation. In 1942, Vichy handed over foreign Jews to deportation to the extermination camps. The extent to which these deportations were carried out by the French authorities was concealed post-war, but most of those deported in 1942 were not under German control until handed over for movement out of the country. Fewer than 3 per cent of those deported survived. Vichy, however, did not have the same attitude toward French Jews at this stage. They were not rounded up until 1943–4, and their survival rate was higher in part because more were able to take shelter within France.

Outside Trieste, the concentration camp at San Sabba is an Italian national monument and museum. It operated from 1943 to 1945 and about 5,000 people were killed there. San Sabba was the sole concentration camp in the Mediterranean. A longer-term perspective is provided by the Jewish Museum in Athens.

Wartime Destruction

The Germans also proved brutal occupiers for much of the non-Jewish population. This was particularly the case in Marseille, which offended them as a centre of resistance and also because it was cosmopolitan. Hitler ordered the 'purification' of the city, and, aside from the repression of opponents and the deportation of Jews to slaughter, the Old Port was emptied of its people and dynamited, with 1400 buildings destroyed. The German treatment of resistance activity was also extremely harsh and left a lasting legacy of dislike, notably, but not only, in Greece. Indeed, this harshness was seen across occupied Europe, and there were massacres of civilians in Italy and the Balkans.

Fighting between regular forces also produced much damage, for example at Salerno. So, even more, did bombing, as by the Allies at Cagliari, Trapani, Pantelleria and Monte Cassino, and by the Germans and Italians on Malta.

Sicily and the Mafia

After the Allied landings in 1943, the Americans opened the prisons, declared the Mafia to have been political prisoners, and gave them roles in local governments. Brigands reappeared claiming to be pro-American patriots fighting for Sicilian independence. After the war, the Italian army destroyed the bands by January 1946, with only one major band remaining active until its head, Salvatore Giuliano, was killed in July 1950. He became the subject of Italian films as well as an opera. In March 1946, special autonomy was conceded to Sicily.

Retrospect

With the hindsight of 2020, the Mediterranean campaigns in the Second World War can appear not only far less consequential than those on the Western and Eastern Fronts in that war, but also as somehow unimportant. That is mistaken. The campaigns provided the Allies with vital experience in fighting the Germans and in amphibious operations, prevented Axis advances into the Middle East, thereby offering defence-in-depth for the Indian Ocean, and involved the deployment of significant Axis forces, not least the very large numbers of German and Italian troops captured in Tunisia in 1943. The results of the war there also looked toward the post-war world, with the Soviet advance into the Balkans in 1944, the end of the Italian Empire in 1942–3, and the weakness of its British and French counterparts, especially the last.

10. From 1945 to the Present

The old European section of Istanbul glittered at the end of the broad half-mile of bridge with the slim minarets lancing up into the sky and the domes of the mosques, crouching at their feet, looking like big firm breasts. It should have been the Arabian Nights, but to Bond, seeing it first above the tops of trams and above the great scars of modern advertising along the river frontage, it seemed a once beautiful theatre-set that modern Turkey had thrown aside in favour of the steel and concrete flat-iron of the Istanbul-Hilton Hotel, blankly glittering behind him on the heights of Pera.

James Bond, the most famous Briton of his generation, initially a Cold War warrior, did not focus on the Mediterranean in Ian Fleming's novels, although he went there in *From Russia, With Love* (1957), as detailed in this quote. Once translated to the screen, Bond went more frequently to the Mediterranean, as in the 1963 film of that novel and in *On Her Majesty's Secret Service* (1969), and notably so from the 1970s: Egypt and Sardinia in *The Spy Who Loved Me* (1977) were followed by Venice in *Moonraker* (1979), Greece and Spain in *For Your Eyes Only* (1981), Monte Carlo and North Africa in *Never Say Never Again* (1983), Gibraltar in *The Living Daylights* (1987), Istanbul in *The World Is Not Enough* (1999), Venice in *Casino Royale* (2006) and Rome in *Spectre* (2015). For Bond and other films, the Mediterranean is the backdrop for wealthy people on spectacular yachts, and the setting for exotic cities. The impact of film in an increasingly visual society was of great significance in strengthening the impression created by holiday brochures. It never rained in either. Nor were there traffic jams, or rubbish.

Ironically, Istanbul under Recep Tayyip Erdoğan, its elected ruler from 2003, was to be changed far more in the early twenty-first century than Fleming suggested. This was not least with a third bridge across the Bosphorus (named after Sultan Selim I); a 76-km (47-mile) rail tunnel in part under it; a massive new 29.5-square-mile airport, intended to be the world's biggest aviation hub, which was opened in 2019; and Turkey's biggest mosque.

1945–65

The Second World War left Europe in ruins and on the front-line of the rapidly developing Cold War between American and Soviet-led alliance systems. The Mediterranean was to be a focal zone for the Cold War. In a continuation of the rapid changes of the war years, the politics of the region changed radically during the post-war period. Initially, the war might simply have appeared to be a resetting of the European world order, with Britain and France restored as the major imperial powers. Italy had lost that status, but a pro-Allied regime had been established there in 1943. Italy had been driven from Libya in 1942, and in 1947 relinquished all claims there; but, from 1943, there were British and French areas of administration, the entire coast being in the British area. Moreover, British intervention in 1944 helped ensure that the Royalists gained control of the cities in the early stages of what became the Greek Civil War. In Sétif in eastern Algeria, support in 1945 for independence from France was brutally suppressed with the killing of many Algerians.

Athens in 1944

British troops intervened against ELAS, the left-wing Greek People's Army of Liberation. A British soldier recalled:

> The enemy was just the same as any other Greeks as far as we knew, they didn't have any uniform as such . . . It was a situation that was completely different to the way we had been used to fighting . . . As an average infantryman, one of the first questions that you ask is 'Which way is the front?' so that you know if the worst comes to the worst which way you can go to get out of the bloody place. In this sort of situation, which is a typical urban 'battlefront', it's all around you.

Success in 1943–5, however, proved a short-lived recovery for Anglo-French imperialism. Although determined to keep control of North-West Africa, France granted independence to Lebanon (1943) and Syria (1946), and Britain likewise decided to do so for Palestine and Transjordan (1948). The management of Arab–Jewish tension was proving too difficult and onerous, notably in the face of Jewish migration from Europe, especially of Holocaust survivors. Calls for an independent Jewish state were supported by the United States. On the pattern of what had already been seen with India in 1947, Britain could neither maintain the peace nor negotiate an agreed close. Its departure was followed by full-scale war between Arabs and Jews in 1948–9.

Post-war imperial exhaustion extended to Britain making it clear in 1947 that it could no longer maintain the anti-Communist cause in Greece and Turkey, and turning to the United States for help in both. This issue had become more urgent as the Cold War escalated and as the Communists established control of Yugoslavia and Albania, and sought both to take over Greece and to establish bases at the Dardanelles. Moreover, there were serious pinch points of tension at Trieste, where Britain and the United States backed Italian territorial claims against Yugoslavia, in a dispute only settled in 1954, and in the Corfu Channel. There, in 1946, a force of British warships passing through international waters was shelled by Albanian shore batteries and, when a demonstration passage was subsequently organised to uphold the law of the sea and Britain's naval prowess, two destroyers were badly damaged by mines laid by the Albanians.

That year, the *Roosevelt*, a 45,000-tonne American aircraft carrier, was sent to the eastern Mediterranean to bolster Western interests. The battleship *Missouri* was also sent. From late 1947, there was at least one American carrier in the Mediterranean.

The Greek Civil War, 1944–9

Communist failure in Greece in 1949 reflected divisions and growing Royalist strength. Stalin's rift with Tito in 1948, in response to his anger with the latter's independence, closed Yugoslav bases to the Communists. Meanwhile, the Greek army learnt to be proactive and effective in counterinsurgency conflict, while it also benefited from Anglo-American support, including American Helldiver aircraft, and from the inclusion of social and economic policies in strategy. The army was helped by the extent of popular support, as well as by the Communists' adoption of more conventional methods of fighting in order to create a proto-state. It proved impossible for the Communists to recruit the manpower anticipated, the Soviets did not provide the heavy weaponry sought, let alone intervene, and the Communists' reliance on position warfare helped lead to their defeat. Both sides killed prisoners and civilians whom they deemed hostile.

The late 1940s became a struggle over control of the British system, of empire both formal and informal. Independence for Palestine in 1948 was followed in 1948–9 by the first of the Arab–Israeli wars, a conflict in which Israel survived an attempt to destroy it, while Egypt gained the Gaza Strip and Jordan the West Bank of the River Jordan. The Arab attacks were poorly coordinated. The Israelis benefited from the determination borne of a conviction that their opponents intended genocide; the Arabs certainly at least intended what was later to be termed ethnic cleansing. In the event, refugees fled and were driven from areas taken over by both Arabs and Jews.

Libya became independent in 1951 under King Idris. The airbase near Tripoli built by the Italians in 1923 became, as Wheelus Air Base, a major American facility. The British also based aircraft in Libya.

In Egypt, the overthrow of the monarchy in 1952 in a coup was followed by a radical nationalist government. Britain agreed in 1954 to withdraw its troops by June 1956, the government then nationalised the Suez Canal and, in the Suez Crisis of 1956, Britain and France launched a military intervention that both failed and greatly compromised their imperial prestige. Once ashore, British and French forces made progress, but Colonel Abdel Nasser, the Egyptian dictator, in effective control from 1954, was not overthrown and international pressure, notably by the United States, led to the abandonment of the intervention. The Israelis had to withdraw from Sinai and the Gaza Strip, which they had captured in concert with Britain and France.

The focus is often the iniquities of the Western powers, but this is a partial account. Imperialism was also seen with non-Western states, notably Egypt, in particular its attitude to Sudan, Yemen and Libya. In addition, the coup in Egypt in 1952 was followed in 1953 by an abolition of democracy, in the shape of the 1923 liberal constitution, and of political parties, and by the harsh treatment of rivals by special tribunals. The former government was blamed for failure in the war with Israel in 1948–9, and charges of treason were widely distributed. In addition, the Muslim Brotherhood, accused of instigating civil war, was outlawed in 1954 and persecuted. The military seized total control, which it used to its own profit. Meanwhile, the state socialism followed by the Egyptian government could not produce significant economic improvement.

The Fleet and Suez, 1956

The denial to Britain of the use of airbases in Libya, Jordan and Iraq, hitherto friendly states, encouraged a reliance on naval power, as did carriers being closer to Egypt than bases in Cyprus and Malta, such that aircraft could replace their fuel and load weapons more rapidly. Aircraft from three British and two French carriers destroyed the Egyptian air force, preparing the way for the first helicopter-borne assault landing from the sea, which was launched from two British light carriers. However, the subsequent operation was fatally compromised by the political situation.

The Suez invasion was the culmination of an assertive British policy in the Middle East, one directed against the Soviets and the challenge of Arab nationalism, and intended to show continued British relevance. The Baghdad Pact in 1955, which, by the end of the year, linked Britain, Turkey, Iraq, Iran and Pakistan, showed how Britain's Mediterranean presence was part of a wider geopolitical commitment, a different form of imperialism. This policy also led to plans for intelligence operations designed to overthrow the governments of Egypt and Syria, plans that were not brought to fruition.

The Suez Crisis, however, revealed British dependence on the United States. Concerned about the impact of the invasion on attitudes in the Third World, the American government refused to extend any credits to support sterling, blocked British access to the International Monetary Fund until she withdrew her troops from Suez, and was unwilling to provide oil to compensate for interrupted supplies from the Middle East. The damaging Anglo-French backdown proved particularly problematic for Britain's stance in the Middle East, with Iraq's pro-Western monarchy falling victim to a left-wing military coup in 1958.

From 1954 and 1955 respectively, France and Britain faced nationalist insurgencies in Algeria and Cyprus. France granted independence to Morocco and Tunisia in 1956 in order to focus on Algeria, and that ensured that the future King Hassan II of Morocco (r. 1961–99), and not the French, played the key role in suppressing a rebellion in the Rif region of northern Morocco. Treated by the French as part of France itself, Algeria, its largest colony, had the largest French settler population, most of them adamantly opposed to the indigenous nationalists who sought independence. The French government, notably from 1956, sought a middle way, that of military firmness against the nationalists (which encouraged intervention in Egypt in the Suez Crisis), while also attempting to win the support of the bulk of the indigenous Muslim population by introducing reforms. French counterinsurgency policies included sealing the borders, focusing on the people as the prime sphere for operations, using the army for police tasks, forcibly resettling approximately a quarter of the peasantry into guarded camps, and employing considerable brutality, notably reprisals, as at Philippeville in 1955, and torture. These policies contained the National Liberation Front (FLN), but could not end the rebellion. The last, in turn, undermined attempts at reformist and technocratic social engineering.

As part of the Cold War, the FLN benefited from support by the Eastern Bloc: money, arms and international recognition.

Involving terrorism, counterinsurgency warfare, and the complex interplay between events in Algeria and wider international developments, the struggle also offered a template for many of the issues seen during decolonisation. Brutal itself, the FLN, rather than the French, was responsible for the majority of deaths of Algerian Arabs and Berbers. This killing deliberately destroyed the prospects for a middle way. The apparently intractable nature of the struggle built up political pressure in France for a solution, as did the large-scale call-up of reservists, which enabled France to deploy over half a million troops, as well as about 200,000 *harkis*, loyal Muslim militia. This became what was at the time the longest struggle in the Mediterranean since the Second World War

Despite the hopes of the settlers, Charles de Gaulle, who came to power in France in 1958, proved willing to cut the link with Algeria. Seeing France's destiny as European, rather than colonial, he also thought that acquiring nuclear status would make it unnecessary to retain Algeria as a source of North African troops. On 4 November 1960, de Gaulle proclaimed the future existence of 'an *Algérie algérienne* ... an Algerian republic'. High-level talks with the FLN began in February 1961. An attempt in 1961 by rebellious generals based in Algiers to overthrow de Gaulle, invading France to that end, totally failed, and independence was granted in 1962. De Gaulle had not had an emotional commitment to Algeria, and granting independence to other French colonies in North Africa and, in 1960, sub-Saharan Africa made hanging on to Algeria appear inappropriate.

One consequence of Algerian independence was yet another erosion of ethnic and religious heterogeneity in the Mediterranean. Over 900,000 Algerians of European descent left, with their land, property and businesses then put under state control. The Jews in Algeria fled to France or Israel. The *harkis* who went to France were the least well treated among the immigrants, and many were kept for years in resettlement camps. The *harkis* who stayed in Algeria were mistreated with terrible brutality. Algeria was changed in specific ways as well. Thus, the Neapolitan fishermen left the Algerian port of Stora for good, and the church was converted into a mosque.

Multiple identities and other loyalties were not to be permitted. The Arabisation of Algerian government and education was fostered by bringing in bureaucrats and teachers from Egypt and Syria. However, whatever the rhetoric of modernisation, socialism and Third World Solidarity, military control from the FLN and factionalism were key elements of the new politics. Separately, Copts in Egypt and Jews across the Arab Middle East came to be badly treated. The latter fled to Israel.

Conversely, heterogeneity was seen with Muslim movement into Europe, so that by 2016 there were 5.7 million Muslims in France, making up over 8 per cent of the population. Most are of Algerian extraction, as in Belleville in Paris, in the heavily immigrant and poverty-struck northern districts of Marseille and in the North African quarter of Perpignan, which are areas of social exclusion. The complexity of the Mediterranean as a region of diasporas was enhanced as a result of the outcome of the Algerian war. Tourists can visit North African shops, markets, cafés and restaurants, for example in Perpignan. In contrast, there were 2.9 million Muslims in 2016 in Italy and 1.2 million in Spain.

There was a measure of terrorist violence from these communities. In particular, a truck attack by an Islamic extremist on Bastille Day celebrations in Nice in 2016 led to eighty-seven deaths. That year, Manuel Valls, France's Prime Minister, described Islam as a problem. France has banned the *burqa*. However, *jihadist* action is very much that of a minority, and mosques across the Mediterranean, for example the largest one in Rome, seek to keep relations acceptable.

Cyprus, a military base to compensate for the loss of Egypt, provided greater opportunities for the British in counterinsurgency warfare in the 1950s than Malaya and Kenya, in part because there was far less tree cover, while the area of operations was smaller and aircraft were based more closely. The new governor, Field-Marshal Sir John Harding (who had replaced a civilian), saw the situation in large part in a military light. However, lacking adequate intelligence, the British were unable to separate the EOKA (*Ethniki Organosis Kyprion Agoniston*) insurgents from the civilian population and to protect the latter from often murderous EOKA intimidation. As a result, EOKA could be checked but could not be destroyed, and was not deprived of its means of regeneration.

Setting a precedent for the cession of independence for territories with a small population, Britain gave independence to Cyprus in 1960. Spain left Spanish Morocco in 1956, although retaining Ceuta and Melilla as enclaves; as Britain does Gibraltar. That well-justified comparison is not welcome to Spain, which maintains a claim to Gibraltar despite a marked lack of support there.

In 1958, the USA sent 14,000 marines to Beirut to protect the Lebanese government from what it claimed was the threat of international communism, but, in practice, was the populist pan-Arabist Nasserism that led in 1958–61 to the United Arab Republic of Egypt and Syria. This pan-Arabism was weakened by the nationalism of the individual Arab regimes and by the failure of their socialist economic policies. The union with Egypt was overthrown by a coup mounted by a group of Syrian officers in 1961.

Malta was granted independence by Britain in 1964. A referendum in Malta revealed a large majority in favour of integration with Britain, which would have resulted in representation in Parliament comparable in the French with such territories as Martinique. However, this approach was not pursued, just as earlier interwar ideas of union with Italy had not been pursued.

There was also political continuity in the late 1940s and 1950s. Spain continued to be a dictatorship under Francisco Franco, and the small-scale insurrectionary attempt to overthrow him in the late 1940s failed. In Greece, the Communists were defeated in the civil war that ended in 1949. Founded in 1949, NATO had Italy as a member, but was not particularly Mediterranean. This changed in 1952 when Greece and Turkey joined.

Western dominance of the Mediterranean was scarcely unchallenged, but, notably because of the Soviet–Yugoslav rift in 1948, was stronger than had appeared the case immediately after the Second World War. Moreover, the Mediterranean was part of the wider framework of Western strength. For example, in the event of war with the Soviet Union, it was planned that British Canberra bombers would fly from Cyprus, over Turkey and the Black Sea, to attack industrial cities in Ukraine.

Albania: A Maverick State

Conquered by Italy in 1939 and occupied by Germany in 1943, albeit facing a resistance movement, Albania was liberated in 1944 with much of the old élite compromised by collaboration. The ruthless Communist leader Enver Hoxha, who became Communist General Secretary in 1943, seized power in 1944, wiped out his Communist rivals (many by apparent suicide) and the non-Communist nationalists, took credit for the liberation from German control, and ruled as dictator until his death in 1985. His harsh and unbending totalitarian regime survived in part by changing its foreign sponsors. Allied with Yugoslavia, which treated Albania as a dependent and exploited its oil and mineral resources, Hoxha followed the Soviet Union when it broke with Tito in 1948, only, in turn, to break with the Soviets in 1961 because he disapproved of Khrushchev's rejection of Stalin and the cult of personality. Instead, Hoxha turned to China, which provided economic and financial help.

The Communist model of totalitarian state control, personality cult, collectivisation and state atheism remained insulated from reformist pressures elsewhere in Eastern Europe, which was kept at a distance for fear of ideological contamination. Under its paranoid leadership, Albania was heavily fortified, not least with thousands of individual pillboxes constructed as part of a simple surveillance and defence system. The *Sigurimi*, the security service, had about 10,000 agents. Very few tourists were admitted, and what they could see was very much restricted and supervised.

1965–75

Tension in the Mediterranean escalated from the mid-1960s, as the United States and the Soviet Union embraced the causes of client states, which, in turn, displayed both independence and aggression. Leapfrogging the American containment ring, the Soviets pursued plans for a naval base in Egypt, whose dictator, Nasser, was increasingly hostile toward the United States. The troubled eastern Mediterranean saw two full-scale wars between pro-American Israel and its Soviet-aligned Arab neighbours: the Six Days War of 1967, and the Yom Kippur/Ramadan/October War of 1973. In turn, these were the focus, both consequence and cause, of more continual and wide-ranging conflict. This very varied conflict included Palestinian terrorism and Israeli responses, civil war in Lebanon, where strong divisions had grown anew in intensity after independence, and growing Muslim–Jewish tension in Europe, for example among refugees from Algeria in Marseille.

The Six Days War was essentially fought on land, although the Israeli warship *Eilat* was sunk by Soviet missiles fired from Egyptian missile boats. With the rapid and dramatic conquest of the Gaza Strip and Sinai, the Six Days War advanced Israeli's border to the Suez Canal. Jordan and Syria were also defeated. In Libya, mob attacks were mounted on the American and British embassies in Tripoli in response to inaccurate claims that these powers had backed Israel. The Soviet Union had made preparations to intervene against Israel but, to pre-empt the possibility, the American Sixth Fleet was sent into the war zone. The rapid build-up of the Soviet navy in the late 1960s challenged the American position in the Mediterranean, which was weakened by the Vietnam commitment, as the Soviets appreciated during the 1970 Jordanian crisis.

In the Yom Kippur War of 1973, both sides deployed missile boats, the Israelis sinking at least nine Egyptian and Syrian ships and driving their navies back to harbour. This was important to Israel given the pressure it was under from Egyptian and Syrian land attack in the unexpected conflict and the vulnerability of the Israeli coastal cities of Haifa and Tel Aviv to attack. Neither side had carriers. In the event, the land attacks were repelled. The war was a focus for the wider confrontation of the Cold War. Indeed, there was a stand-off between the Sixth Fleet and the Soviet Fifth *Eskadra*.

More generally, there was a sense of the West under strain and in retreat. An Egyptian-backed, anti-Western, revolution in Libya in 1969 resulted in a radical pro-Soviet regime under Colonel Muammar Gaddafi influenced by Nasserite ideas. Colonel Muammar Gaddafi's pan-Arab ideas led in 1969 to the Arab Revolutionary Front with Egypt and Sudan in 1969 and in 1970 Syria stated it would join. Gaddafi wanted a single Arab state but, instead, in 1971, a Federation of Arab Republics was established. Floating on money from Libyan oil, which had been discovered in 1959, this involved Egypt, Libya and Syria. Subsequently, both Egypt and Libya, and Egypt and Syria, planned unions without effect. The Federation was not implemented. Pan-Arabism was an aspect of the widespread search for a new identity. In Israel, this focused on religion, while in Lebanon there was interest in a supposed descent from the ancient Phoenicians, even though that was highly tenuous and a misunderstanding of historic circumstances.

Greek nationalism in Cyprus was an instance of the same process. In 1974, a Turkish invasion of Cyprus left the island divided until today, and with a Turkish Cypriot statelet, officially the Turkish Republic of Northern Cyprus, proclaimed in 1983, that is only recognised by Turkey. In Greece, the military had seized power in a coup in 1967, 'the colonels' retaining control until 1974. The last two events were linked. The Greek *junta* had sought to strengthen its wavering domestic popularity by backing the longstanding demand for *enosis*, union with Cyprus, an independent state with a Greek-speaking Christian majority, but where the Turkish Muslim minority were protected by the Turkish Cypriot role in the governing 'partnership' arrangement. Sectarian conflict broke out in 1963. In July 1974, with Greek backing, this government was overthrown in a coup by EOKA-B, the self-styled successor to EOKA, and replaced by another that was designed to implement *enosis*. Moreover, the 'ethnic cleansing' of Turks was begun by the Greeks.

However, a rapid military response by Turkey – an invasion of much of the island, which was accepted by the United States – led to the humiliation of the far weaker Greek *junta*. The Turks had long prepared for an intervention, and, from 1967, the 39th Marine Infantry Division was ready 40 miles (64 kilometres) to the north at Mersin on the Turkish coast. The Turks benefited from air superiority and from nearby bases, and the Greeks, many keener to crush nearby Turkish Cypriot enclaves, failed to focus on the Turkish beachhead, which allowed the Turks to build it up and then advance from it. In the end, the Turks were able to enforce a de facto partition of the island.

Its authority gone, the Greek *junta* handed over power to Constantine Karamanlis, a conservative who had been Prime

Minister from 1955 to 1963. His New Democracy Party won the elections in November 1974, and a new constitution was introduced in 1975. A political pattern similar to that of Western Europe was established, and, in 1981, Greece joined the EEC (European Economic Community).

Yet, in divided Cyprus, about 165,000 Greek Cypriots had been driven from the Turkish zone, continuing the ethnic consolidation already seen since independence. Different histories were on offer and this remains the case. Turkish Cypriots were told to forget the idea of a united Cyprus. Regarding them as insufficiently Turkish, the Turkish government deployed a public memorialisation intended to inculcate identification with Turkey: flags, statues and, from the 2000s, under the Erdoğan government, the building of mosques. İşbank, the biggest Turkish bank, had fourteen branches in Northern Cyprus by 2012. In Greek Cyprus, still the Republic of Cyprus, in contrast, there was an emphasis on the territory and individual properties that were lost, and the relatives who had been killed, as well as the slogan 'I don't forget.' In the late 2010s, an effort was made to unearth the bodies of those murdered and 'disappeared' during the conflict.

The situation in the western Mediterranean was far less volatile, notably because Franco's death in 1975 led in Spain neither to a coup nor to revolution, but, rather, to a largely orderly transfer of power to a democratic system. This transfer was entrenched when a small-scale, attempted right-wing military/police coup in 1981 was a total failure.

1975–90

The last stage of the Cold War saw continued tension, but the Israel–Egypt peace settlement lessened the potential for international breakdown. Libya continued to be volatile, leading to a short war with Egypt in 1977, but was essentially contained. In geopolitical terms, Soviet allies – Libya and Syria – were offset by Western allies – Egypt and Israel, between which the United States had negotiated peace in the Camp David Accords of 1978. Under these, Israel withdrew from Sinai. Relations between the two states were normalised in 1980. The following year, in response, President Anwar Sadat of Egypt was assassinated by the Egyptian Islamic Jihad. However, his pro-Western successor, Hosni Mubarak, continued the agreement with Israel. Libya and Syria were also affected by the deployment of NATO forces; after the end of its commitment to the Vietnam War, the United States was better able to deploy warships in the Mediterranean.

Affected by civil war from 1975 to 1990, Lebanon was a focus of instability, and Israel's invasion in 1982 marked a new stage in a descent into chaos. In August 1982, the Israeli candidate, Bashir Gemayel, was elected President of Lebanon, but he was assassinated the following month, destroying the basis for a settlement between Israel and Lebanon. Israel now found itself with an onerous commitment and with local allies who required support. The slaughter, in September 1982, by Israel's Lebanese allies, the Phalange militia, of Palestinians in the Sabra and Shatila refugee camps in Beirut, and the Israeli bombardment of the city, caused the crisis to escalate both within Lebanon and internationally.

In 1982, a multinational Western force was sent to Lebanon to try and bolster its stability, but the troops soon became targets. In 1983, the US Sixth Fleet bombarded militia positions on the hills near Beirut, but neither the Americans nor French could prevent the destruction of their headquarters in Beirut by lorries full of high explosive driven by suicidal guerrillas. The British, more attuned to terrorist moves, thanks to their experience in Northern Ireland, blocked a comparable move. A sense of political impotence led to the withdrawal of the Western force in 1984.

In turn, the Israelis withdrew from Lebanon in 1985, bar for a security zone along the frontier with Israel; and withdrawal from there followed in the face of the Hezbollah movement. The collapse of Israeli influence in Lebanon was matched by Syrian success and, in 1989–90, the Syrians played an important role in bringing the Lebanese civil war to an end. It was agreed that the Christians should have half of the seats in Parliament, which over-representation in terms of population ratio was a way to get them to accept defeat.

There was no comparable conflict elsewhere in the Mediterranean. Yugoslavia was stable, and Italy saw off the challenge from the Red Brigade terrorist movement as well as from far-right political violence. France had no recurrence of the internal instability of 1968, while the Spanish coup attempt in 1981 totally failed, and did not recur. Thanks to this, Spain joined the European Economic Community in 1986.

Britain retained its position in Gibraltar and the two sovereign bases in Cyprus; but the military presence in Malta was withdrawn, and Malta, instead, increasingly looked to Libya. There was discussion in the early 1970s of the possibility of NATO's presence in Malta being replaced by the Soviet Union, China or Libya. Malta had provided Britain with a base for tracking Soviet submarines in the Mediterranean. As a result of the alignment, the Libyans were informed in 1988 of the arrival of American bombers trying to make reprisals for the destruction of Pan Am Flight 103. The Americans and Libyans had already clashed in the Gulf of Sidra in 1981, when two Libyan jets fired on two American ones, which shot them down. Libya had claimed the Gulf as a closed bay and part of its territorial waters in 1973, leading the Americans to conduct Freedom of Navigation operations, which the Libyans considered provocative.

1990–2000

Problems in the 1990s focused on Yugoslavia, where the serious economic difficulties of the 1980s had already exacerbated nationalist tensions and encouraged a politics of envy and grievance that challenged the precarious inter-republican balance of the country. Divisions between the republics were matched by tensions within, and, in 1991, conflict began as the Serbian-dominated Yugoslav army sought to suppress Slovene and Croatian moves towards independence. Having failed to maintain Yugoslavia, the Serbs sought to force through a Greater Serbia. Religious and ethnic rivalries helped define the sides in a period of episodic conflict that lasted until 1999, a conflict that included Western military intervention, first in the Bosnian crisis and then in that in Kosovo. The French carrier *Foch* and the British *Invincible* supported the air assault on Serbia in the Kosovo crisis, while Italy provided airbases for NATO aircraft. At the same time, the crisis was contained and did not become a wider international struggle.

In neighbouring Albania, the fall of Communism at the end of the Cold War was followed by largely fraudulent economic opportunism that included pyramid schemes that collapsed in 1997 with many robbed of their savings. Clan loyalties came to the surface anew in feuds, but the crisis did not intensify or spread.

There was a counterpart crisis in the Muslim Mediterranean to that in Yugoslavia, but one that was very different both because there were not the federal system and fissiparous cultures of Yugoslavia, and due to the lack of comparable international intervention. In Algeria, under pressure from the expression of growing discontent and opposition in terms of Islamic fundamentalism and Berber activism, the regime opened the political system in 1989, only for the Islamic Salvation Front (FIS) to win the first round of parliamentary elections in late 1991. In the response, the army, in effect in a coup, cancelled the second round. *Le Pouvoir* (the Power), a clique of generals, businessmen and politicians, ran the country, fighting an Islamist insurrection in which probably 44,000 people were killed (although estimates have been as high as 200,000). Opposed to Islamists, both France and the United States provided the government with support. The FIS was banned and many of its members arrested, which resulted in a guerrilla movement that, in turn, divided between the very violent radicals of the Armed Islamic Group (GIA) and the FIS. Talks between the latter and the regime failed in 1994, leading to increasingly anti-societal violence by the GIA. This led FIS elements to declare a unilateral ceasefire with the government in 1997. From 1999, the combination of amnesty and repression produced a reduction in violence, so that the radicals became a minor force from 2002. In the event, there was no significant reform.

In 1997, meanwhile, the army overthrew Turkey's first Islamist Prime Minister, Necmettin Erbakan, but with no resulting violence on the Algerian model. Libya, Egypt and Syria remained under authoritarian control. Israel faced the *Intifada*, a popular Palestinian resistance movement that began in 1987, stopping in 1993 with the signing of the first Oslo Accord. It was followed by another *Intifada* in 2000–5. Rockets were launched from Gaza into Israel and, in response, Israel mounted attacks into Gaza, notably in 2004, 2008–9, 2012 and 2014.

2000 onwards

The location of crisis was different in the 2000s. The 'War on Terror' from 2001 accentuated tensions within the Middle East, but the latter had their own dynamic. Thus, in Lebanon in 2005, mass protests against Syrian influence, after a car bomb attributed to the Syrians killed Lebanon's leading Sunni politician, obliged Syria to withdraw its troops and , in the 'Cedar Revolution', led to the anti-Syrian March 14 coalition gaining power, which it held until 2009. However, in place of the nationalist optimism of 2005, divisive sectarian politics remained crucial, as did Syrian interventionism, including the assassination of those opposed to Syrian influence.

Despite continued tension in the former Yugoslavia, notably in Kosovo, but also in Bosnia and Macedonia, conflict was
contained. In 2006, Montenegro became independent from the
rump federal union with Serbia without any international crisis,
although Russia subsequently tried to intervene in its politics to
prevent Montenegro from joining NATO.

In Albania, democracy broke down in 2009, as the opposition,
claiming that a general election had been fraudulent, boycotted
Parliament. In 2011, in the capital, Tirana, Republican Guards
opened fire on an opposition rally, killing four. The government
claimed it was thwarting a coup. In both Albania and Lebanon,
there was to be a prefiguring of the disillusion seen with the Arab
Spring.

Across the Mediterranean, as more generally, fiscal problems
centred on the 2008 financial crisis greatly accentuated economic
and political difficulties. This was notably so in the Eurozone as it
was impossible to devalue the currency, while fiscal policy was set
by the strongest economy, Germany. The situation was particularly
serious in Greece, where there was a politico-fiscal crisis, linked to
the size of the public debt, and the austerity measures necessary
from 2010, and, even more, 2015, to obtain bailout loans: of 110 billion euros in 2010, 108 billion euros in 2011 and 86 billion euros
in 2015. With GDP falling by 28 per cent between 2008 and 2016,
the crisis greatly strained the social fabric. Unemployment rose
greatly, to 28 per cent, businesses went bankrupt, there were violent anti-austerity protests, and many fed at soup kitchens. Many
were not paid for the work they did. Racial violence rose as a result
of the crisis, with Golden Dawn, an anti-immigrant party, winning
parliamentary seats for the first time. Foreign control was driven
home, as the 'troika' of the European Commission, the IMF and
the European Central Bank pressed the need for public expendi-
ture cuts. In 2018, economic growth returned and unemployment
fell to 18 per cent; but there were still major problems, not least
continued underinvestment.

Elsewhere in the Christian Mediterranean, there were also serious economic and social tensions. The combination of an end to appreciable growth with fiscal austerity exacerbated unemployment in Italy, France and Albania. In Spain, where a property boom had helped drive the economy, the 2008 crash hit both the housing market and the banking sector. The unemployment rate by 2013 was over 27 per cent. The crisis in Spain spread to encompass the political system and helped exacerbate Catalonia's anger about its position within Spain. The existing political system was also gravely weakened in Italy. Popular resentment across the EU states was bred by the handling of the 2008–9 recession and the subsequent euro crises.

More widely, economic problems, notably a lack of work and income that allegedly caused a crisis of masculinity, as well as the mistreatment of women, and economic mismanagement, notably related to subsides and the price of bread, were important to the disaffection that led to the 'Arab Spring' that began in Tunisia in December 2010. Politics were also the fore in the shape of a rejection of the totalitarianism of Arab states, and the accompanying corruption and economic mismanagement. In Tunisia, corruption and police brutality under Zine El Abidine, dictator from 1987, was focused by Mohamed Bouazizi, a fruit vendor, who, having been robbed by the police, set himself alight. The crisis escalated and the dictator fell in 2011.

To optimists about the 'Arab Spring', democratisation appeared an option. Although not generally seen as part of the process, Israel had withdrawn its settlements and troops from Gaza in 2005. In 2011, Muhammad VI of Morocco relinquished some of his powers in a successful attempt to lessen tension (followed by providing more food and fuel subsidies in 2012), although there, as elsewhere, democratisation led to rivalry between Islamists and secularists. In 2011, President Bouteflika of Algeria dealt with protests by providing subsidies and pay rises. There was no rising.

Hopes of reform and democratisation, however, were swiftly dashed in most countries. In Libya, chaos followed the overthrow of Colonel Gaddafi in 2011, in a civil war begun with a rebellion, on the side of which NATO intervened. The French carrier *Charles de Gaulle* played a role in the NATO air operations over Libya, as did American and Italian carriers. Italian airbases were also used. Despite the major problems these attacks faced, due to a lack of reliable reconnaissance information, they first countered Libyan army units and then seriously damaged them, destroying aircraft, tanks and the Libyan navy. It took a long time to prevent the Libyan army from launching attacks, and there were concerns that the lengthy operation had failed or become attritional. Initially too small, the commitment did not succeed as originally anticipated. Nevertheless, after a sizeable escalation, the NATO air umbrella provided crucial support for the Libyan insurgents who eventually advanced to attack the capital, Tripoli, and to overthrow the regime. NATO air reconnaissance detected Gaddafi's flight, and the militia then hunted him down. The subsequent chaos, however, ensured that the Libyan joke in 2013 was 'The only road to paradise is the one to the international airport.'

In Egypt, the military ruler, Hosni Mubarak, was overthrown by a popular revolution in 2011. A government dominated by the Muslim Brotherhood took over in 2012. The first democratically elected President in Egypt was elected that year, with Mohamed Morsi narrowly beating Mubarak's last Prime Minister, Ahmed Shafik. Morsi was the first civilian in this role. He promised to build an 'Egyptian renaissance with an Islamic foundation', but was the candidate of the Muslim Brotherhood. Indeed, in December 2012, a draft constitution increased the role of Islam and limited freedom of speech. Massive anti-government protests in July 2013 led to the army overthrowing Morsi and seizing power. The army suppressed pro-Morsi protesters with great violence. Street protests were banned, and tens of thousands of political prisoners are still in jail. Morsi's death in 2019 was treated in Turkey, a centre for Muslim Brotherhood exiles, as an attack on Sunni Islam.

Meanwhile, a bitter civil war had broken out in Syria in 2012. This war did not focus on the Mediterranean part of Syria. Nevertheless, the Assad regime took great pains to retain control over the ports of Latakia and Tartus, which served as a key nexus of cooperation with Russia, and helped maintain Russia's commitment to the regime.

The Mediterranean also became the focus of a wider humanitarian crisis due to refugee movements from Asia and Africa. Syria was a key source of refugees in the former case and Eritrea in the second. The crisis led to a new Mediterranean geography of refugee camps and sites, for example the Altinözü refugee camp just into Turkey from Syria. Warships were deployed in order to try to police the movement of refugees from North Africa. The latter became more pronounced from 2011 when Gaddafi was overthrown. In cooperation with Italy, his regime had limited refugee flows from Libya, but its overthrow led to chaos as competing factions fought for control.

In this context, refugees, alongside economic migrants, were trafficked in large numbers from Libyan ports, such as Sabratha, to Italy, notably to the islands of Pantelleria and Lampedusa. In the first half of 2013, around 8000 illegal immigrants arrived in Italy from North Africa, but, in the first half of 2014, the number rose to over 65,000 and, by mid-August, according to some estimates, to 100,000. In 2014–17, about 600,000 people crossed from Libya to Italy. In 2017, the International Organization for Migration claimed that sub-Saharan African migrants seeking to reach Europe were being seized and sold in Libyan 'slave markets'. Many would-be migrants into Europe can be found in Libya, both in detention centres and living rough.

Crossing in open boats, the migrants are exposed to the sun and generally short of water. The boats are very crowded and, aside from the danger of shipwreck, a certain number die on the crossing. UNHCR, the UN refugee agency, calculated a death rate per 100 arrivals of 1.8 per cent in 2015 rising to 3.4 in the first three months of 2017 due to the traffickers using less effective boats. The traffickers are mostly African. Different Italian administrations and European states have adopted contrasting approaches to the issue, as, over time, have the European Union and other international agencies. Operation Sophia is the European naval force operating off the Libyan coast. In 2018, after Italy closed its ports to rescue ships, nearly 60,000 migrants tried to cross the Mediterranean from Africa to Spain according to UN figures. Some tried to smuggle themselves into Ceuta or Melilla. In June 2019, Southern European leaders called for EU burden-sharing in taking migrants arriving via the Mediterranean.

Israeli–Arab disputes continued to give rise to conflict in Mediterranean waters. The Israeli navy has a superior capability to that of Israel's neighbours, which is necessary given Israel's situation, its dependence on overseas trade and the vulnerability of its coastline. However, the focus on Israeli public and governmental attention is on the army and air force, which are more frequently involved in combat and deterrence. Moreover, the army is required for the control of the occupied area. Israeli warships have been affected by the increased capability of land defences: in 2006, the corvette *Hanit* was hit by a radar-guided missile fired by Hezbollah from southern Lebanon. Three years later, Hamas fired missiles at Israeli warships bombarding its positions in the Gaza Strip. These warships have been used to blockade the Strip. There is, however, no capacity for amphibious operations comparable to that seen in the Second World War.

Environmental Change

Environmental change is not always negative. The use of DDT as an insecticide and land drainage had unpleasant consequences, but also banished the debilitating disease of malaria, for example from Sardinia. Nevertheless, change, and notably global warming, had an increasingly negative impact from the late twentieth century. Drought has hit Mediterranean countries in many years, including 2005–8 and 2014–18. Water shortages have led to the depletion of natural aquifers, and to the movement of salt to the surface, a movement which affects soil fertility. The more persistent differential availability of water within, and between, countries led to schemes to move water, with attendant political strife over dams, river flows and aquifers. There is scant emulation in the Arab lands of Israel's use of drip irrigation.

Climate warming is an issue. Summer heatwaves affected water availability, pushed up fire risks, and led to spikes in death among the elderly in particular, as in 2004 and 2006–7. In 2007, temperatures in Greece reached 45 °C, while Albania declared a state of emergency in the face of large numbers of heat-related conditions. In 2019, the temperature in southern France reached 45.9 °C, a degree above the previous high for the same area in 2003. The extreme heat proved a disaster for the vines.

In part, this situation was a matter of environmental change, and in 2019 the French government ascribed the heatwave to human-made climate change. In the heat, pollution levels rose in Marseille. Public policy and social trends were also significant. In France, in 2003, more than 15,000 lives were lost in the record heatwave. The death of old people through heat-related conditions reflected not only the poor state of governmental care for the elderly, but also the breakdown of social cohesion as adult children left the responsibility for their aged parents to the state and, instead, went on holiday. In Greece in 2007, forest fires were in part linked to arsonists working for property developers, with forests, where building is not supposed to take place, reclassified as farmland once they had been cleared by fire. In the mid-2000s, southern and central Greece lost much of its forest cover, and, in 2007, the planned development of a road along the coast of the western Peloponnese was linked to arsonists concerned to acquire land cheaply so that they could subsequently resell it at a profit. Control over land interacted with climate change. As a further reminder of the need to focus on human agency, arson in some areas, for example in Provence in the early 2000s, was traced to boredom and alienation among part of the population.

In Catalonia in 2019, however, a large-scale forest blaze was believed to have begun when a pile of manure at a chicken farm spontaneously combusted in the extreme heat. Marc Castellnou, the head of forestry unit in the Catalan fire service, said: 'One of the reasons forest fires spread faster now is that many people have left the countryside to live in the cities. Rural life does not exist any more and the forests have grown out of control so it is harder for us to bring them under control.' In Greece, 102 people were killed in a fire that wrecked a seaside suburb.

Global warming and pollution affect marine life, notably with cyanobacteria ('blue-green algae') blooms in the Adriatic and plastic across the Mediterranean. Plastic fishing nets are a problem, for example off Greece where they have affected seahorse communities. Two tonnes of abandoned plastic fishing nets were removed in early 2019 from the waters off Stratoni, north Greece, where there is the densest colony of long-snouted seahorses in the Mediterranean. In the western Mediterranean, the disposal of plastic under which crops are cultivated creates difficulties for marine life. Factory fishing, particularly by Spain, is also a major problem, hitting fish stocks across the Mediterranean, as well as aggravating relations with Gibraltar.

Cities and industrial plants on coasts lead to pollution, for example the large phosphate plant at Gabès in Tunisia that kills people, wildlife and plants alike. Overfishing and pollution from the oil drilling in the Gulf of Gabès, notably oil spills, hit fishing in Tunisia's Kerkennah islands to which tourists no longer go. Catches off the islands there are getting smaller, including a marked reduction in the weight of octopus that are caught.

Bottom trawlers uproot seabed flora and harvest the smaller fish. In addition, it is not safe to drink from polluted rivers, such as the Nile. Although air pollution on Spain's Mediterranean coast is not bad, the situation is less happy on Italy's, especially near Naples, and is also poor in Cyprus, Athens and Valletta. This has led to restrictions on traffic flows in Athens.

In agriculture, there are problems as a result of the demise of mixed agriculture in favour of monoculture and the accompanying lessening of biodiversity. Agricultural practices led to soil degradation. Thus, the emphasis on early ripening varieties of avocados, strawberries and other crops that enjoyed a big profit margin in urban shops, especially in Northern Europe, led to the removal of soil-retaining tree crops, such as olives, from slopes. There was also an emphasis in some areas, such as Tuscany, on a scenic landscape in which the clutter of a crowded agrarian working past was replaced by a less populated, more manicured, world, one appropriate for tourists and second-home owners.

Energy demands are another source of tension. Albania, which had no private cars under the Communist regime that ended in 1991, rapidly became a car society and as the population of the capital, Tirana, grew, its facilities such as street paving and sewage improved. More generally, while Communist, Albania had been open to the influence of Italian television from across the Adriatic, and this encouraged a stylisation of fashion in terms of Italian cafés and clothing. From 1991, both became common in Albanian cities, while second-hand Mercedes cars did so on the roads. There had been a shortage of adequate investment under the Communists, and the problem continued with a major lack of power-generating capacity. As a result of frequent power cuts there in the 2000s, many companies and concerns acquired their own generators, the practice also seen in Lebanon, although small-scale generation is generally a far less efficient system than its large-scale counterpart. Greece turned to wind turbines.

In Istanbul in 2013, the urban environment proved a focus of political discontent, with large-scale rioting due to a government plan to redevelop Gezi Park, one of the few green spots in the central part of the city. Moreover, the Erdoğan government pressed ahead with plans that will threaten the freshwater sources for a city that yearly grows by about 300,000 people; due, in part, to Turkey's high rate of population growth and, in part, to movement from the countryside.

While the environment was changing, so also was population structure, although this was greatly complicated by large-scale migration. The general trend of the latter was into Europe from Africa and Asia, as well as from Eastern and Southern to Western and Northern Europe. Economic opportunity and political conflict played significant roles. The conflicts in the former Yugoslavia ensured that by 1995 there were nearly 350,000 Bosnian refugees in Germany. High immigration could lead to upward revision of short, medium and long-term estimates for population. Thus, for Spain, there was an upward revision of medium-term estimates, from 45 million in 2008 to close to 50 million by 2015.

Immigration was particularly sensitive due to real and/or projected falls in the indigenous population including in Spain, Italy, Croatia, Greece and Malta. These falls were linked to stagnant labour markets and a related lack of optimism, notably among the young, so that in Spain in 2012 youth unemployment was 57 per cent, and in Naples by 2019 it was over 40 per cent. Fairly or not, these rates were associated with a fall in the birth rate as a product of despair among the young. The falling birth rate was not limited to Catholic countries, as it was also seen in Greece, while, with a total fertility rate of 1.9 children per woman in 2017, France had the highest rate in Europe and was close to replacement level. The high rate in France owes much to consistently supported pro-family policies, which are not matched in other countries, including Italy.

Italy's Population

In 2018, the number of births fell to the lowest since records began in 1861. Births fell 4 per cent from 2017, to just under 440,000. Deaths outnumbered births by 193,000, the fourth consecutive annual fall in the overall population. Stripping out migrants, the Italian population shrunk by 677,000 in 2015–18. The decline in births began in the 1980s, so that whereas in 1964 the number of children per woman was 2.7, by 1995 it was only 1.19. Poor welfare provision and working conditions are a factor. The number of working Italians between the ages of fifteen and thirty-four was about a third fewer than in 1998. At the same time, emigration, especially among the young, has risen, with 157,000 leaving Italy in 2018. It is estimated that there are about half a million Italians in London. Twenty-three per cent of the Italian population is aged sixty-five or more. This puts enormous pressure on public finances, not least due to generous pensions. Italy by 2019 had the second highest debt-to-GDP ratio in the EU after Greece. Economic prospects are threatened.

Despair for some is opportunity for others, and immigration has continued. Thus, in Italy, there were about 200,000 Muslim immigrants entered annually between 1993 and 2003 and by 2018 8.7 per cent of the Italian population were immigrants. Immigration rose greatly as a matter of concern in the 2010s as a result of the Syrian crisis. This was notably so from 2015. Thus, that year, when Germany opened its borders, there was fear in the intermediate countries. About half a million migrants for example went via Slovenia, where opposition to immigration was registered in the results of the 2018 parliamentary election. So also in the 2019 European elections, notably in France, Italy and Greece, although far less so in Spain. Matteo Salvini, Italy's Interior Minister in 2018–19, made Italian nativism, demographics and politics crucial to his successful political presentation. In 2019, his League won 34.3 per cent of the Italian vote in the European elections.

Religion was not the sole issue, nor a stagnant indigenous population. Most Syrian refugees live within the Islamic world, notably in Syria, Turkey, Lebanon and Jordan. About 6.5 million are internally displaced, while close to a million Syrian refugees are in Lebanon. By 2019, fired up by unemployment rising to 15 per cent, polls in Turkey indicated growing opposition, for example in the Mediterranean port-city of Mersin, to the 3.6 million Syrian refugees. Irrespective of war, there are major economic pressures across much of the Mediterranean due to rising population.

As a separate pattern, there was migration within cities, and notably from upland areas, including mountainous ones, and cliff coastlands, to cities. Political change played a role. In Communist-era Albania, those in collective farms generally were not permitted to leave the farms, which ended long-established migration patterns, not least seasonal migration. Once Communist rule ended, there was significant migration to Albania's cities, notably Tirana, and overseas. About a third of the Albanian population left, mostly to seek work, sometimes in crime. The majority went to Greece, where net emigration in the 1960s and 1970s changed to net immigration from the 1990s. There was concern about Albanian immigration, and, in 2007, a nationalist right-wing party gained ten seats in Parliament. The interplay between diaspora and national identities continues to remain important to Mediterranean history.

Across the Mediterranean, relatively unprofitable agricultural areas declined, not least as improved communications and freer trade in food accentuated this lack of profitability. In place of mountain farming, there was a preference for lower and gentler slopes where the growing season was longer and it was easier to use machines. Tourism could only be a substitute in some of the mountainous areas. Moreover, average farm size was generally too small to generate much profit, and this hit living standards and thus the domestic market for manufactured goods and service. As a key aspect of structural reform, attempts were made to encourage consolidation, both among individual holdings, which were often highly fragmented, and between them. However, farm size remained a major problem, not least in Greece, affecting the potential for mechanisation by limiting local investment capital. This was/is also an issue in southern Italy.

Agrarian policies after 1945 had emphasised the creation of owner-occupied individual farms, as in Greece, but the viability of this social order was challenged by mechanisation and by competition within the EU. Mass migration from the agricultural economy from the 1950s has left many traces on the landscape, including ruined buildings and farms, and also abandoned terraced land once used for arable cultivation or orchards, but now given over to pasture. Specific problems in particular regions reflected technological changes. Thus, the rural cork industry in Provence was hit by the manufacture of plastic-based corks.

In contrast to the Christian Mediterranean, where population levels are falling (particularly in Italy) or static, population rose greatly in Islamic countries, notably in Algeria, Egypt and Turkey. By 2018, Egypt's population was close to 100 million and was rising by 2.5 million each year. The previous decline in the birth rate has stalled, in part due to opposition from Islamic fundamentalism. By 2018, Algeria had 42 million people, with a median age of twenty-eight and youth unemployment of over 22 per cent. The growth of population in the region challenged economic prosperity, and kept wages low, depressing economic demand. Moreover, there was a high rate of male underemployment and unemployment, irrespective of very serious labour discrimination against women.

Resource pressures were focused by population movement into the cities, and the resulting need to purchase staples, notably bread and cooking oil. The ability of governments to subsidise staples therefore became a key social and political issue. Strains linked to population growth were a major contributory factor in the 'Arab Spring' that began in December 2010, with regimes overthrown in Tunisia, Egypt and Libya in 2011, followed, in 2019, with what was called a 'New Arab Spring' focused on Algeria and Sudan.

Changing the government did not ease economic or environmental fundamentals, a point also true for Greece, Italy and Spain. In Tunisia, where the economy remained stagnant, with the commonplace characteristics of inflation, low wages and an overlarge public sector, there was rioting in 2018 because a rise in the value-added tax led to an increase in food prices. This rise was a condition of a 2016 IMF loan package to help deal with the deficit. However, living standards fell. In June 2019, the candidate topping the polls ahead of elections was banned from standing. In Egypt, where General Abdel Fattah al-Sisi has been in power since 2014, external debt and taxation similarly rose, unemployment remained high, while fuel subsidies and domestic consumption were cut. The resource, social and political problems posed by a rapidly rising population, and by the variability of future water supply from the Nile as a result of climate changes, notably climatic oscillations, are becoming more acute.

Alongside change, there is consistency in patterns and practices, for example the strength of Egyptian bureaucracy. Thus, in Albanian villages, there are insistent blood feuds. Moreover, under the Communists and subsequently, the pre-Communist subordination of women in Albania remained insistent despite the language of equality, and an expansion in the education of women. One of the major exceptions, but, again, an aspect of the vitality of pre-Communist practices, was that of 'sworn virgins', women who were allowed to retain a degree of independence and, crucially, to own property, because they swore to remain unmarried. As an indication of the subordination expected to flow from marriage and of the role of public symbolisation, only these women were permitted to smoke in public.

Discrimination remained a major issue in the Islamic world. Aside from serious issues in the world of work, the legal position of women suffered in religious courts, which continued to handle issues of marriage, divorce and child custody. Sexual harassment is a major problem, as is violence against women. Masculinity is frequently confused with such violence, and that is employed in particular against independent-minded women.

At the same time, religious-linked contrasts should not be pushed too far. There are similarities between Christian and Muslim societies. It is not only in Muslim societies that women are subordinated. In Croatia in the 1990s, nationalists sought to use pro-natalist propaganda and policies in order to build up their 'people', advocating a trinity of 'home, nation and God'. The government ignored the need for women to work. The public culture, however, was somewhat different in 2013 when Croatia joined the European Union. It is also a member of NATO, alongside Montenegro and Albania. The last, indeed, spends a relatively high proportion of its GDP on defence.

Across the Mediterranean, consumerism has been a driving force in society, the economy, the fiscal system and politics, creating pressures for each, and, indeed, also for the environment. Thus, in Thessaloniki, the poor continue to shop in city-centre markets, travelling by bus or walking, but the wealthier clog the roads by driving to suburban supermarkets.

Over the long-term, there has been higher per capita wealth across the Mediterranean, as well as greater access to education. Each contributes to an individualism and breaking down of old social bonds that challenge previous patterns of behaviour. Yet, Northern Europe is more dynamic, meritocratic, mobile and growing than Southern Europe and also does not have falling birth rates comparable to the latter. This contrast on dynamism raises questions about the effectiveness of all the Mediterranean societies, whether European, African or Asian. By far the most dynamic economically is Israel.

Turning to the Mediterranean as a whole, the size of the public sector is a major problem, and in the Christian as well as the Islamic Mediterranean; in Cyprus, the civil service is both the biggest employer and pays high salaries. So also with corruption in Mediterranean societies, as in Egypt, Montenegro, Slovenia and Spain – a far from exhaustive list – or criminality, as in Albania. Corruption makes it very difficult to enforce regulations for example on traffic, waste disposal or pollution. Moreover, unemployment is high across the Mediterranean, as is underemployment; the latter ensures that hotels often have relatively large staffs. Thus, despite its relatively good growth rate and falling poverty, compared to most of North Africa, Morocco has high youth unemployment, which leads to migration, legal and illegal, to Spain.

Religious division remains a major political, social and cultural barrier within, and between, countries. This division is most strongly felt for minorities persecuted by radical Islamists, as in Egypt, where Cairo's Coptic cathedral was bombed during Sunday Mass in 2016. About 10 per cent of the Egyptian population, the Copts have been frequently attacked by Islamists in the 2010s, including by terrorist bombings. So also with attacks on Christians in Algeria. In Syria, in contrast, the Assad regime drew heavily on support from minorities – Christians, Shi'as and Alawites – while the opposition is largely Sunni. They are the bulk of the refugees from Syria, and much of their property has been seized.

Government in the Middle East tends to lack popular consent, at least in the sense of a ready willingness to obey the law. This situation leads to attempts to win compliance, particularly by food subsidies, as in Algeria, Egypt and Libya, to quieten the people, but, at the same time, encourages oppression. The secret police are a key adjunct of government, and one that instils a degree of fear in society.

However, the failure of government other than to maintain control is repeatedly apparent. Thus, a lack of investment results in power shortages, as in Lebanon and Egypt, exacerbates water supply issues, and causes terrible internet connections, which is a problem in much of the Arab World. In some states, the control is non-existent (Libya) or very limited (Lebanon).

The relative significance of religious attitudes is a problematic issue, not least the degree of anti-scientific commitment seen in education policy in some countries, for example Turkey in the 2010s. The readiness to question and challenge established practices and interests is overly limited as is the willingness to prefer flexibility over corporatism when confronted by global economic changes. Despite the weakness of government regulation as a means to encourage or help economic expansion, it was still the reflex position of most European governments, and across the range from agriculture via industry to services.

Visiting Earlier Cultures

Earlier cultures are generally understood in terms of archaeology and the remains of buildings. Yet, cultural legacies can also be seen. This is particularly the case with some religious and/or ethnic enclaves, such as Copts in Egypt, Syriacs who survived Turkish massacres in 1915, or the monasteries of Mount Athos in Greece, which can be viewed from the sea. There are also pre-Islamic elements in the Islamic world, as with the legacy of Berber culture in North Africa. In Tunisia, local saints are venerated in shrines in a tradition that went back to Berber and sub-Saharan roots, only to fall foul of Muslim reformists in the nineteenth century and of Islamists today: variously as superstitious and idolatrous. Many of such Tunisian shrines have been attacked since the 2011 revolution.

Tourism

The films of the 1950s helped make the supposed life of the Riviera more prominent, with travel part of the consumerism of the post-war West. *Et Dieu ... créa la femme (And God Created Woman)*, a 1956 film, launched Brigitte Bardot and made St-Tropez much better known, notably in the United States. The resort became known for hedonism and topless sunbathing.

More generally, the economic 'Long Boom' from the late 1940s to the early 1970s saw a major rise in tourism, one that included its extension down the social scale to reach not only the middle class but also the working class. This process was greatly enhanced by innovations, notably the linkage of jet aircraft to the package industry. Lax planning controls and the cheap price of land were also key enablers, and a series of tourist resorts took off. Helped by the climate and the sandy beaches, these developments caused a particularly rapid rise in tourism in the 1960s. The number of international tourists in Spain, mostly on the Mediterranean coast, rose from 4 million in 1959 to 14 million in 1964 and 76 million in 2015. Domestic tourism was also important, and notably so in France where a series of resorts were built from the 1960s, such as La Grande-Motte in Languedoc and the Baie des Anges near Antibes. Modernist architecture, often very unattractive, can readily be seen, for example at Palavas near Montpellier. Another social context for overbuilding, in this case for the wealthy, can be seen in Monaco. In North Africa, resorts were developed in Tunisia from 1960, notably Hammamet and Djerba. The 1989 Tunisian National Development Plan established new tourist resorts, including Port El Kantaoui.

Cruises

The Mediterranean remained the centre of the growing cruise-ship industry in the late twentieth century, and this continued to be the case in the early twenty-first despite the expansion of cruising in the Caribbean and the new industry created by East Asian demand for cruising. The Mediterranean had the appeal of a number of recognised stops in close proximity, of strong product recognition around the world, of an absence of typhoons and hurricanes, and of ready access to European and North American passengers.

The industry, however, was long buffeted by politics, notably the Arab–Israeli Wars and the civil wars in Lebanon. Nevertheless, although Beirut, today a highly dynamic city, remained off the standard itinerary, Israel was visited by liners. Cruising options were affected by more wide-ranging political issues. In the 2000s instability in Somalia contributed to a major rise in Somali piracy that included attacks on cruise ships. Insurance premiums rose. This situation affected cruise-ship routes through the western Indian Ocean, a process accentuated by instability in Yemen, and, therefore, Aden ceasing to be a cruise destination. Although 'repositioning cruises' without passengers continued through the Suez Canal and the Red Sea, links between Mediterranean and Indian Ocean cruise itineraries fell. Instead, the Mediterranean circuit was often that of liners in the Caribbean for the winter, a repositioning cruise at the end of the winter, the Mediterranean for spring and early summer, then the Baltic, and then the Caribbean. Alternatively, some liners stayed year-long in the Mediterranean.

In the 2010s, the instability linked to the Arab Spring, combined with terrorist attacks on tourists, greatly affected cruise visits to North Africa. Instead, cruise ships concentrated in the eastern Mediterranean on Greece, Turkey and Cyprus, although instability in Turkey discouraged some cruise companies from visiting Istanbul in the late 2010s. Libya, which had been of growing importance as a destination in the 2000s, notably with visits to Roman sites, went totally off the radar as a result of civil war from 2011. Syria, never popular, likewise from 2012. Both have remained unvisited by liners.

Tunisia was hit by terrorism in 2015, not least in the attack on the Bardo Museum, a gem, with excellent exhibits, notably mosaics, to see without having to walk far, and, as I discovered earlier that year, a welcome contrast to the archaeological museum of the crowded and large category, such as Naples. Twenty-two people were killed in that attack, and, at another on a beach resort in Sousse, thirty-eight were killed. These attacks led a million people to cancel holidays, caused about seventy hotels to close, and saw tourism revenues drop by nearly half from 7 per cent of GDP. However, Russian security and political concerns about Egypt and Turkey led to bans on travel there in late 2015, and, as a result, about 600,000 Russian tourists visited Tunisia in 2016. In 2018, Britain lifted its travel ban on Tunisia, which led to the reopening of tourist flights.

Tourism flows reflect events elsewhere. Thus, the Yugoslav crises of the 1990s led to tourists staying away, notably with cruise ships not visiting war-scarred Dubrovnik. Subsequently, tourist numbers greatly rose in Croatia, and Dubrovnik became a very crowded cruise-ship destination in the 2010s, as it remains. Tourism revenues rose in Greece in 2013 due to instability in Egypt and Tunisia. Tourism to Egypt had risen after the government adopted more supporting policies from 1975, including easing visa restrictions. The number of tourists in Egypt rose from 0.1 million people in 1951 to 1.8 million in 1981 and 5.5 million in 2000, to peak at 14.7 million in 2010. Instability led to decline to 9.5 million in 2013. There was a recovery, from 5.4 million tourists when figures plunged in 2016, to 8.3 million in 2017, followed by strong recent gains to produce 4 per cent of GDP and to employ one in ten workers. Nevertheless, there was an attack on a tourist bus in May 2019. The Mediterranean coast of Egypt is not a tourist destination.

Affected by political instability and the war in Syria, Lebanon ceased to be a major destination for Western tourists, although, as a reminder of the multiple flows that went into the tourist picture, it remained attractive to tourists from the Arab world. However, political disputes in the Arab world affected this, with travel there from the United Arab Emirates banned from 2012. In 2018, the largest percentage rises in tourism in the eastern Mediterranean were in Israel and Montenegro, although, in large part, these rises reflected lower bases than the figures for Turkey, Greece and Croatia, each of which remained major destinations. Turkey did particularly well with tourists in 2018, attracting 39 million tourists; although a dispute with Saudi Arabia led to the latter discouraging tourism there in 2019.

In the Western and Central Mediterranean, Spain, France and Italy were the countries overwhelmingly visited by cruise liners in the 2010s, with Barcelona, Marseille, Nice, Naples, Venice and Dubrovnik the key ports. Civitavecchia is the cruise-ship port for Rome. Monte Carlo is another very popular cruise destination: the Port Hercule in Monaco was greatly expanded from 2004 by use of a large floating breakwater.

In North Africa, Moroccan ports that are visited are on the Atlantic, notably Casablanca and Tangier. Eco-resorts are being built on the north coast, and road and rail links improved with the rest of Morocco, but this is not a cruise-ship destination. The fortified Spanish enclave ports of Ceuta and Melilla do not tend to attract cruises, or even many tourists. Algeria was regarded as unsafe for a while, but became a destination anew in the late 2010s. From west to east, the destination ports are Ghazaouet, Algiers and Béjaïa. Close to the Moroccan border, Ghazaouet is the port for Tlemcen and El Mansourah. The major sites in the former are the eleventh century Great Mosque and the deconsecrated Sidi Belhassen Mosque, which is a museum containing mosaics, carvings and pottery. From Algiers, the pyramid-shaped Mausoleum of Mauretania and the Roman ruins at Tipaza are visited, and, from Béjaïa, the Roman remains at Djémila, as well as Berber villages.

The size of some cruise ships was dramatised on 13 January 2012 when the 114,137-tonne *Costa Concordia* struck a rock off the

Italian island of Giglio, partially sinking. The response and evacuation were chaotic. Launched in 2015 in Trieste and costing £372 million, it had a capacity for 3780 passengers and 1100 crew; 3229 and 1023 were abroad, and 32 died. Less dramatically, on 2 June 2019, the 66,000-tonne MSC *Opera*, which can carry nearly 2700 passengers on its thirteen decks, lost control in the Giudecca canal in Venice, and hit the quayside and a moored tourist boat. In 2013, the Italian government had already banned ships of over 96,000 tonnes from the centre of Venice, but the law was overturned on appeal. The city of Venice wished, and still wishes, to stop the ships entering along the Giudecca canal. In 2017, in response, the Italian government said that it would halt the 500 cruise ships that sail down the Giudecca canal each year by routing them around the side of the Venice lagoon, which would allow them to reach the port of Marghera on the mainland without coming near Venice. However, by June 2019, nothing has been done, much to the anger of the *No Grandi Navi* (No Big Ships) movement. Aside from safety, the wake produced by the ships was a major issue in Venice, as it damaged fragile canalside buildings. At the same time, the considerable income the city derives from cruise ships, as well as the profits from bunkering and provisioning, makes the issue more complex. As its resident population has long been falling, Venice would die without tourists.

The growing size of cruise ships has ensured that the ports that can take the large boats, such as Barcelona, Dubrovnik and Venice, have many thousands of people added to their daytime population. By 2018, Venice hosted over 25 million visitors a year, 14 million staying for only one day. Many of them were cruise passengers. In 2018, the city decided to introduce an entry fee for short-stay tourists, similar to that in the Aeolian Islands.

The situation is very different for smaller cruise ships; and itineraries have been developed to provide another experience at this scale. Thus, Crotone (Italy), Otranto (Italy), Sarandë (Albania) and Kalamata (Greece) are all now destinations. In part, such ports are for nearby destinations: Otranto for Lecce, Sarandë for Butrint, Kalamata for Mystias, and Trapani for Erice. So also for St-Florent and L'Île-Rousse, both in Corsica, Bandol and Cavalaire-sur-Mer, both in Provence, and Anzio, Portoferraio and Giardini Naxos in Italy, the last three for Rome, Elba and Taormina respectively.

Traditional Turkish gulets, wooden vessels, provide a way to visit shallow coastal waters, including seeing underwater remains, for example in the bay of Kekova. These ships provide a way to see the coastline as it would have been visited in the past.

The contrast between large and small cruise ships is likely to become more significant, as visitors returning to the Mediterranean seek to visit places that are new to them. The companies face the challenge of devising itineraries that are of interest both to first-time and to experienced passengers. Cruising offers mass tourism, a higher-priced more distinctive activity, and the overlap of the two.

As an alternative to cruise ships, there are also numerous ferries. Some, in part, reflect political links, notably from Spain to Ceuta and Melilla, or Trapani to Pantelleria and Porto Empedocle to Lampedusa. Most ferries are commercial. Thus, from Marseille, Toulon, Nice, Genoa, Livorno and Savona, it is possible to sail to Corsica. From Corsica, Marseille, Genoa, Livorno, Civitavecchia, Naples, Palermo and Trapani, it is possible to sail to Sardinia. Ferries are also very important for the Balearics, the Adriatic, Sicily, Malta and the Aegean. The longstanding route from Brindisi to Greece and Albania is served by ferries: to Vlorë in Albania, and Igoumenítsa, Corfu, Cephalonia and Patras in Greece. From Bari, it is possible to go to Durrës in Albania, Bar in Montenegro, and Cephalonia, Corfu, Igoumenítsa and Patras.

Politics pose greater problems elsewhere, for example for Cyprus. There are ferries from Alanya, Mersin and Taşucu in Turkey, to Kyrenia in Turkish Cyprus, and from Greece and Israel (but not Turkey) to Cyprus. With or without a car, ferries offer the possibility of a bespoke cruise.

Ferries, however, will not be the choice of most tourists, no more than the local stopping trains that can show you so much of coastal regions, and notably so in Italy. That is a pity, as life in the slow lane is a good way to enjoy the Mediterranean. Moreover, it returns us to the experience of travellers and tourists in the past. At sea, the slow lane underlines the significance of current and wind, and, therefore, the relationship between different bodies of water, and between them and the land. The slow lane also ensures that sites can be seen at a speed that captures their varied facets.

Distance is a clearer factor if moving slowly. Thanks in part to that, air travel is important in getting to the Mediterranean, but is not the best means for transport when there. By sea, the distances that are readily apparent are not only those from west to east, but also those created by the secondary waters, as in travelling from Alexandria to Istanbul, or from Haifa to Trieste, crossing, respectively, the Aegean and Adriatic as well. Those waters greatly extend the north–south transits.

These distances are such that, alongside often potent similarities, there are instructive contrasts in the Mediterranean. It joins three continents, a range of cultures and a wealth of histories. The visual impact of this variety is unsurpassed for a sea of this size. It is easy to see why the Mediterranean remains the foremost cruise destination for those interested in history and culture.

Conclusions

The extent to which the Mediterranean is a unit has engaged attention both in its own right and as part of the longstanding debate over European identity. In the preface to the influential French *Larousse Encyclopedia of World Geography* (1967), originally published in French in 1959–62, Pierre Deffontaines (1894–1978) pressed for the unity of the Mediterranean basin, although the value of this somewhat geographical determinism was not encouraged by the argument that the Eurasian plains from the Oder to the Pacific should also be treated as a single unit.

His argument accorded with that of Fernand Braudel (1902–85) in *La Méditerranée et le Monde Méditerranéen à l'Époque de Philippe II* (*The Mediterranean and the Mediterranean World in the Age of Philip II*), a hugely influential work which appeared first, in French, in 1949. Braudel's career indicated the role of the Mediterranean as it included a spell from 1923 to 1932 as a schoolteacher in Algeria, which he loved, and archival work in Dubrovnik from 1936 before becoming a prisoner of the Germans during the Second World War, during which he wrote a draft. Similarly, Deffontaines, from 1939 to 1964, was Director of the French Institute at Barcelona, an aspect of 'soft power', which was very important in the Mediterranean, and notably for the Papacy and for France.

Braudel provided a total and unitary vision, but the structural, more geographical, dimension of his great work, with its stress on long-term factors, did not readily cohere with the chronological political section dealing with the late sixteenth century, the Age of Philip II of Spain (r. 1556–98). The problem of the relationship between structure and agency is a fundamental one for scholarship, while structural factors are not simply 'little touched' by time (or events), as Braudel misleadingly suggested.

Braudel was much stronger on the Christian Mediterranean than on its Muslim rival, but there has been a finer balance since in scholarship, not least as more research has become available on Muslim countries over the last millennium, for example on Egypt. There has also been an engagement with deeper political currents, so that rivalries and factionalism can be related to more than Braudel's *histoire événementielle*. He had described the history of events as the 'crests of foam that the tides of history carry on their strong back', and, in the preface to the much-revised second edition, published in 1966, asked, 'Is it possible somehow to convey simultaneously both that conspicuous history which holds our attention by its continual and dramatic changes – and that other, submerged, history, almost silent and always discreet, virtually unsuspected either by its observers or its participants, which is little touched by the obstinate erosion of time?' In fact, human life is readily transformed by politics, as the history of the Mediterranean demonstrates clearly, not least with reference to religion.

Not just French geographers and historians, but also modern commentators have proved particularly interested in the idea of the Mediterranean as a cultural and political unity and a sphere for activity. The argument for a united Mediterranean basin, seen in 2008 in French President Nicolas Sarkozy's plan for a Mediterranean Union, was frequently made in Southern Europe, especially when EU (European Union) funds were sought for North African states on the grounds that their stabilisation, especially that of Morocco and Algiers, would alleviate pressures such as immigration in Spain and France. A colonial overhang by both powers was also at stake, as also with Italy in Libya, although the latter was far less pressing than the fraught relationship between France and Algeria. Libyan stabilisation, however, became a far more acute issue. It remains a country divided by civil war.

France also saw its influence in North-West Africa as a way to lessen the added influence won by Germany as a result of the end of Communist control in Eastern Europe.

Yet, such calls for action and aid also reflected the questionable nature of the suggestion of a Mediterranean unity, for they drew on the idea that there was a difference between North Africa and Southern Europe that had to be stabilised in order to contain the serious challenge in Europe posed by immigration and Islamic consciousness. Whatever the geographical basis, the idea that the Mediterranean can be treated as a value system, a goal or an ideology, is problematic. Difficult enough for Europe, despite the structure of the EU, this argument, at the Mediterranean level, flies in the face of the multiple tensions bound up in the overlapping worlds of religion, ethnicity, politics and nationalism.

Indeed, as I write (June 2019), the government of Turkey, increasingly authoritarian since surviving a 2016 coup attempt, has just failed to overturn the recent election results in Istanbul, Gaza and Israel are exchanging fire, and there is continuing bitter civil war in Libya. The military-based Egyptian government, where President Abdel Fattah al-Sisi is now due to stay in office until 2030, has ordered the makers of television dramas to produce scripts that glorify the military and promote conservative family values. Military prosecutors police authors in Egypt.

Mediterranean Gas

America's Geological Survey has estimated natural gas reserves of 122 trillion cubic feet under the Mediterranean from the coast of Gaza to southern Turkey, a figure comparable to that of Iraq. Significant finds began in the early 2000s, with the Gaza Marine field, and others followed, for example the Aphrodite field between Cyprus and Israel found in 2011. However, taking gas from 1500 metres below the seabed is costly. In addition, there are issues over how and where to move it: by pipeline or by means of liquefication (Egypt has two liquefaction facilities: at Damietta, a key site in the Crusades, and Idku) and thence by sea. Finds of gas encouraged more exploration that led to disputes over drilling rights, notably between Cyprus and Turkey, which claims most of the Cypriot waters south of the island. In 2018, Turkish warships blocked access by an Italian drilling ship licensed by Cyprus. France's Total company also is licensed and, in May 2019, France agreed to upgrade Cyprus's Evangelos Florakis naval base. Also in 2019, Turkey and one of the rival Libyan governments agreed maritime zones that ignored internally recognised Greek and Cypriot counterparts.

There is, moreover, maritime territory disputed between Israel and Lebanon. In June 2019, Hezbollah accepted UN talks, brokered by the United States, designed to sort out the Israel–Lebanon maritime border. Lebanon is desperate, with little to export, a lack of generating capacity, and the economy and public finances close to collapse. Israel has stopped Palestine from developing Gaza Marine. In addition, other countries made finds, notably the Zohr and Noor fields in the Egyptian zone, and the Leviathan and Tamar fields off Israel.

There has been consideration of a pipeline from Israel, Egypt and Cyprus via Crete, mainland Greece and Italy to European markets, which would be the world's longest undersea pipeline and offer an alternative to Russian sources. This, the 'Eastern Mediterranean Pipeline', was strongly backed in 2018–19 by Mike Pompeo, the American Secretary of State, who called the region 'a key strategic frontier'. The route via Turkey, in contrast, appears closed by political uncertainties, including disputes over Cyprus, poor relations between Israel and Turkey, and American suspicion of the latter.

Of the Mediterranean's historic cities, several are firmly off the tourist itinerary. Thus, ruled by Hamas since 2007, Gaza, aside from violence, suffers from power shortages that keep it dark at night and stop lifts from working. In addition, desalination plants there do not work, in part due to Egyptian and Israeli blockades of fuel, sewage is not treated, the hopes that led earlier in the decade to the building of hotels have proved abortive, and there is a shortage of water, including for irrigation. Both salt and sewage are seeping into the overused aquifer. Relations with Israel lead frequently to conflict involving Gaza. There is also conflict in northern Sinai to the south-west of Gaza where the Egyptian army has been fighting *jihadists* since 2015, and notably so in the city of Rafah, demolishing many houses to that end. This area is certainly not a tourist destination.

Very differently, long-standing tension over the idea of Turkish accession to the EU is a continuing feature. Edmund Stoiber, the Prime Minister of Bavaria, who narrowly lost the election for the German chancellorship in 2002, argued that Turkish accession would be an excessive fiscal and therefore economic burden. Frits Bolkestein, an EU commissioner critical of Turkish accession, in 2004 compared the large-scale immigration that he predicted would follow accession with past political challenges from the Ottoman (Turkish) Empire, declaring 'the liberation of 1683 will have been in vain', a reference to the second Turkish siege of Vienna.

The Islamicist, as well as authoritarian, direction of Turkish government under Recep Tayyip Erdoğan has further challenged the secular character of much of European society. However, in other directions, he has been willing to consider major change, as in his unfulfilled project for a 30-mile (50-kilometre) canal parallel to the Bosphorus that is designed to divert tanker traffic to a safer alternative between the Sea of Marmara and the Black Sea.

Cyprus is another continuing difference between Turkey and the European Union. When, as a condition of accession talks, the Turkish government signed a protocol extending its customs

union with the EU (its biggest trading partner) to the new members that had joined the EU in 2004, including Cyprus, it issued
a statement that this did not imply recognition of the Greek-
Cypriot government. Croatia joined the EU in 2013, and there are
currently accession negotiations elsewhere in the Balkans. There
is no such prospect for Turkey.

Meanwhile, there has been no unification in Cyprus to match
the earlier one of Germany, and understandably so as the divisions in Cyprus run more deeply. In 2004, while the Turkish
Cypriots voted in favour, the Greek Cypriots voted heavily against
a UN reunification plan that had been seen by the EU as important to accession by Cyprus, only for the EU to accept the accession
of Cyprus in terms of the Greek-Cypriot part of the island. The
EU saw this government as the sole legitimate representative of
the island. Cyprus and Greece strongly oppose Turkish accession
to the EU.

Identity is a matter of competing histories and current rivalries. The imperial experience adds tension, as when there was
criticism in Algeria in 2013 of a joke by François Hollande,
President of France in 2012–17, which was interpreted as reflecting racism and repeating stereotypes. Within France itself, there
are tensions about the treatment of Algeria when it is treated in
effect as a colony, tensions that have played a more prominent
role over the last two decades than they did hitherto. Italian
imperial rule was an issue thereafter in relations with Libya.
In Britain, in contrast, there is not comparable sensitivity about
its Mediterranean past due to the greater prominence, instead,
of slavery and India as issues. Most modern Britons would be
surprised to be told that Britain had been an imperial power in
Egypt and Israel.

There is criticism of Western imperialism in the Islamic world,
but far less of past Islamic empires. Thus, there is scant mention
in Turkey of the treatment of Armenians and Greeks in the 1910s
and 1920s, and critical discussion of it is harshly treated. The

Erdoğan government, and its Justice and Development Party (AK), have taken interest in the Ottoman legacy much further than the previous Kemalist administrations; although this is very much a partisan account of this legacy, which is presented as an example of a heroic Islamic past. The neo-Ottoman approach affects public commemoration, sport, fiction, films and museums. The 1453 Panorama Museum in Istanbul is the most popular in the country for Turks, but not for foreign visitors. Maps depicting the extent of the Ottoman Empire are displayed in public.

In turn, views that could be regarded as critical of past glories led to anger, as with *Magnificent Century* (2011–14), a popular television series that depicted Süleyman the Magnificent as a womaniser and a drunkard. Turkey's interest in Syria is largely related to particular security issues, but can in part be considered in terms of a historical image of a greater past, which, for example, led to praise for Selim I, the conqueror of Syria in 1516. In the poll for Istanbul's mayoral election in June 2019, Erdoğan's AK Party sought to discredit the eventually successful opposition candidate, Ekrem Imamoğlu, by claiming that he had a secret Greek heritage and that the opposition wanted to turn Istanbul back into Constantinople, thereby making it less Turkish and Muslim.

There were also obvious contrasts in terms of the current integration of Mediterranean countries within wider networks. Thus, Lebanon and Syria are both to a degree part of an Iranian-based Shi'a system. In contrast, Israel is closely linked to the United States.

Integration is not only political. There have been high rates of Northern European investment in housing near the Mediterranean. This is especially so from Britain and the Netherlands in Spain and France. In the 2000s, as the result of a strong pound, cheap borrowing and large-scale building in Spain, there were over one million British homeowners in Spain. Russia, in turn, has provided settlers in Cyprus, where over 50,000 former Soviet citizens live, and Montenegro. Living in the Mediterranean offers warmth, year-round golf, lower taxation and a cheaper life-style. In Agatha Christie's *Death on the Nile*, Mrs Alderton likes Majorca because 'it's cheap'. The related movement of people led to appreciable shifts of pension income to the Mediterranean, as many of those who moved there were retired. The development of communities of foreign retirees was different to tourism, but both reflected a separation of the Mediterranean: between what was wanted by foreigners and what by locals, and between aspirations and a more problematic reality.

There is no comparison for Europeans in Egypt or Algeria, or for Arabs. Indeed, wealthy Arabs prefer to buy property on the Mediterranean coast of Spain and France, although Beirut retains an appeal.

Investment in housing helped make control over permission to build a murky issue, bringing together politics, business, law and crime. Xenophobia also played a part, not least in Greece and Spain, in each of which foreign homeowners were accused of taking land and breaching planning regulations, and notably so in coastal areas such as Corfu.

The future is shot through with uncertainty. For example, China, which had earlier helped build dock facilities in Malta, is interested in developing Mediterranean ports in Greece and Italy as part of its global 'Belt and Road' strategy, particularly Piraeus, Athens's port. In 2019, Italy signalled its support for this strategy, which has implications for its ports, notably Genoa, Naples and Trieste. The last provides ready access to Central Europe as does no other major port. Chinese containers are prominent in Athens and Naples.

At the same time as uncertainties, there are many continu-ities. Clan politics remain significant in many areas, whether Libya or Montenegro. So also with geopolitics, as in Egypt's attempt to dominate Cyrenaica (eastern Libya) and Gaza. As another instance of continuity, or, at least (and the distinc-tion is important), a presentation of continuity, the strength of assumptions about nationhood has encouraged hostility to immigration. Thus, the arrival of about 50,000 migrants in Spain in 2018 helped Vox, a populist party founded only in 2013, to make political gains in 2018–19.

Differences between Christendom and Islam provide a measure of continuity, as with poor relations between Greece and Turkey. Yet, in practice, there are also many similarities between the Christian and the Muslim Mediterranean, and this was also true of the past and will be so in the future. Today, in Italy as in Egypt, a sedentary lifestyle is contributing to more obesity, while, in both, drug addiction is rising, and feeds a major Mediterranean trade. This includes flows across the Mediterranean by speedboat, notably from Albania to Italy and from Morocco to Spain, providing a regular night-time scene in the Strait of Gibraltar. Rubbish is a major problem in many cities, whether Beirut, Istanbul, Naples or Rome, as is terrible traffic, including in each of those cities. A dependence on remittances from those working at a distance is important in Mediterranean cities from Barcelona to Beirut. So also with high debt-to-GDP ratios, for example in Egypt, Italy and Spain.

Even more clearly as a common factor is climate change. Summer temperatures are rising and, alongside droughts, the hotter heatwaves are hitting crop yields. Aquifers are being drained as groundwater is pumped up to help with falls in rainfall. River flows are falling. Water availability is moving from planning into nightmares. At the same time, there are differences in the severity of the issue, which is much worse in Egypt than in France or Croatia. In part, there are contrasts that are environmental, in character as well as reflecting population figures, but civic culture and public policy are also major issues. Thus, the strong French state, with its outcome-orientated engineering ethos of public works, is not matched in Egypt.

Contrasts in these and other matters reflect a range of factors; and it is important to be wary of any ethnic, religious or environmental determinism. Political culture, the key issue, is in part a matter of contingencies. It is certainly not predetermined. Indeed, the future of the Mediterranean has the fascination of uncertainty. This is not adequately captured if a Braudelian emphasis is adopted, with its focus on the constant or semi-constant nature of environmental, more particularly geographical, opportunities and problems. Such an approach might have been pertinent for societies dominated by the seasons, by simple organic power systems for transport and energy (porters, horses, galleys, wind-powered ships, wood fuel), and by a worldview defined by religious systems in which there was direct intervention by gods, while time was in part settled by the certainty of an apocalypse.

Modern circumstances and culture are different. The future does not appear likely to be a repetition of the past, nor a return to it. An emphasis on change, however, necessarily also directs attention to changes in the past. Part of the fascination of the Mediterranean is that the strength of the historical record is such that we can see this process. It is an area where history is particularly present, and one that has been of fundamental importance for humanity. The blue sea, in storm as in repose, is one that sets us wondering and encourages us to wander.

Selected Further Reading

Abela, Joan, *Hospitaller Malta and the Mediterranean Economy in the Sixteenth Century* (Woodbridge, 2018).

Abulafia, David, *The Great Sea: A Human History of the Mediterranean* (London, 2011).

Abulafia, David (ed.), *The Mediterranean in History* (London, 2003).

Aissaoui, Rabah and Claire Eldridge (eds), *Algeria Revisited: History, Culture and Identity* (London, 2017).

Astarita, Tommaso, *Between Salt Water and Holy Water. A History of Southern Italy* (New York, 2005).

Bennison, Amira, *The Almoravid and Almohad Empires* (Edinburgh, 2016).

Braudel, Fernand, *The Mediterranean and the Mediterranean World in the Age of Philip II* (London, 1972–3).

Brummett, Palmira, *Mapping the Ottomans: Sovereignty, Territory, and Identity in the Early Modern Mediterranean* (Cambridge, 2015).

Buttigieg, Emanuel, *Nobility, Faith and Masculinity: The Hospitaller Knights of Malta c. 1580–c.1700* (London, 2011).

Cohen, Julia Philipps and Sarah Stein, *Sephardi Lives: A Documentary History, 1700–1950* (Stanford, CA, 2014).

Cline, Eric, *1177 BC: The Year Civilization Collapsed* (Princeton, NJ, 2014).

Crane, Sheila, *Mediterranean Crossroads: Marseille and Modern Architecture* (Minneapolis, MN, 2011).

Davis-Secord, Sarah, *Where the Worlds Met: Sicily in the Early Medieval Mediterranean*, (Ithaca, 2017).

Fevziu, Blendi, *Enver Hoxha: The Iron Fist of Albania* (London, 2016).

Fox, Robert, *The Inner Sea: The Mediterranean and Its People* (London, 1991).

Gaggio, Dario, *The Shaping of Tuscany: Landscape and Society between Tradition and Modernity* (Cambridge, 2017).

Gallant, Thomas, *Experiencing Dominion: Culture, Identity, and Power in the British Mediterranean* (South Bend, IN, 2002).

Genc, Kaya, *Under the Shadow: Rage and Revolution in Modern Turkey* (London, 2016).

Goffman, Daniel, *Izmir and the Levantine World, 1550–1650* (Seattle, WA, 1990).

Göçek, Fatima, *The Transformation of Turkey: Redefining State and Society from the Ottoman Empire to the Modern Era* (London, 2011).

Greene, Molly, *A Shared World: Christians and Muslims in the Early Modern Mediterranean World* (Princeton, NJ, 2000).

Harris, William (ed.), *Rethinking the Mediterranean* (Oxford, 2005).

Heather, Peter, *Rome Resurgent: War and Empire in the Age of Justinian* (Oxford, 2018)

Holland, Robert, *Blue-Water Empire: The British in the Mediterranean since 1800* (London, 2012).

Horden, Peregrine and Nicholas Purcell, *The Corrupting Sea: A Study of Mediterranean History* (Oxford, 2000).

Hosler, John, *The Siege of Acre: 1189–91: Saladin, Richard the Lionheart, and the Battle that Decided the Third Crusade* (New Haven, CT, 2018).

Hurlburt, Holly, *Daughters of Venice: Caterina Corner, Queen of Cyprus and Woman of the Renaissance* (New Haven, CT, 2015).

Isabella, Maurizio and Konstantina Zanou (eds), *Mediterranean Diasporas: Politics and Ideas in the Long Nineteenth Century* (London, 2016).

Kaegi, Walter, *Muslim Expansion and Byzantine Collapse in North Africa* (Cambridge, 2010).

König, Daniel, *Arabic-Islamic Views of the Latin West: Tracing the Emergence of Medieval Europe* (Oxford, 2015).

Kostis, Kostas, *History's Spoiled Children: The Formation of the Modern Greek State* (London, 2018).

Kundahl, George, *The Riviera at War: World War II on the Côte D'Azur* (London, 2017).

Lough, John, *France Observed in the Seventeenth Century by British Travellers* (Stocksfield, 1985).

McCormick, Michael, *Origins of the European Economy: Communications and Commerce,* AD 300–900 (Cambridge, 2001).

McDougall, James, *A History of Algeria* (Cambridge, 2017).

Malcolm, Noel, *Agents of Empire: Knights, Corsairs, Jesuits and Spies in the Sixteenth-Century Mediterranean World* (London, 2015).

Manning, J. G., *The Open Sea: The Economic Life of the Ancient Mediterranean World from the Iron Age to the Rise of Rome* (Princeton, NJ, 2018).

Mansel, Philip, *Levant: Splendour and Catastrophe in the Mediterranean* (London, 2010).

Metcalf, Michael, *Byzantine Cyprus 491–1191* (Nicosia, 2009).

Moe, Nelson, *The View from Vesuvius: Italian Culture and the Southern Question* (Berkeley, CA, 2002).

Murray-Miller, Gavin, *The Cult of the Modern: Trans-Mediterranean France and the Construction of French Modernity* (Lincoln, NE, 2017).

Nasiali, Minayo, *Native to the Republic: Empire, Social Citizenship, and Everyday Life in Marseille since 1945* (Ithaca, NY, 2016).

Porch, Douglas, *Hitler's Mediterranean Gamble. The North African and the Mediterranean Campaigns in World War II* (London, 2004).

Pryor, John, *Geography, Technology, and War: Studies in the Maritime History of the Mediterranean 649–1571* (Cambridge, 1988).

Quinn, Josephine, *In Search of the Phoenicians* (Princeton, NJ, 2018).

Rapoport, Yossef and Emilie Savage-Smith, *Lost Maps of the Caliphs* (Oxford, 21019).

Rowland, Ingrid, *From Pompeii: The Afterlife of a Roman Town* (Cambridge, MA, 2014).

Schneer, Jonathan, *The Balfour Declaration: The Origins of the Arab–Israeli Conflict* (New York, 2010).

Theroux, Paul, *The Pillars of Hercules: A Grand Tour of the Mediterranean* (London, 1995).

Tibble, Steve, *The Crusader Armies, 1099–1187* (New Haven, CT, 2018).

Tyerman, Christopher, *How to Plan a Crusade: Reason and Religious War in the High Middle Ages* (London, 2015).

Winter, Michael, *Egyptian Society under Ottoman Rule, 1517–1798* (London, 1992).

Wolff, Larry, *The Singing Turk: Ottoman Power and Operatic Emotions on the European Stage from the Siege of Vienna to the Age of Napoleon* (Stanford, CA, 2016).

Woolmer, M., *A Short History of the Phoenicians* (London, 2017).

Zavagno, Luca, *Cyprus between Late Antiquity and the Early Middle Ages (ca. 600–800): An Island in Transition* (London, 2017).

Zuiderhoek, A., *The Ancient City* (Cambridge, 2017).

Index

INDEX

Michael II 75
Michael VIII Palaiologos 76
Middle East 233, 239, 246–7, 249, 259, 274
migration 201, 225, 268–70, 274, 284–5, 287, 291
Milazzo 109
Mildmay, William 142–3
Milos 5, 22, 34, 135
Minoan culture 25
Minorca 43, 108, 109, 161–2, 180
Minos 25
Mitchel, Andrew 12
Molesworth, John 12
Monaco 14, 276, 279
monasteries 67
Mongols 60, 71, 75–6, 83
Mont Cenis pass 11
Monte Carlo 205–6
Montenegro 211–12, 260, 273, 279, 289, 290
Monto, George 171
Moriscos 115, 117
Morocco 50, 60, 97, 122, 127, 128, 149–51, 191–2, 222–3, 247, 250, 261, 274, 279, 284, 291
Morsi, Mohamed 262–3
Mozart, Wolfgang Amadeus 146, 153
Così fan tutte 144, 145, 147
Idomeneo 8
Müezzinzade Ali Pasha 118–19
Muhammad 57
Murad II 108
Murad III 121
Muslim Brotherhood 246, 262–3
Muslims 43, 57, 59–61, 63, 66, 71, 80, 82, 85–7, 99–100, 115, 122, 128, 131, 196, 216, 221, 247–9, 252, 254, 258, 269, 275, 284, 291
Mussolini, Benito 169, 222, 228–9, 235, 236
Müteferrika, Ibrahim 158
Mycenae 25–6

Naples 6–8, 77–9, 82, 104, 143–7, 153, 166–7, 178, 181–2, 189, 194, 199–200, 203, 207, 267–8, 290
rising 1647 132
Napoleon Bonaparte 11, 149, 156, 164, 172, 173–5, 177–9, 189, 194
Napoleonic Wars 179–80
Narmer 24
Nasser, Abdel 245, 252
National Liberation Front (FLN) 247–9

nationalism 218–19, 221–3, 230, 245–7, 250, 254, 257–8, 273, 285
NATO 251, 256–8, 260, 262, 273
Navarino Bay, battle of 182
navigation 88–9, 96, 102, 124–5
Naxos 103
Negroponte 98–9
Nelson, Horatio 148–9, 180–1, 193
Neolithic period 21
Netherlands 289
New Arab Spring 272
newspapers 138
Nicaea 74–6, 77
Nice 81–2, 204, 205
Nicholls, Norton 145
Nicias 31
Nicolay, Nicholas de 108
Nicosia, Cyprus 109, 116, 125
Nightingale, Florence 206
Nile, battle of the 148–9, 174
Nile Valley 24
Nine Years War 137
Normans 61–2, 64, 68, 72, 74, 78, 85
North Sea 213, 214
Northall, John 144–5
Numidians 40
Nunes, Pedro 125
Nuragic culture 28

obsidian 4–5
Ochakov Crisis 170
Odoacer 54
Odysseus 17–18, 20
oil 209–10, 224, 229, 235, 251, 253, 266
Opera (cruise ship) 280
Operation Dragoon 236–7
Operation Torch 235
Oran 114
O'Reilly 151–2
Orthodox Christianity 74, 82
Oruç 100
Ostia 50
Ostrogoths 54–5
Otranto 98–9, 109, 280–1
Otto of Bavaria 184, 186
Ottoman Empire 287, 289
Ottoman Turks 58, 77, 89–92, 171, 289

P&O 202
Pain 189, 276
Palaeolithic period 21
Palermo, Sicily 7–8, 57, 61, 62, 80, 85
Palestine 204, 216, 220–2, 243, 245, 259

303